NEW ESSAYS ON THE NATURE OF RIGHTS

This original collection of jurisprudential essays furthers our understanding of the nature of rights. In Part 1, Halpin considers the value of Hohfeldian neutrality when theorising about law in general, and legal rights in particular, and Kurki focuses on Hohfeld's operative notion of power. In Part 2, Kramer rebuts Wenar's objections to his Interest Theory of rights, and May provides a comparative defence of the Interest Theory against Wenar's Kind-Desire theory of claim-rights. Penner then pursues legal doctrine, focusing on whether judges hold the powers of their office as rights, an issue over which Wenar and Kramer have clashed. Sreenivasan, utilising a novel test case involving pure public goods, argues that the third party beneficiary objection to the Interest Theory is fatal. McBride builds on Sreenivasan's Hybrid Theory of claim-rights to construct his new Tracking Theory of rights. Cruft then argues that the best extant versions of the Interest and Will Theories of rights cannot avoid a form of circularity, and Van Duffel argues that meeting four adequacy constraints, which he proposes, counts in favour of any theory of rights. In Part 3, Andersson proposes a tie breaking procedure for rights conflicts in the applied realm of politics, and Steiner concludes by alleging that Kant's principle of right, a standard of corrective justice, has distributive implications.

New Essays on the Nature of Rights

Edited by
Mark McBride

•HART•
PUBLISHING
OXFORD AND PORTLAND, OREGON
2017

Hart Publishing
An imprint of Bloomsbury Publishing Plc

Hart Publishing Ltd
Kemp House
Chawley Park
Cumnor Hill
Oxford OX2 9PH
UK

Bloomsbury Publishing Plc
50 Bedford Square
London
WC1B 3DP
UK

www.hartpub.co.uk
www.bloomsbury.com

Published in North America (US and Canada) by
Hart Publishing
c/o International Specialized Book Services
920 NE 58th Avenue, Suite 300
Portland, OR 97213-3786
USA

www.isbs.com

HART PUBLISHING, the Hart/Stag logo, BLOOMSBURY and the Diana logo are trademarks of Bloomsbury Publishing Plc

First published 2017

British Library Cataloguing-in-Publication Data
A catalogue record for this book is available from the British Library.

ISBN: HB: 978-1-50991-014-4
ePDF: 978-1-50991-016-8
ePub: 978-1-50991-015-1

Library of Congress Cataloging-in-Publication Data

Names: McBride, Mark, (Law teacher), editor.

Title: New essays on the nature of rights / Edited by Mark McBride.

Description: Portland, Oregon : Hart Publishing, 2017. | Includes bibliographical references and index.

Identifiers: LCCN 2017017561 (print) | LCCN 2017022466 (ebook) | ISBN 9781509910151 (Epub) | ISBN 9781509910144 (hardback : alk. paper)

Subjects: LCSH: Law—Philosophy. | Law and ethics. | Law—Methodology. | Jurisprudence.

Classification: LCC K258 (ebook) | LCC K258 .N49 2017 (print) | DDC 342.08—dc23

LC record available at https://lccn.loc.gov/2017017561

Typeset by Compuscript Ltd, Shannon
Printed and bound in Great Britain by Lightning Source UK Ltd

To find out more about our authors and books visit www.hartpublishing.co.uk. Here you will find extracts, author information, details of forthcoming events and the option to sign up for our newsletters.

PREFACE

This collection arose out of a conference on 19–20 May 2016 in Singapore at the National University of Singapore (NUS)—kindly funded by my NUS Start-Up Grant (WBS Number R-241-000-126-133). The conference was held under the auspices of the recently founded NUS Centre for Legal Theory—several members of which both helped in my organisation of the conference and participated in the conference itself. Administratively, thanks go to Kris Zhao for assistance at the conference. Special thanks go to Wendy Wee for her patient administrative support during—but especially in the build-up to—the conference.

CONTENTS

LIST OF CONTRIBUTORS

Anna-Karin Andersson is Researcher at the Department of Global Public Health and Primary Care, University of Bergen.

Rowan Cruft is Senior Lecturer in Philosophy at the University of Stirling.

Andrew Halpin is Professor of Law at the National University of Singapore.

Matthew Kramer is Professor of Legal and Political Philosophy at the University of Cambridge.

Visa Kurki is PhD candidate at the Faculty of Law, University of Cambridge.

Mark McBride is Assistant Professor of Law at the National University of Singapore.

Simon Căbulea May is Assistant Professor of Philosophy at Florida State University.

James Penner is Professor of Law at the National University of Singapore.

Gopal Sreenivasan is Professor of Philosophy at Duke University.

Hillel Steiner is Professor of Political Philosophy at the University of Manchester.

Siegfried Van Duffel is Associate Professor at the School of Humanities and Social Sciences, Nazarbayev University.

INTRODUCTION

The nature of rights—legal and moral—has long been of interest to philosophers. But within contemporary debates over rights, one can justifiably see *A Debate Over Rights*, as a seminal book which, in 1998, set the agenda and context for subsequent writing on rights, within which this current collection must be situated. In that 1998 book, three leading contributors to the debates (two of whom are contributing to the current volume) spoke forth. Those contributors—Matthew Kramer, Nigel Simmonds and Hillel Steiner—clashed over many matters, but also shared sufficient common ground such that a genuine debate was had. And one can see a continuation of the clashes—including a perceived need to transcend those clashes—and common ground in this current collection. Finally, though it was not the central focus of the 1998 book, extensions of rights' theorising to, broadly speaking, the political realm were countenanced. And that element extends to the current collection.

I have thus chosen to carve the essays up into three categories: (Hohfeldian) common ground; clashes over theories of rights; and extensions to the political realm. It almost goes without saying that there are other ways one might carve the essays up. And relatedly, as one would expect, there is significant overlap (which I shall, on occasion, note in the context of specific essays) in these three categories.

Common ground, first. Most significantly, in both this and the 1998 book, all contributors adopt the analytical framework of Wesley Hohfeld as a means to bring clarity of exposition to their espoused positions. They use Hohfeld's logical framework to articulate and defend their theories and also to critique the theories of others.

Given the foundational role of Hohfeld's schema, it is natural to begin this collection with the essays of Andrew Halpin and Visa Kurki—each of whom devotes sustained attention to Hohfeld. Halpin's principal (and, to this writer, laudable) aim is to preserve the neutrality of Hohfeld's analytical scheme—neutral, in the sense of not determining any controversial position in the germane debates—at three levels: legal disputes, legal doctrinal theory and (what he calls) guild ideology. Halpin uses these levels to build up to a fourth locus of Hohfeldian neutrality—the domain of legal rights. And, though the foregoing might be considered the heart of Halpin's essay it serves as a prolegomenon to his elaboration of his own *Dispute Theory* of rights, and consideration of the political realm. Kurki, meanwhile, while still training his focus on Hohfeld, operates at a less panopticonical level than Halpin. Kurki's starting—and ending—point is Hohfeld's operative notion of *power*. Specifically, Kurki, after detailed consideration of philosophers' objections to the broad notion of power with which Hohfeld operates, seeks to defend preservation of Hohfeld's expansive notion, provided it is supplemented by a notion of *competence*, picking out an important subset of Hohfeldian powers.

Clashes, second. Kramer's 1998 articulation and defence of his *Interest Theory* (IT) of rights is deservedly considered a landmark piece. After a *tour de force* through Hohfeld, Kramer set out, and defended, for the first time, his IT—an IT which he has subsequently refined and modified. Then in the 1998 book, by turn, Simmonds and Steiner (by differing methods), sought to articulate and defend their *Will Theory* (WT) of rights against IT. So, two main 'games in town': IT, on which protection of the interests of the putative right-holder is at the core of a right; and WT, on which *control* of the putative right-holder over another's duty is at the core of a right. Assess their merits and demerits; and then take your pick! Since the 1998 book, two central, and related, dialectical developments can be charted: a continuation of the IT v WT debate, and an effort to transcend the starkly dichotomous choice (IT or WT) which served as a background to the 1998 skirmishes. These two dialectical developments are continued in this collection, though in a novel form.

The next essay in this collection is Kramer's. At its heart, Kramer's essay is an effort to rebut Leif Wenar's recent objections to Kramer's IT (in its capacious, and non-capacious variants) and, in the process of doing so, to contest that Wenar's own theory of (claim-)rights—Wenar's recent efforts to transcend the IT v WT debate—is a promising alternative to Kramer's IT. Predictably, in the course of Kramer's relentless efforts to impugn Wenar, we get a clear state-of the-art restatement of Kramer's IT.

Given the centrality of rebutting Wenar to Kramer's project, it is natural to follow up Kramer's essay with two others—Simon Căbulea May's and James Penner's—with a similar focus. Moreover, given that May grapples in detail with many of the same Wenarian examples as Kramer, and approaches them in a similar spirit to Kramer, it is natural to take May first. At its core, May's essay is a comparative defence of (a *justificatory*, Razian) IT against Wenar's *Kind-Desire Theory* of claim-rights. Methodologically speaking, May sets up two desiderata for a theory of claim-rights: extensional adequacy; and capability of explaining claim-rights' significance in social life. On each score, May argues IT fares better than Wenar's theory. Penner, meanwhile, whilst also grappling with Wenar, does so in a rather different spirit. Penner's central focus is on whether judges hold the powers of their office as rights. This is an issue over which Wenar and Kramer have clashed: Wenar claiming IT cannot account for the (putative) fact that judges do; Kramer claiming IT can so account. But the shared premise in this debate is the belief that judges *do* hold the powers of their office as rights. And Penner, upon adopting (what he takes to be) a Razian version of IT, contests this fact. What distinguishes Penner's essay is his efforts to bring fine-grained legal doctrinal analysis to bear on this issue, and on associated issues over legal (and moral) powers more generally.

Gopal Sreenivasan's essay is next in this collection. Sreenivasan, in a recent series of carefully worked out papers, has articulated and defended his own novel theory of claim-rights—his own novel means of transcending the IT versus WT debate. That theory is the *Hybrid Theory* of claim-rights (and a subsequent contributor—myself—engages sustainedly with that theory). Sreenivasan's current contribution presupposes, rather than defends afresh, his theory. His platform for theoretical discussion is the (partly political) question whether individuals can hold a claim-right to any pure public good—with his sharpening example being *herd immunity* against contagious infectious disease. This question, and example, provides a springboard for Sreenivasan's main claim: that the *third-party beneficiary* objection to IT is fatal.

The final three essays located in this category are Mark McBride's, Rowan Cruft's, and Siegfried Van Duffel's. It is natural to take McBride's essay first: it builds on Sreenivasan's theory to construct a new theory of rights—the *Tracking Theory* of rights. McBride begins by confronting head-on the most prominent putative counterexample to Sreenivasan's theory—offered by Kramer (and Steiner). In the course of fleshing out a hybrid theorist's response to that counterexample, McBride modifies Sreenivasan's theory, and concludes by formalising what merits being called a new (Nozick-inspired) hybrid theory of rights.

The concluding essays in this part—Cruft's and Van Duffel's—squarely enter the methodological realm. Cruft, the next author in this volume, pursues a theme from his previous work on rights, viz that, while learning lessons from the IT versus WT debate, we must look beyond it for a fully adequate theory of rights. He pursues this theme in a novel direction in this volume, by proposing that the best extant versions of IT and WT cannot avoid a form of circularity (which he pinpoints in his contribution). While being up front that he has not completed the job of finding a fully reductive (non-circular) theory of rights, Cruft concludes by pointing in the direction that any such search must take. It is natural to end this category with Van Duffel's methodologically focused essay. In brief, this essay proposes four (non-exhaustive, extensional and intensional) adequacy constraints on any theory—conceptual analysis—of rights, with the extent to which any theory meets such constraints being a count in its favour. Insofar as Van Duffel's constraints are accepted, it is an interesting question the degree to which the theories of rights espoused by the philosophers in this collection meet said constraints.

The political realm, finally. While, as noted, extensions to the political realm did not take centre stage in the seminal 1998 book on rights, such extensions bubbled under, and occasionally bobbed to, the surface. And this volume concludes with two contributions—from Anna-Karin Andersson and Hillel Steiner—in the realm of politics, respectively, looking at tie-breaking procedures for rights conflicts in the applied realm, and alleging that Kant's *principle of right* (paradigmatically a standard of corrective justice) has distributive implications. In brief, Andersson, arguing from a central commitment to *respect for persons*, proposes that certain rights conflicts (eg, A and B urgently need a new heart, and only one heart is available) should be adjudicated by considering to what extent individuals involved in the conflict have promoted certain values prior to the occurrence of the conflict. Steiner, meanwhile, prosecutes the above claim through engagement with Ernest Weinrib. Each of Steiner and Weinrib operates with a shared Kantian perspective, but Steiner contests Wenrib's claim that Kant's principle of right is independent of distributive justice.

What next? The hope is that this collection can serve as a point of departure for further jurisprudential debate on all the above dimensions (in much the way that the 1998 book did): Hohfeldian analysis; clashes over theories of rights; and extensions to the political realm. Theorising over the nature of rights is alive and well. Long may it continue.

Mark McBride

1

The Value of Hohfeldian Neutrality when Theorising about Legal Rights

ANDREW HALPIN*

I. Introduction

The present essay is an offshoot from a broader project in which I suggest that the Hohfeldian scheme of analysis has been misunderstood at a very basic level during the whole course of its reception over the past hundred years; and, that the theoretical debate over property in the law has been contested between two entrenched positions whose intellectual plausibility is dependent on sustaining the false understanding of Hohfeld (either as a foundation or as a target), and is in both cases nullified by a corrected understanding of Hohfeld's scheme of analysis.[1]

The central argument of that project is founded on a simple point that, contrary to the received view of his work, Hohfeld intended his scheme of analysis to pay equal attention to legal relations and aggregate legal positions. A number of consequences follow from this simple point; notably, the reductionist understanding of Hohfeld is discredited, and his assumed support for the bundle of sticks[2] approach to property is revealed to be unfounded. What is proposed as a completed Hohfeldian scheme of analysis, relying on a dual-level analysis that incorporates both legal relations and aggregate levels, is shown to possess greater resources for providing clarity where current doctrinal argument is confused, and for unlocking the prevailing deadlock between rival theoretical views on property.

One of the minor, less developed themes of that project is the neutrality of Hohfeldian analysis, which goes hand-in-glove with the ability of Hohfeld's scheme of analysis to represent both sides to a dispute. Such neutrality can be

* I am grateful for helpful comments on an initial draft of this essay from the participants at the conference held in May 2016 and for subsequent discussion with Mark McBride. I also gratefully acknowledge the financial assistance of the National University of Singapore research fund (R-241-000-107-133) in supporting the research for this essay.

[1] The project is being pursued as a book with the provisional title, *Hohfeld Reconsidered: A Century of Misunderstanding*. The present work draws significantly from that broader project.

[2] Or, bundle of rights—I employ the sticks version but treat the two as synonymous here.

discerned in a number of locations. First and foremost, in *representing both sides to a legal dispute before a court*. This basic neutrality follows from two characteristics Hohfeld claimed for his analytical scheme: its exhaustive ability to represent all the different dominant positions (colloquially and indiscriminately referred to as rights) claimed in a legal action, as against the subordinate positions of the other party to the dispute; and the possibility of representing the denial of the claimed relationship by claiming its opposite or negation within an alternative legal relationship between the parties found within Hohfeld's scheme of analysis. The tendency is to focus more on the correlative relationships between dominant and subordinate positions, and less on the opposite relationships by which the claimed legal advantage can be denied. Yet if this second characteristic is always present alongside the first, it follows that the Hohfeldian scheme is equally capable of representing both sides to a legal dispute, and that the outcome of that dispute is not itself determined by an application of Hohfeldian analysis.

It also follows that efforts to resolve a legal dispute by bringing Hohfeldian analysis to bear in favour of one party alone amount to a misrepresentation of Hohfeld's scheme, or even a demonstration of its failure to make the practical impact upon the law that Hohfeld himself wished for it. I comment briefly on this point below with regard to legal disputes involving property. However, the importance of this point for the focus of the present essay extends beyond the use of Hohfeld for the accurate representation of legal disputes. If the Hohfeldian analytical scheme is considered sound and also capable of illuminating theoretical discussion on the nature of (legal) rights, then the broader point can be made that for any position that is asserted to be a right within a theoretical analysis of rights that embraces Hohfeld, it follows that the denial of that position should also be capable of being represented within that same theoretical analysis. There may, of course, be additional premises within the theory of rights that promote the adoption of one of these positions as a legal right rather than the other, but this additional work will have to come on top of the analytical work derived from Hohfeld since that is capable of representing both positions. The primary purpose of this essay is to work through the full implications of this point.

A digression on the parenthetical legal I placed before rights. Hohfeldian analysis has been employed to develop theories of rights that are not restricted to the legal domain—notably, moral and political rights are included. For simplicity, the main argument of this essay will proceed to discuss legal rights alone, and then in the concluding reflections I shall comment on how the findings from the legal domain might apply to rights in other normative domains.

The second location for Hohfeldian neutrality occurs in what I shall loosely call *legal doctrinal theory*, that is to say, a theory developed to elucidate a doctrinal area of law. Given the recognition that the role of legal doctrine is to systematically portray an area of law in such a way that the answer to any potential dispute within that area can be clearly inferred from the body of doctrine—or, at least, that is the aspirational role of legal doctrine, then doctrinal theory will aim to further that role by bringing theoretical insights to assist the current state of the practical understanding of legal doctrine. I, again, draw on my previous work on property to illustrate the neutrality of Hohfeldian analysis between opposing doctrinal theories of property law. And again, the use of Hohfeldian analysis on one side of the theoretical dispute is regarded as a misrepresentation of Hohfeld's scheme, or even a demonstration of its failure.

The third location for Hohfeldian neutrality concerns a general understanding of law as opposed to an understanding of a specific area of legal doctrine, but is still very much within a practice-oriented perspective, rather than a realm of theory that is more removed from practical concerns.[3] It involves theorising about a general rudimentary aspect of practice in a way that expresses the divergent views of practitioners on that issue, and at a level on which practitioners themselves can reasonably be expected to engage. We might then label this as *guild ideology*, referring as it does to important ways in which practitioners reflect upon and articulate their own practice.[4] The obvious illustration is the dispute between formalism and realism in portraying the practice of law. The demonstration of Hohfeldian neutrality in this location is historically more charged in that Hohfeld himself can be judged to have taken a partisan position in this dispute. Nevertheless, it will be argued below that Hohfeld's own views were at odds with his analytical scheme which can be shown to be strictly neutral in this location too.

The main thrust of the present essay is to suggest that Hohfeldian neutrality in the way it can be seen in these three locations, as being capable of representing both sides of a dispute, also applies to a more general or abstract theoretical concern with the nature of legal rights in particular and of rights more generally. That is to say, that a Hohfeldian analytical framework is capable of representing both sides to a theoretical dispute over the nature of (legal) rights. As such, it cannot be relied on by either side as partisan support for that theoretical outlook. If this primary objective can be delivered, it then opens up more interesting lines of enquiry, on which I shall offer some preliminary and rather tentative observations in the conclusion.

The first of these lines of enquiry raises questions about theorising over the nature of a (legal) right. If a commonly employed analytical resource (the Hohfeldian scheme) is incapable of differentiating between opposing theoretical accounts of a right, then on what basis can judgement be made between opposing views? To pursue this investigation, there needs to be a preliminary refinement of the expressed neutrality of the Hohfeldian scheme between two opposing theoretical accounts of a right. If the Hohfeldian scheme has any analytical traction it must be capable of pointing out some potential deficiencies, some analytical flaws, in any theoretical account. The expression of neutrality must, accordingly, take place after a basic threshold of analytical clarity has been passed. This refinement can

[3] I am not sure that there is a single way of making the contrast. Pure theory, general theory of law, system-independent theory, grand theory would all fall on the other side in that they remain indifferent to such practitioner attitudes.

[4] For wider discussion of guild ideology, see Halpin (2006: 159).

be understood as expecting a theory of rights to respect the basic analytical distinctions found within the Hohfeldian scheme. Once this requirement has been observed, the importance of Hohfeldian neutrality is not limited to a case where there exists within the literature an opposing theory of the nature of a right that has passed this basic threshold of analytical clarity, so providing us with neutrality between two opposing accounts. The reach of neutrality here is far more destructive of a proclaimed analytical superiority for a particular theory of legal rights, in that it would equally favour a purely hypothetical alternative account to the single account being championed—which is to say it would favour no theoretical account at all.

A controversial inference that can be drawn from this line of enquiry is that the theoretical pursuit of the nature of a (legal) right is misguided in seeking a uniform understanding of that nature and the rights that fall under it, where that is intended to analytically rule out opposing instantiations of rights. This would appear to follow from the possibility of an alternative theoretical account being analytically left open favouring different instantiations of rights (hypothetically, at least) by Hohfeldian neutrality. This inference is explored, at a very general level, in relation to the will-interest debate over the nature of rights and the more recent progeny that debate has produced.

If this controversial inference is accepted, a second line of enquiry is then called upon to grapple with the startlingly obvious point that when we talk about rights we are talking seriously about closure and restriction; we are saying that not everything goes. If taking a particular set of (legal) rights seriously cannot be based on the correct degree of analytical rigour, to find the winning theory of rights, then where does the restrictive character of rights come from? I characterise a plausible alternative to meet these demands as the dispute theory of rights (although we shall see this is something of a misnomer), and at this point engage in a little more detail with some illustrative representations of the rejected theories. More pointedly, in relation to the subject of this essay, I shall suggest that the arguments to be offered here in order to maintain Hohfeldian neutrality in this fourth location of *theories of (legal) rights* can be expanded to provide a plausible account of the restrictive character of rights that is tied into their practical emergence as a set of legal rights.

In order to fully flesh out this argument, it will be necessary to provide some details of how the completed dual-level scheme of analysis (recognising legal relations and aggregate levels) can be expanded to allow for a third level of grander theoretical or ideological concerns. I have been working on this expanded scheme in another setting of considering the analytical issues in making historical and comparative studies of property,[5] but for present purposes the salient point is that

[5] 'An Appropriate Analytical Scheme for Historical Perspectives on Property'—a preliminary draft was presented at the Seminar on History and Theory of Property Law held at the Centre for Law and Society in a Global Context, Queen Mary University of London, on 12 April 2016, and a final draft will be incorporated in the broader project mentioned in n 1.

the legal relations level of analysis linked to the aggregate level is a necessary feature of any plausible *legal* understanding of property rights. It is this feature that I shall argue is the dominant factor in establishing the restrictive quality of a set of legal rights, while keeping any theoretical account of (legal) rights contingent upon other factors.

The structure of the present essay follows this rather meandering introduction and can be summarised as follows. Following the introduction (section I), section II considers the key elements of Hohfeld's analytical scheme. Section III examines three locations of Hohfeldian neutrality: (a) a legal dispute; (b) legal doctrinal theory; and (c) guild ideology. This prepares for the fuller investigation of a fourth location of neutrality in theory of legal rights, in section IV. Section V amplifies this additional identification of neutrality in proposing a dispute theory of rights. The concluding reflections in section VI consider the implications of this study for efforts to produce a uniform theory of legal rights, and respond to the question over its application to moral and political rights.

II. The Key Elements of Hohfeld's Analytical Scheme

Hohfeld had two very clear aims for his analysis of fundamental legal conceptions and the jural (or legal) relations in which they were established. First, the conceptions were supposed to provide a definitive classification of the four different types of legal rights held by parties, which had been found in a state of muddled confusion created by the indiscriminate use of a single term, 'right'.[6] So, Hohfeld provides us with:

(1) *X*'s **claim-right** (or, simply, **right**) to the conduct of *Y*.
(2) *X*'s **privilege** (or, **liberty**) to engage in his or her own conduct.
(3) *X*'s **power** to change a legal relation of *Y*.
(4) *X*'s **immunity** against having a legal relation of his or her own changed by *Y*.

The parenthetical synonyms in (1) and (2) have subsequently gained wider currency in the discussion of Hohfeld's scheme, and we shall follow the commonly preferred usage below.

Second, these four types of rights were supposed to assist in clarifying the practical legal positions of the parties to a legal dispute,[7] without which there would be

[6] Hohfeld (1919: 35–36). Page references throughout this essay are to this book version of Hohfeld's work, a republication after his death of his two seminal articles: Hohfeld (1913) (this article was sufficient to establish Hohfeld's analytical scheme regarding his arrangement of fundamental legal conceptions, or legal relations—to introduce a preference we shall justify below) and his subsequent article, expanding on certain points introduced in the first (Hohfeld 1917).

[7] The setting of 'judicial reasoning' presupposes a legal dispute. See also ibid, 26 ('the solution of practical, everyday problems of the law'); 36 ('application in concrete cases'); 63 and 66 ('the solution of concrete problems of litigation').

no clear understanding of what precisely was at stake between the parties.[8] To further this aim, the four types of rights had to be linked with the subordinate positions of the parties over which they are exercised, within a legal relation. Each legal relation is constituted by the correlative relationship formed from a dominant position (one of the four types of right) together with its subordinate position, so:

(A) *X* has a **right** to the conduct of *Y* and *Y* is under a **duty** to perform that conduct.
(B) *X* has a **liberty** to engage in conduct and *Y* has **no-right** that *X* refrain from it.
(C) *X* has a **power** to change a legal relation of *Y* and *Y* is under a **liability** to have that legal relation changed.
(D) *X* has an **immunity** against having a legal relation changed by *Y* and *Y* has a **disability** to change it.

The correlativity between dominant and subordinate positions in every case is demonstrated by their interdependence, by the fact that each may be fully explained in terms of the other. *X* has a right against *Y* over specific conduct of *Y* just when *Y* is under a duty to *X* to perform that specific conduct; *Y* has a duty to *X* to perform specific conduct just when *X* has a right against *Y* over that specific conduct of *Y*. And so on, for liberty/no-right, power/liability and immunity/disability.[9]

However, the full capacity of Hohfeld's scheme to clarify what is at stake in a legal dispute depends also on another relationship he identified between his fundamental legal conceptions (or the legal positions they represent). One of the four correlative relations, (A), (B), (C) or (D), may be used to express precisely what is being claimed by one party in a legal dispute, but if it is a dispute we also need to know what is being denied by the other party. This requirement could have been met by placing simple negations of the first party's claims in the mouth of the opposing party. *X* claims a right over *Y*'s conduct; ie, that *Y* owes *X* a duty. *Y* responds by denying *X*'s claim: *X* has no-right over *Y*'s conduct; ie, *Y* owes no-duty to *X*. Hohfeld's scheme became a little more elaborate at this point in talking of relationships of 'opposites' between the legal positions.[10]

Considering the precise nature of a Hohfeldian opposite or negation[11] would take us into one of the more technical aspects of Hohfeld's scheme, which happily need not detain us here.[12] The key point being made by Hohfeld is that if one party to a legal dispute is claiming what can be represented by one of the four correlative relations, (A), (B), (C) or (D), then the position of the opposing party can

[8] ibid 35–36 ('inadequacy and ambiguity of terms unfortunately reflect, all too often, corresponding paucity and confusion as regards actual legal conceptions'); 43 ('obscured by the very indefinite and rapidly shifting meanings with which the term 'right' is used').

[9] ibid 36, 39.

[10] ibid 36.

[11] ibid 39. Hohfeld casts his opposite as a 'mere negation'.

[12] The issue is not pertinent to our present concerns as it does not affect the common understanding that a Hohfeldian liberty involves the negation of a duty, which is enough in order to proceed with the elementary application of his scheme.

be represented by an alternative from these relations, described as its opposite or negation. Specifically, a claim in the form of (A) will be denied by making a claim in the form of (B), with due adjustment for the party who is now dominant; and similarly for (C) and (D). To take the former case:[13]

> *The denial (or 'opposite') of an (A) claim by X—*
>
> *X* has a right to the conduct of *Y* and *Y* is under a duty to perform that conduct
>
> is a *(B)* claim by Y—
>
> *Y* has a liberty not to engage in that conduct and *X* has no-right that *Y* perform it.

And similarly for the latter case:[14]

> *The denial (or 'opposite') of a (C) claim by X—*
>
> *X* has a power to change a legal relation of *Y* and *Y* is under a liability to have that legal relation changed
>
> *is a (D) claim by Y—*
>
> *Y* has an immunity against having that legal relation changed by *X* and *X* has a disability to change it.

Hohfeld (1919: 38–39) himself describes the relationship of opposite as occurring between the fundamental legal conceptions or individual positions (a liberty is the opposite of a duty, etc), but since these cannot exist outside their correlative relationships, a fuller representation, as given here in (A)–(D), requires the legal relations to be mentioned.[15]

These two core aspirations for Hohfeld's scheme stand out immediately and unequivocally. His analytical scheme purports to be capable of providing clear distinctions between different legal positions, and then to use the differentiated positions to clarify the specific point of conflict between parties to a legal dispute. Although it follows that the resolution of that dispute will necessarily be expressible in terms of a Hohfeldian relation, since judgment will favour the relation proposed by the one party or its opposite argued for by the other party, what cannot be derived from the Hohfeldian scheme is the way in which judgment will go. In that respect, the Hohfeldian scheme is wholly neutral.

[13] More fully, the claim and denial could also be found the other way around: the denial (or 'opposite') of a (B) claim by *X*—*X* has a liberty not to engage in particular conduct and *Y* has no-right that *X* perform it—is an (A) claim by *Y*—*Y* has a right to that conduct of *X* and *X* is under a duty to perform that conduct.

[14] Again, more fully, the claim and denial could also be found the other way around: The denial (or 'opposite') of a (D) claim by *X*—*X* has an immunity against having a particular legal relation changed by *Y* and *Y* has a disability to change it—is a (C) claim by—*Y* has a power to change that legal relation of *X* and *X* is under a liability to have that legal relation changed.

[15] Hohfeld referred to the conceptions themselves as 'the lowest common denominators' (1919: 63–64) but no single conception could exist for Hohfeld without the presence of its correlative within a legal relation, so that it is the relations and not the conceptions that form the atomic particles of law in the Hohfeldian scheme (to employ another metaphor), with the two correlative conceptions in each relation amounting to subatomic particles (to extend the image further).

III. Three Locations of Hohfeldian Neutrality

A. A Legal Dispute

Despite the quality of neutrality being regarded as self-evident for the Hohfeldian scheme of analysis in the setting of a legal dispute, once the basic features of that scheme have been grasped as portrayed in the previous section, it has to be admitted that this has not been universally accepted. The thinking behind the opposing viewpoint is that by representing the problem of a legal dispute in Hohfeldian terms, that then creates a partisan representation of the problem favouring one party over the other; that a non-Hohfeldian representation will provide a different perspective on the issue favouring the other party. It is important to stress that if such an opposing viewpoint is plausible it attacks the primary objectives of Hohfeld's scheme and the key features of that scheme as he presented it. To put it bluntly, a Hohfeldian scheme that can only feature on one side of a legal dispute is not the analytical scheme Hohfeld himself devised. Supporters of the opposing viewpoint thus have a double burden to clarify how exactly the Hohfeldian scheme cannot express the other side to the legal dispute, and how the non-Hohfeldian analysis is itself restricted to the one side alone.

The burden is not discharged merely by showing that more than the Hohfeldian scheme offers is required in order to resolve the dispute. The requirement of additional resources to achieve that is completely consistent with Hohfeldian neutrality. And, the recognition of a need for such additional resources does not in itself work out to the advantage of one party rather than the other. These matters can be briefly illustrated here by taking the example from property law of a case that has been put forward by Hanoch Dagan as one whose resolution turned upon whether a Hohfeldian analysis was applied or not.[16] The US Supreme Court case of *Craft*,[17] according to Dagan (2011), reveals in the majority and dissenting speeches how a *Hohfeldian bundle of sticks* approach leads to a different outcome from a *Blackstonian rigid forms* approach to property. I shall point out here how both sides can be expressed in Hohfeldian terms, and thus also the eventual outcome; that on both sides additional resources to Hohfeldian analysis are required to advance the argument in the form of normative argument; and how it is the outcome of that normative argument which determines the winner, and the eventual selection of the appropriate Hohfeldian representation of the outcome.

The case of *Craft* concerned a form of marital property, tenancy by the entirety, which creates a type of joint ownership between the spouses, typically over the matrimonial home; and the possible subjection of that property to a federal tax lien against the property of the husband. The technicality at the heart of the

[16] A far more detailed discussion of these matters, and the illustration, is found in the broader project mentioned in n 1.

[17] *United States v Craft* 535 US 274 (2002).

dispute concerns the nature of the joint ownership involved in a tenancy by the entirety. This can be treated in two very different ways. In the one, each party to the joint ownership enjoys an individual proprietorial interest in the matrimonial home, which could accordingly be subjected to a lien affecting one party's property. In the other, the proprietorial interest is not held individually and the joint ownership has to be legally terminated before individual proprietorial interests can be created; so, while the tenancy by the entirety continues the matrimonial property cannot be subject to a lien affecting one party's property.

The issue at stake in the case of *Craft* can be expressed as a dispute between two opposite Hohfeldian relations. On the Wife's side, as favoured by the dissenting minority, there is an assertion of a (D) relation, providing a Hohfeldian immunity (in both the husband and the wife) against the prospective power of the tax authority to exercise a lien against the property constituting the tenancy by the entirety, so defeating that prospective power and leaving the tax authority with a disability. For the Internal Revenue Service (IRS), favoured by the majority, there is asserted an opposing (C) relation amounting to recognising the power of the tax authority to exercise a lien against the property and correlatively a liability (again, in both husband and wife). The case is resolved by recognising either a (D) relation, or its negation, a (C) relation, and as it happened in the Supreme Court the (C) relation prevailed by a majority. So, the practical significance of Hohfeldian analysis lies both *potentially* when the dispute is still active (in terms of asserting opposing Hohfeldian relations) and as a matter of *outcome* when the dispute is resolved (in terms of a favoured Hohfeldian relation).

It might be suggested that the legal dispute revolves around accepting or dismissing a particular legal relation but, of course, the mere assertion of a legal relation is incapable of resolving the dispute. The dispute might be settled by showing how the one legal relation fits into the proper doctrinal understanding of that area of law, but even then there needs to be *doctrinal argument* which cannot be undertaken at the legal relations level alone. The question is whether the contentious legal relation is consistent with the doctrinal understanding of the party's aggregate position as a holder of a tenancy by the entirety, as opposed to, say, the property being in the sole name of the husband with the wife being in residence, with or without a beneficial interest. This sort of enquiry and the argument that follows can only be undertaken at the aggregate level. A tenancy by the entirety, a beneficial interest in the matrimonial home, etc, are not fundamental legal conceptions and appear nowhere in Hohfeld's set of fundamental legal relations, (A)–(D).

If doctrinal argument is required as an additional resource to Hohfeldian analysis, then it can be deployed on both sides. It is not the case that on one side one has Hohfeldian analysis and on the other side doctrinal argument. In the actual case of *Craft*, it appears that it was not so much doctrinal argument (that seemed to be indeterminate) but *normative argument* that swayed the Supreme Court. If normative argument provides the additional resource, it is again capable of appearing on both sides. In *Craft*, there are indications that the majority and dissent were swayed by different normative considerations: respectively, a concern that the Grand Rapids property would escape the claims of the IRS entirely;[18] and the rejection of that concern[19] accompanied by a concern that protection should be given to the wife against her husband's indebtedness.[20] Again too, this resource must operate at the aggregate level. The normative argument for providing the IRS with an effective revenue stream is not made by baldly asserting a power to exercise a lien, but through a consideration of the normative significance of the aggregate position of the IRS with respect to the source of this particular revenue, including the past default of payment by the husband, and any prospective revenue that might be forthcoming from the Grand Rapids property. Similarly, the normative argument for securing independent financial security for the wife is not made by baldly asserting an immunity against the IRS, but through a consideration of the normative significance of her aggregate position, including the expectations present when the tenancy by the entirety was set up, and the wider social importance of providing her with financial security in this way.

Once judgment is delivered, the legal point will be resolved by deciding in favour of one side on the contested legal relation, but that outcome (the IRS has a power with a corresponding liability on each of the husband and wife, as the majority decided) will be located in the aggregate legal position (the tenancy by the entirety), and in that clarified form (now including the liabilities) it will reflect the successful normative (or doctrinal) argument. In the same way, an aggregate position modified in a different manner (a tenancy by the entirety with immunities) would have reflected the dissenting argument had it been successful. Throughout this process Hohfeldian analysis is neutral as to portraying the different sides of the legal dispute and in portraying the eventual outcome.

B. Legal Doctrinal Theory

Indirectly, the discussion in section III.A casts doubts upon the prevailing viewpoint in property theory that Hohfeldian analysis favours one of the two dominant approaches to understanding property rights, namely the bundle of sticks approach, given Dagan's reported attempt to restrict Hohfeld through an endorsement of that approach to one of the sides to the dispute in *Craft*. We now turn to consider directly this aspect of Hohfeldian neutrality.

The general misapplication of Hohfeld we have already noted, in support of one side of a practical legal dispute, is distorted further when Hohfeld is invoked on one side of a theoretical debate over property. For one thing, Hohfeld's analytical scheme was produced with an avowed disinterest in theory. His concern w 'practical, everyday problems of the law' was accompanied by an express reje of 'a merely philosophical inquiry',[21] and reinforced by other statements

[18] 535 US 274, 285 (2002).
[19] ibid 301.
[20] ibid 289–90.
[21] Hohfeld (1919: 26).

characteristics at all as against non-proprietary interests protected by the law.[28] At the very least, the flexibility of the bundles approach opens up a vista on countless types of property. The individual sticks, standardly taken within this view to represent independent Hohfeldian legal relations, can be bundled together, as Hanoch Dagan (2011: 30) puts it, in 'a limitless number of permutations'.

The disengagement between these two approaches occurs when their respective tendencies harden into exclusive and exclusionary understandings of property in the law. It is hard to say precisely why this should have happened. Blackstone's formulation of dominion certainly encourages an extreme position on property, but nobody in the common law world takes seriously the idea of 'sole and despotic dominion ... in total exclusion of the right of any individual in the universe',[29] in an absolute sense.[30] Yet on the forms side the thinking behind this image has prevailed to the extent of marginalising as secondary any legal give and take between the property holder and other members of the community. The importance of asserting the relationship between property holder and property remains paramount, even when that relationship is expressed so as to mention the other members of the community, as it is with the right to exclude others. The others in this formulation are firmly positioned outside the enjoyment of the property by the property-holder; there is no compromise, no interaction even, between the interests of the property holder and the interests of the others.

Little wonder then that the bundles brigade have nothing to say to the forms folk, since their whole preoccupation is with the relationships, the communal compromises, involving interests of both property holders and others. Why they should similarly harden that tendency so as to avoid recognition of discrete forms of property may simply be a matter of critical reaction,[31] but certainly there is no evidence of them offering their insights as a means of qualifying or tempering the forms approach. Net result, deadlock.

The illumination provided by the dual-level analysis on this state of affairs is, first, to demonstrate the analytical inadequacies of each approach. Although taking the bundles approach as Hohfeldian is, as we have mentioned, a misrepresentation of Hohfeld, it can be said that what the bundles approach can feed into

[28] See Singer (2009: 1032): 'the bundle-of-rights idea could suggest that property has no meaning whatsoever as a legal category'. This draws on the earlier observation made by Grey (1980: 81) that the bundles approach 'has the ultimate consequence that property ceases to be an important category in legal and political thought'.

[29] See n 25 above.

[30] See Burns (1985); Dagan (2011: ch 2); Alexander and Peñalver (2012: ch 7); Van Der Walt (2009). Beyond the common law world, one can find clear opposition to entertaining the idea in the first place, as reported by Michelon (2014: 283):

> Article 27 of the 1917 Mexican Constitution famously disposed that '[t]he Nation shall at all times have the right to impose on private property such limitations as the public interest may demand, as well as the right to regulate the utilization of natural resources which are susceptible of appropriation, in order to conserve them and to ensure a more equitable distribution of public wealth'. More succinctly, but in the same vein, the Brazilian Constitution states both that 'XXII—the right of property is guaranteed' and that 'XXIII—property shall fulfill its social function'.

[31] Merrill (2012: 155): 'Those who persist in calling property a bundle of sticks are ... too hostile to the institution to try to describe how it really works and why'.

a genuine Hohfeldian analysis operates on the legal relations level alone. This is the hallmark of the reductionism supported by the bundles approach. In contrast, the forms approach, which typically makes no pretence of satisfying Hohfeldian analysis, could, if pushed, be directed to furnishing material for the aggregate level analysis. However, any serious interest with the legal relations level is strenuously denied.[32]

So, if we are persuaded that the completed analytical scheme, incorporating the dual-level analysis, is required to properly represent Hohfeld's scheme of analysis and is necessary to depict property in the law, then it follows that each of the dominant theoretical approaches to property in the law is fundamentally flawed, and that neither is Hohfeldian. At this point, we should note that the completed scheme of analysis does provide opportunities to promote the underlying concerns of either approach. Exploration of established forms of property is available at the aggregate level. Consideration of diverse connections between the property holder and other members of the community is provided at the legal relations level. However, the further illumination provided by the dual-level analysis spells out how irredeemably flawed each approach is.

The dual-level analysis does not simply insist on the recognition of two levels of analysis; it demonstrates their interaction and mutual interdependence. This is seen notably in the way that both levels interact in representing a doctrinal or normative disagreement over property in the law, and in effecting its resolution. The account of this interaction, illustrated by the case of *Craft* above, demonstrates the need for aggregate positions to supplement legal relations in order even to express normative or doctrinal aspects of property in the law. So, the indictment against each of the dominant approaches is not simply that it denies one of the levels on which property needs to be analysed (the forms approach denying the legal relations level, and the bundles approach denying the aggregate level). More than this, by denying any link between the level of analysis that it is prepared to operate on (aggregate level for the forms approach, legal relations level for the bundles approach) with the other level, each offers a flawed understanding of property even on its preferred level of operation.

Correcting these analytical inadequacies by embracing a dual-level Hohfeldian analysis does not favour one theoretical approach to property over another. Nor does it establish a new theoretical approach to property to displace all rivals. What it does do is to provide a common venue in which opposing theoretical approaches can be conveyed, both as to the normative or doctrinal significance of their postulated aggregates and as to their impact upon a contested legal relation in a legal dispute. For example, take a case of public access through a private beach,[33] which can be approached through a theory of property which adopts a

[32] For examples of the avoidance of the legal relations level of analysis, see Fennell (2012) and Smith (2012b). Douglas and McFarlane (2013) follow Smith's modularity with the same effect.

[33] See *Uston v Grand Resorts, Inc*, F 2d 1217 (9th Cir 1977), discussed in Alexander and Peñalver (2012: 133–34).

rigid exclusionary ideology of property, or through one that takes a more flexible understanding of social responsibility to the holding of property. In either case, the completed Hohfeldian scheme offers the opportunity to attach the differing normative perspectives to an aggregate level understanding of the private ownership of the beach, and equally the opportunity at the legal relations level to advance one or other of the two opposing positions on the outcome of the legal dispute: an (A) relation imposing a duty to keep off the beach; or the opposing (B) relation providing a liberty to cross the beach by members of the public to gain access to the sea.

C. Guild Ideology

A useful way of illustrating the different expectations that can be associated with Hohfeldian analysis in terms of understanding the general practice of law is provided by tracing the changing attitudes towards Hohfeld from the American Legal Realists. There is a fascinating commentary on differing perceptions of the use of Hohfeld's analysis in a discussion by Gerald Postema (2011: 104–06) of their response to Hohfeld. Postema points out that Hohfeld was initially embraced by the American Realists. They welcomed Hohfeld's analysis as being capable of destroying established legal categories by collapsing them into generic legal relations. This provided valuable ammunition against a formalist portrayal of legal doctrine, which proceeded by a process of logical deduction from established legal categories. Take away the fixed legal categories, and legal formalism is deprived of its premises, it was thought. The legal field is then opened up to far greater possibilities. We have already encountered possibly the most famous illustration of this line of thought. Hohfeld could be used to demolish an established category of property, and to recognise alternative collections of legal relations as property, metaphorically captured as bundles of sticks. And, as has already been remarked, this has been viewed as opening up a vast number of possible cases of property in place of the established category.

Thus, Hohfeld was welcomed as a card-carrying member of the American Realists. But Postema interjects that such an interpretation of Hohfeld was without foundation. From an ideological perspective, the progressive reforms espoused by the Realists may have required the overthrow of vested interests protected by the law, such as property, but the analysis of such legally protected positions into their constituent legal relations says nothing either way about the desirability, value, or social necessity of the established arrangements. As Postema (2011: 105) puts it, '[Hohfeld's] analysis was entirely neutral with respect to ideological matters'.

Moreover, within an analytical perspective, the legal relations provide the 'atomic components' of the law but are incapable of generating any insight on how those components should be brought together. Postema (2011: 106) expresses it very clearly:[34]

> Hohfeld was silent about combinatorial principles, but from silence it is not possible to infer that there are no such principles or that they are drawn from entirely extra-legal (merely political) considerations of policy. Similarly, from the fact that the atomic components do not by themselves generate logical connections among them, it does not follow that they are not and cannot be connected in some way, by virtue, say, of some features of law in general or structures and principles of certain departments of law, or other considerations.

We might want to qualify Postema's claim of absolute silence over combinatorial principles,[35] in the light of the position adopted on the simple point mentioned in section I, and speak instead of Hohfeld's near silence on aggregate legal positions, for it is precisely at the aggregate-level analysis that 'combinatorial principles' will come into play. Nevertheless, Postema's key point is well made. At the legal relations level of analysis, the Hohfeldian approach offers nothing to favour one combination of legal relations or another; and, at that level, nothing is said as to what factors or 'principles'—legal, political, social, or otherwise—might be at play in determining which combination of legal relations prevails in the law.

Accordingly, a pro-Realist expectation for Hohfeld's analytical scheme at the legal relations level is not supported; but, on the other hand, neither is it ruled out. Within this gap, it is perhaps understandable that the Realists presumed on Hohfeld's support, particularly if his expressed sympathies were progressive.[36] Yet, a Realist understanding of law is incompatible with Hohfeld's own ambition for his work, which is fleetingly though boldly expressed at the conclusion of his first article (1919: 64):

> But if all these relations are reduced to their lowest generic terms … [b]y such a process it becomes possible not only to discover essential similarities and illuminating analogies in the midst of what appears superficially to be infinite and hopeless variety, but also to discern common principles of justice and policy underlying the various jural problems involved. An indirect, yet very practical, consequence is that it frequently becomes feasible, by virtue of such analysis, to use as persuasive authorities judicial precedents that might otherwise seem altogether irrelevant. If this point be valid with respect to powers, it would seem to be equally so as regards all of the other basic conceptions of the law. In short, the deeper the analysis, the greater become one's perception of fundamental unity and harmony in the law.

The antagonism is evident in the culmination of a discovery of 'fundamental unity and harmony in the law'. Even more so, when this harmony is effected through a

[34] The clarity can be advanced further by noting the point made above that the fundamental elements (atomic components) of the law are the legal relations rather than the conceptions. For the conceptions do generate logical connections between themselves (eg, rights and duties can mutually be inferred from each other), but the legal relations do not, affirmatively, or combinatorially, as Postema puts it. There are only logical inferences of negation, as has been mentioned above.

[35] Similarly, Postema (2011: 103): 'although Hohfeld's analysis puts the question of the combinatorial principles clearly in view, he offered nothing towards answering it'.

[36] ibid 105.

greater use of 'judicial precedents' centred on the identification of the 'basic conceptions of the law'. This makes it clear that the 'common principles of justice and policy' mentioned earlier in the excerpted passage, which might suggest a Realist concern with extra-legal influences, are rather to be apprehended by means of a systematic exposition of legal doctrine.

Something like this realisation appears eventually to have hit Karl Llewellyn (a former student of Hohfeld at Yale). Postema cites the reference by the historian Natalie Hull to Llewellyn's observation in the course of his 1955 'Lectures on Jurisprudence' that if Hohfeld had completed the work on his analytical scheme then war would have broken out between the Realist project and Hohfeld's analysis.[37] Similar reservations were expressed by Arthur Corbin.[38]

Hohfeld's ambition for a legal unity and harmony that is not dependent on extra-legal factors involves a vision of law, and the use of legal materials, that is ultimately formalist. However, this formalist vision of law is predicated by Hohfeld wholly on the legal relations level of his analytical scheme in the passage where the ambition is expressed. And if Postema is correct in portraying the limitations of what can be entailed by the scheme of legal relations alone, then it cannot support Hohfeld's formalism any more than it can support a Realist anti-formalist vision of law. These are matters of complete indifference for that part of Hohfeld's analytical scheme.

Nothing Hohfeld himself states about the fundamental legal relations, (A)–(D), or about the correlative positions found within them, contradicts Postema's observations. The very tentative aspiration for a completed analytical scheme commences with Hohfeld (1919: 64) pointing out that the fundamental conceptions of power and liability can be found in a variety of what amount to aggregate legal positions: 'conditional sales of personalty, escrow transactions, option agreements, agency relations, powers of appointment, etc'. From this his lofty ambition proceeds, on the assumption that the common elements of power and liability in these diverse settings will bring with them a unified harmony of law, justice and policy. As an argument, this would be as convincing as moving from the realisation that all the words in a newspaper contained the common elements of the letters of the alphabet to reaching the conclusion that all the articles in the newspaper were united in providing a coherent and consistent view of the world.

But Hohfeld does not make an argument. He proclaims a vision. What is significant is that his vision discloses a view of law which derives a legal formalism primarily from a deeper grasp of the fundamental legal relations. Notwithstanding his insistence at that very point of the need for an additional aggregate-level analysis,[39] his unwarranted conviction[40] that the legal relations level of analysis

[37] Hull (1997: 107, fn 109). Similarly, Twining (2012: 97), on Llewellyn's waning enthusiasm for Hohfeld, referring to the same lecture.

[38] Hull (1997: 105).

[39] Hohfeld (1919: 64, fn 100). This constitutes the most explicit endorsement by Hohfeld of the need for the dual-level analysis, but is by no means the only evidence of his support for it.

[40] I delve further into the possible reasons for Hohfeld's conviction in the broader project mentioned in n 1.

will deliver the major accomplishments of his completed scheme can account for his continuing preoccupation with that level, and his subsequent neglect of the aggregate-level analysis.

In the absence of the fulfilment of Hohfeld's formalist vision for law, the lack of a comprehensive and consistent body of legal doctrine will ensure that as a practising lawyer one has further opportunities to venture outside the arrangement of legal materials as merely composed of legal relations, and explore the political, social and normative aspects[41] of the parties' conflicting interests which can only be done by considering their aggregate positions, as landlord or tenant, spouse or creditor, etc. This, at least, follows if one adopts an anti-formalist, realist understanding of law.

If one is inclined to be less realist and more formalist, then any degree of formalism short of the perfectionism embraced in Hohfeld's vision still leads to the need for aggregate-level analysis in encountering practical legal problems. There are two arguments to support this conclusion. In a less than perfect body of legal doctrine where there are disputes over competing formalist views of the law, it can be argued that it is impossible to resolve those disputes from within a wholly formalist setting; however the decision is reached between them, it cannot but help dealing with extra-legal considerations involving different perspectives on justice and policy which can only operate at an aggregate level.[42]

If this first argument which seeks to breach formalism is rejected by somehow introducing a purely formalist venue for staging and resolving the conflicting formalist views, then still the requirement for an aggregate-level analysis can be demonstrated by a second argument. From all that has been previously said about the legal relations level analysis, it is clear that the dispute between the two formalist views must involve the assertion and denial of a particular legal relation connecting the two parties: the assertion of one legal relation and the counter-assertion of its negation or opposite. But, as we have seen, the mere assertion of a legal relation cannot amount to any argument in favour of it. And this holds even if that argument is made on doctrinal grounds alone. In order to make an argument the legal relation in question will have to be linked into a doctrinal account of its significance. And doctrinal significance cannot be found over an individual legal relation any more than a political, social or normative significance can. In the same way that these considerations require an aggregate-level analysis, so too do doctrinal considerations. Whether, for example, an individual right-duty relation to pay a sum of money is doctrinally required is a meaningless question, until one can link it into a doctrinal understanding of, say, a contractual obligation which necessarily involves the aggregate positions of the contracting parties—and, if the doctrinal situation is more specialised, then different aggregate positions of landlord and tenant, purchaser and vendor of land, husband and wife, adult and minor, etc, etc.

[41] I use this triple expression loosely here to indicate that non-doctrinal (non-legal) factors may encompass policies and values of different kinds.

[42] For an argument along these lines, see Halpin (2013).

We may conclude then that, not simply at the legal relations level but also within a completed Hohfeldian scheme incorporating the aggregate level of analysis, Hohfeldian analysis is capable of equally portraying more or less realist and more or less formalist-doctrinal understandings of the practice of law; and remains neutral as between them.

IV. Establishing Neutrality in a Fourth Location: Theory of Legal Rights

These three locations of the neutrality of the Hohfeldian scheme of analysis are at least suggestive that when it comes to devising a theory of legal rights Hohfeldian neutrality will apply here too, thus again requiring 'additional resources' to determine the outcome of the dispute between competing theories; to resolve which theory of legal rights is favoured, and to make it clear on what basis that favour is bestowed. One perfunctory argument to enhance this suggestivity is to take a theory of legal rights as amounting to a broader instance of legal doctrinal theory, as encountered in section III.B, and then to infer that Hohfeldian analysis in this broader context will share the characteristic of neutrality that was established in the narrower context of a specific doctrinal theory, such as one covering property rights.

As an introduction to a more involved argument to establish the neutrality in this fourth location, it is worth pausing on the significance of this cursory point. The neutrality of Hohfeldian analysis with respect to legal doctrinal theory amounts to a finding that there does not exist (or, at least, Hohfeldian analysis does not provide) an analytical resource that is capable of providing greater clarity to our doctrinal understanding of law in a way that supersedes working through the elementary resources (normative or doctrinal) that underpin that area of law. Take the example of the dispute over public access to the ocean through a private beach. One theory of property rights might favour one outcome to the dispute where another theory favours the other. Neither theory is ruled out by the Hohfeldian scheme any more than any outcome is ruled out, as we saw in section III.A. The promotion of one doctrinal theory or one outcome has to resort to the strength of arguments that can be derived from basic normative or doctrinal considerations.

That is to say, the working out of legal disputes either in the instant case or at a (doctrinal) theoretical level is not a purely analytical matter (although clarity of analysis can assist greatly), but is rather a matter of exploring the normative and doctrinal positions adopted by the law. That such positions are not analytically fixed but contingent upon the circumstances of the society and the legal tradition in which the law is found is evident from the variations that can be observed across time and across jurisdictions. Family law organised around the central idea of *patria potestas* is not an analytical failure, but an expression of family law reflecting the allocation of power and authority in the ancient Roman patriarchal society. So too with the Roman law on slavery.

If we want to suggest that a general theory of legal rights is any different, then one of two implications follows. First, we may be implying that such a theory is analytically elevated and cut off from the world of legal disputes; it is of such rarefied abstraction that it does not touch upon the material points of conflict found in legal disputes. I find it difficult to see how this could remain a theory of rights (particularly, legal rights) in any valuable sense. In any event, contemporary attempts to theorise (legal) rights clearly do grapple with the material points of conflict found in legal disputes in expounding their theories. Alternatively, we may be implying that by moving from particular doctrinal theory to a general theory of (legal) rights we are opening up additional theoretical resources which are capable of addressing and resolving the issues in legal disputes, without having to fall back on the arguments derived from basic normative or doctrinal considerations mentioned above. The question then arises as to what the nature of this additional resource might be.

If the general theory of rights were itself a normative theory, in the sense that it provides an account of rights from a specific normative outlook (libertarian, neo-liberal, dignity-based, etc) then the presence of an additional resource within that theory would be obvious. Moreover, such a resource would normatively promote the resolution of disputes in accordance with the outlook adopted in the theory and neutrality would not be an issue. It may well be that such normative bias of a theory of rights would sit with its deployment of Hohfeldian analysis, but in this case the lack of neutrality does not attach to the Hohfeldian element but to the particular normative premises adopted; there is nothing to prevent the Hohfeldian element being found in an alternative normative theory with different normative premises. In fact, for any thorough normative theory of legal rights we would expect this to be the case, given the acceptance of the need for such a theory to deal with the material points of conflict found in legal disputes, and the recognition of the Hohfeldian scheme as providing an effective analytical framework for representing the points of conflict found in legal disputes. So far, no threat to Hohfeldian neutrality.

More perplexing is the case where the additional resource within the general theory of rights, that can be relied on to resolve the issues in legal disputes without falling back on basic normative or doctrinal considerations, is considered to be analytical—and, is regarded as Hohfeldian in character. The fundamental challenge here is to show how the neutrality of the Hohfeldian scheme found in the three previous locations can suddenly become transformed to provide (a theoretical account of) the determination of legal rights, which amounts to determining the resolution of legal disputes: the dispute is resolved in favour of the right-holder.

I suggest here reasons for doubting that this challenge can be met. Within this section, I engage with the fascination between will and interest theories of rights at a very general level and argue that no matter where the theoretical emphasis is analytically placed (on will, interest, or some hybridity or substitute) within a theory of rights, a Hohfeldian analytical resource will always permit an alternative without providing the means of determining which should prevail. This stage of the argument is deliberately undertaken in very general terms as the contours of actual theories are constantly changing, and, indeed, we are treated to some of the latest developments in other contributions to this book. Subsequently, in the following section, I do engage with particular details of one iteration of Leif Wenar's theory of rights in order to illustrate in a more precise way how the grounds I offer for doubt can interact with a particular theoretical position.[43]

Recall from section II that under the Hohfeldian scheme no (loosely described) legal right, in whichever specific Hohfeldian form it is found, exists outside a (potential) legal dispute with another party. Each of the four dominant positions correlates to a subordinate position of another party. The aspect of domination varies (requiring your conduct, engaging in conduct myself without your preventing it, an ability to change your position, preventing you changing my position) but in every case it is secured by a subordinate position of the other party. In different ways, the dominant positions provide an advantage to the (loosely described) right-holder. Hohfeld's case is that these four positions represent the only types of rights that can be claimed in a dispute before a court, and where each of these four positions is found the respective subordinate position is found alongside it. So, every case of a legal right involves some type of advantage to the right-holder and at the same time some type of disadvantage to the subordinate party.

The setting for a legal right is then always a dispute involving a conflict of potential advantages which one side will win and the other side will lose. Whoever wins gets the legal right, but equally whoever loses drops the legal right that would otherwise have been gained. This follows from the relationship of opposition between Hohfeld's legal relations, (A)–(D). Where I gain the advantage of requiring your conduct, you drop the advantage of engaging in conduct yourself without my preventing it. Where I gain the advantage of engaging in conduct myself without your preventing it, you drop the advantage of requiring my conduct. Where I gain the advantage of being able to change your position, you drop the advantage of preventing me changing your position. Where I gain the advantage of preventing you changing my position, you drop the advantage of being able to change my position. So, the presence of a legal right, in the setting of a legal dispute, is always the occasion for the absence of a legal right.

Theories of legal rights tend to address the nature of legal rights (what advantages are secured) conflated with the justification for legal rights (why those advantages should be secured).[44] Any of the answers proposed to these questions,

[43] Wenar (2005). I choose this from the many theories of rights available as being in many respects closest to the approach to Hohfeldian analysis I develop in this and related projects, and accordingly as providing the potential for the sharpest expression of difference. The key attribute that keeps Wenar's several functions theory on the other side, together with will and interest theories, is his boast that it constitutes a third theory on the nature of rights: 250, fn 46.

[44] A stimulating take on this point is offered by reading Rowan Cruft's contribution to the present volume as suggesting that the common feature of analytical circularity he identifies within theories of rights conceals normative assumptions.

commencing with furthering the will of the right-holder or furthering the interest of the right-holder, and extending to furthering the several functions, or measure of control that advances interests on balance, or the desires of beings of a particular kind, faces two dilemmas. The first dilemma operates at the *descriptive-analytical* level. If Hohfeld has already accurately and exhaustively portrayed the different types of advantage found in the dominant legal positions of the right-holder, as indicated above, what point is there in seeking some synthesising notion to cover all these cases? Even if it comes off, it will be analytically impoverishing in covering up a significant layer of distinctions that Hohfeld has revealed. As for the prospects of its being pulled off, these appear remote in the context of the particular distinctions Hohfeld has introduced, and remoter still in the light of the convoluted nature of the will-interest debate and its more recent progeny.

The second dilemma operates at the *normative-justificatory* level. Suppose there exists a theory of legal rights that accounts for the nature of all established legal rights in a justificatory way: all legal rights are justified for promoting this (type of) advantage of the right-holder. The problem here is that if the theory is truly general it will also justify all the failed legal rights that were lost when the particular legal rights that prevail within a system of law were established: all the opposite advantages that were lost by the subordinate parties.

The plausibility of distinguishing according to the promoted (type of) advantage between established rights and failed rights is severely diminished when account is taken of two factors. First, as an abstract point, the close mirroring within Hohfeld's opposite relations between winning rights and losing rights, such that the lost right of one person's subordinate position becomes the winning right of another person's dominant position. Second, the empirical variation in which rights turn out to be winning rights or losing rights within different jurisdictions and at different times. How can the same right be justified on one occasion but not on the other? In order to overcome these factors a normative justification of a very specific set of legal rights would have to be mounted, taking us far from the ambition of a general theory of rights. And as with the case considered above of a general theory of rights from a specific normative outlook, it would be the introduction of the tailored normative justifications within the theory that would destroy its neutrality, not affecting the basic neutrality of Hohfeldian analysis in this fourth location.

V. A Dispute Theory of Rights

It is one thing to argue that general theories of legal rights are incapable of analytically establishing the nature of rights in such a way that a particular set of legal rights can be determined, and be justified. This still leaves the problem of how we can analytically identify a set of legal rights as legal rights, and how we can account for the normative or justificatory force of those rights. Furthermore, if, as we have presumed throughout this essay, the Hohfeldian analytical framework is sound and so can be expected to figure in a theoretical representation of legal rights, we are still required to incorporate Hohfeldian insights into any theoretical response we make.

The answer, I suggest, is to abandon completely the search for a uniform nature of legal rights and to commence instead with their practical emergence as a set of legal rights. I call this alternative approach a dispute theory of rights, to emphasise the presence of legal disputes at the heart of this approach, in accordance with the key precepts of Hohfeldian analysis. However, to label it as a theory of rights at all would be misleading, if the use of theory here suggests a quest for a uniform understanding of legal rights. Perhaps more accurately, we should talk of a theoretical framework for identifying and understanding the characteristics of legal rights across the vast variety of instances that exist, varying in the sort of advantages they convey and in the normative justifications for allowing those advantages in different circumstances, in different jurisdictions, and at different times.

Starting at the point of a dispute avoids any preconception as to what a legal right can be. It can be anything over which there can be a dispute, and materialises when that dispute is won. The value of Hohfeldian analysis at this point is in identifying the four basic aspects of human relations[45] that can give rise to a dispute. It does not follow that every incident of human behaviour that happens to fit one of these forms will produce a dispute; one has to await some motivational conflict between the advantages and disadvantages of the parties before a dispute will occur. You engage in scratching your ear in your own home and I, your neighbour, do not require you to do otherwise. Preventing you would be of no advantage to me, so in these circumstances no dispute can arise, and to talk of a legal right here would be otiose.[46]

What might turn out to be a dispute cannot be theoretically predetermined through a theory of legal rights. So, Leif Wenar is tackling the issue the wrong way around when he suggests that we need a theory of legal rights such that a citizen's immunity against the council awarding him a pension should not be recognised as a legal right.[47] It all depends on whether a dispute arises, and, as it happens, a dispute could arise in such a situation. The widow of Mr Brown stands to be paid his council pension, but as Mr Brown died at work due to the council's negligence, as a matter of principle she does not want to receive it. She wants nothing more to do with the council. The council motivated by guilt insists on paying the pension. Now there is a dispute, and if she wins it Mrs Brown will have an immunity against the council awarding her the pension against her will.

45 Admittedly, there is a restriction to two-party human relations, but even so, to get these cleared up would be a phenomenal achievement before moving on to more complex scenarios.

46 The recognition of a dispute-right does not depend on an actual dispute arising before the courts. The common practice of expounding the law in terms of hypothetical disputes suffices. The point is that talk of a legal right becomes otiose when not even a hypothetical dispute could be constructed on the specific facts.

47 Wenar (2005: 249).

In the same iteration of his theory of rights, Wenar treats some rights as 'molecular' or 'complex molecular' rights, as being composed of a number of Hohfeldian relations with other parties (2005: 249). This is insightful in directing out attention away from a preoccupation with independent legal relations towards an aggregate analysis. However, there is a danger here in suggesting that the multiple legal relations ('Hohfeldian incidents') constitute a right, such as the right over one's own body: 'made up of multiple Hohfeldian incidents' (2005: 234). The right over one's body, as an aggregate legal position is not simply constituted by legal relations but, as we saw with the aggregate position of a tenancy by the entirety in section III.A, provides the venue for normative or doctrinal considerations related to that position to play their part in determining the outcome of a contested legal relation. Moreover, for an accurate account of the finer detail of these legal relations, we have to await the emergence of a dispute. Wenar comes close to admitting this in a footnote concession (2005: 234, fn 12) that a general depiction of Hohfeldian incidents is inadequate: the right over one's body is not constituted (in part) by a liberty to move one's body, since some movements will be in conflict with the potential advantages of others and will not be allowed. Just where precisely these qualifications will be made cannot be theoretically predetermined but must await the emergence of a dispute and its resolution.

The real innovation of the dispute theory of rights is that it allows for the practical outworking of legal rights, undetermined by theoretical preconceptions and neutral as between normative predispositions, within a particular legal system, but it still needs to demonstrate that the legal rights emerging are fortified with normative force for that particular jurisdiction. The key to achieving this is to concentrate on a dual-level Hohfeldian scheme whereby individual legal relations as the outcome of a legal dispute are connected to the normative or doctrinal outlook regarding the aggregate position to which those legal relations are attached, within a particular society or jurisdiction. That is not to say that all opportunity for a theory of rights is abandoned. Lower-level doctrinal theory may still interact with the understanding of the aggregate position of the party. The critical point is that such doctrinal theory may itself be contested and is not necessarily determinative of the outcome of legal disputes. A higher-level grand theory or ideology may also be acknowledged if we expand the dual level analysis to a triple-level analytical scheme, allowing for the influence of these grander theoretical ambitions to break through the normative interface at the aggregate level, without necessarily being directly concerned with the details of the positions of the parties at the level of a legal dispute at level (1).[48] The intricate interworkings of these three levels of analysis are explored in greater detail in the broader project I have mentioned.

[48] See Lehavi (2013: ch 1), for a stimulating suggestion that legal renderings of property are distinct from those portrayed in other disciplines (including philosophy). Lehavi explains this as based on different concerns with (broader) values and (narrower) rights—the legal concern with rights feeding into specific structural and institutional features of property in the law.

It may be helpful for present purposes to provide a diagrammatic representation, which follows below in Figures 1–4.

The triple-level analytical scheme provides a framework for effective analytical and normative argument; it does not of itself authoritatively determine the outcome of such arguments. In its application to property, its proper use is as compatible with finding a uniform concept of property in the law of a particular jurisdiction undergirded by a consistent normative outlook on property, as it is with disclosing divergent forms of property informed by a variety of normative outlooks. As it is also compatible with revealing analytically an incoherent state of property law riven by contested normative outlooks.[49] More generally, it does not in itself impose a coherent account (at whatever theoretical level) or a uniform justification of the legal rights found in a particular jurisdiction.

The perceived aggregate, composed of a number of constituent legal relations, may on closer scrutiny be more accurately represented by two putative aggregates, differing over how a contested (but not yet settled) legal relation is to be determined. Bearing in mind that the contested point can be represented as a conflict between two opposing legal relations, as we noted above, we can represent it as $LR_n \vee \neg LR_n$. This point of conflict can then be related to the alternative views of the aggregate (A and B), which both take the established core and adapt it by adding either LR_n or $\neg LR_n$ to it, as in Figure 1.

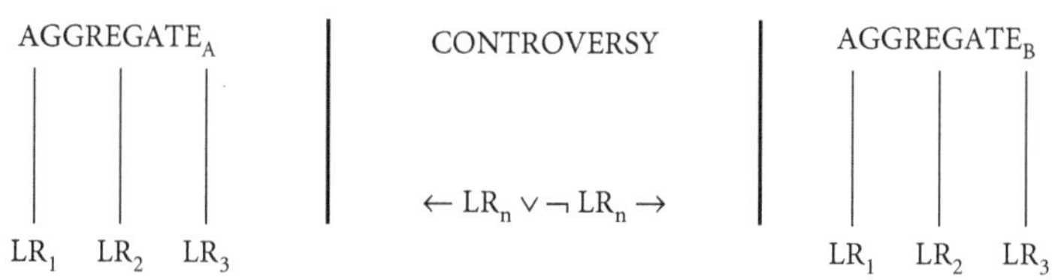

Figure 1: Competing putative aggregates

The controversy represented as 'either LR_n or $\neg LR_n$' will materialise as the affirmation of a legal relation on one side and the affirmation of the legal relation amounting to its negation on the other side, such as an (A) relation and a (B) relation where the controversy is over the recognition of a duty; or a (C) relation and a (D) relation where the controversy is over the recognition of a power, as it was in *Craft*. Where there is no point of controversy at the time in which the law is being considered, the central column of conflict in the above diagram would be omitted, and the two sides merged. However, the potential for emerging controversy should not be ignored.

The diagram in Figure 1 represents the relationship between level (1) legal relations and level (2) aggregate. However, we have noticed that the aggregate level

[49] It is significant that the two recent pluralist approaches to property, found in Dagan (2011), and Alexander and Peñalver (2012), take a perfectionist rather than contested approach to a plurality of approaches to property. However, this is not a necessary outcome once a plurality has been detected.

is not simply constituted by a composite set of legal relations. At the aggregate level, we also find the doctrinal or normative significance of that composition, that is to say, its legal doctrinal status or its significance according to the particular (extra-legal) values prevailing in the society whose law we are considering (for diagrammatic purposes, SOCIO-POLITICAL). These may be regarded as distinct influences upon the aggregate, whose relative importance or unimportance will depend on the guild understanding of law adopted. However, we should acknowledge some interconnection between the two.[50] The socio-political/doctrinal aspect of the aggregate then acts as an umbrella over the composite aspect of the aggregate, providing meaning to established aggregates and offering a venue in which contested, putative aggregates can be resolved. We can portray this in an expanded version of the diagram, in Figure 2.

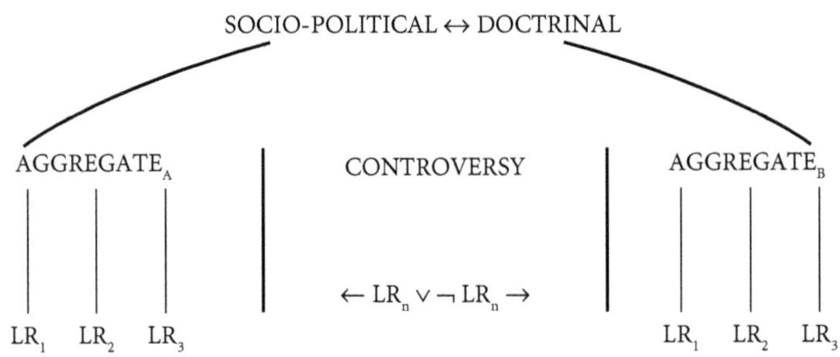

Figure 2: Expanded representation of the aggregate

Note that a purely doctrinal (formalist) rendering of the 'umbrella' would produce a closed legal understanding of the relevant law: doctrinally informed aggregate + constituent legal relations. Whereas recognition of at least some socio-political content within the umbrella directly opens up level (2) to influence from level (3).

To complete the diagram we need to add the third level of ideology or grand theory that may impact upon the socio-political[51] (and through that the doctrinal) aspect of the aggregate, despite being unconcerned with the precise outworking of those socio-political values at the legal relations level. At this point, we can

[50] I point out more fully, in the broader project mentioned in n 1, the connection between the socio-political values and doctrine, and argue in Halpin (2013) that in the face of controversy, doctrine will necessarily yield to socio-political values.

[51] Both ideology and grand theory on level 3 are to be distinguished from the local socio-political values of a particular society on level (2), in being removed from the specific considerations that affect the shaping of a particular society's values as then transmitted through its laws. So, one could identify neo-liberal values as a broad ideology at level (3), and different sets of neo-liberal values worked out in different societies at level (2). Grand theory, similarly, can be identified at level (3) separately from any influence it might have on different societies in different ways at level (2). For discussion of grand theory and property, see Penner and Smith (2013: xix): 'Locke, Hume, Grotius, Kant, and Hegel and their views of the nature of property ... remain a continuing source of inspiration and puzzlement'.

also add to the diagram numbering for the three different levels of analysis, and an indication of the scope of and interfaces between each level. This provides us with a triple-level analytical scheme, as depicted in Figure 3.

A further version of the diagram in Figure 4 provides some sort of demarcation between the strictly legal and the extra-legal normative influences. How starkly this demarcation is to be taken depends on the guild understanding of law adopted, as pointed out above. In practice, anything less than the implementation of a perfectionist-formalist notion of law will afford some active significance to the horizontal interface at level (2) between socio-political and doctrinal, as well as the vertical interface between ideological and socio-political. Even in the absence of an active interface at level (2), a purely formalist notion of law would be the repository of historical normative influences.

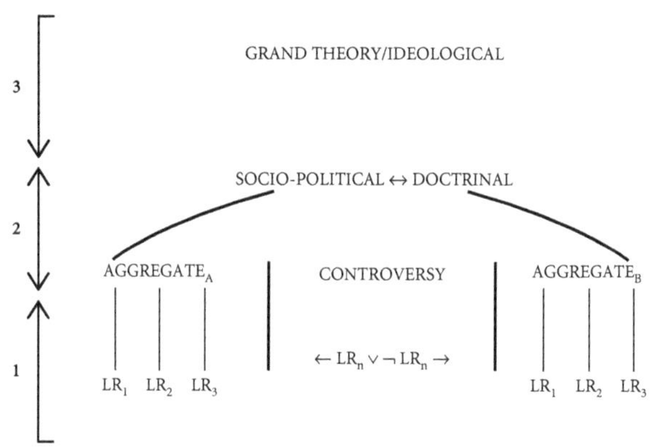

Figure 3: A triple-level analytical scheme

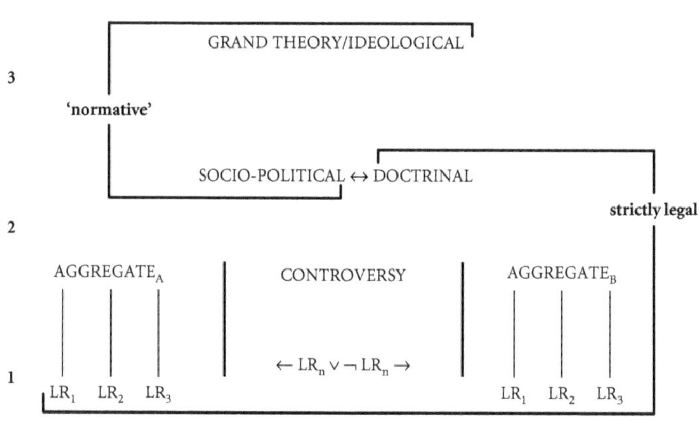

Figure 4: Legal and extra-legal influences

This triple-level analytical scheme does not preclude the emergence of a uniform theory of legal rights, although, from all that has been said above, its arrival is not anticipated any time soon. What it does do in promoting the dispute theory of rights is to allow us to trace the emergence and particular normative justifications of the legal rights that are found in different systems of law. It does this in a way that incorporates Hohfeldian analytical insights in differentiating between different types of legal rights while maintaining the neutrality of the Hohfeldian scheme.

VI. Concluding Reflections

The combination of the dispute theory of rights with the triple-analytical scheme might reasonably be cast as opposing a uniform theory of legal rights, although, as I have just mentioned, it does not render it impossible. What it does provide is the theoretical space to discuss alternative sets of legal rights and alternative normative justifications for legal rights.[52] If our actual experience of legal rights involves us participating in a venue for argument, then a theoretical framework for exploring the nature of that argument and permitting the tracing of different normative outlooks is likely to be more illuminating than a uniform theory purporting to impose a definitive understanding of the nature and normative justification of legal rights. This, ultimately, is the strongest case for adopting the approach suggested in this essay.

If the approach is accepted as a fruitful way of theorising about legal rights, there remains the query lurking in the introduction as to whether a similar approach can be adopted for moral and political rights. A query whose significance is heightened by the efforts here to maintain a faithful representation of Hohfeld's analytical framework, which has generally been regarded as applying as much to moral and political rights as to legal rights.

Simple transferability of the approach developed here is not, I think, an option. The emphasis on dispute is more easily accommodated in the institutional setting of law. Nevertheless, the presence of conflicting potential advantages between the right-holder and other members of the community, and the logical opposition between the granting of one political or moral right to a dominant party and the dropping of another right by a subordinate party, are two features that are transferable to the political and moral normative domains. There is also observable controversy over a number of political and moral rights. In the absence of effective machinery for resolving disputes within those domains the controversies may spill over into the legal domain for resolution.[53] If this is the case, theorising about legal rights should be regarded as a priority.

[52] Recent calls for such a space can be discerned in Stewart (2012) and Hayward (2013).

[53] For general discussion on this point see Halpin (2006).

References

Alexander, G and Peñalver, E (2012) *An Introduction to Property Theory* (Cambridge: Cambridge University Press).

Blackstone, W (1765–69) *Commentaries on the Laws of England* (Oxford: Clarendon Press).

Burns, R (1985) 'Blackstone's Theory of the "Absolute" Rights of Property' 54 *University of Cincinnati Law Review* 67.

Dagan, H (2011) *Property: Values and Institutions* (New York: Oxford University Press).

Douglas, S and McFarlane, B (2013) 'Defining Property Rights' in J Penner and H Smith (eds), *Philosophical Foundations of Property Law* (Oxford: Oxford University Press).

Fennell, L (2012) 'Lumpy Property' 160 *University of Pennsylvania Law Review* 1955.

Grey, T (1980) 'The Disintegration of Property' XXII *Nomos: Property* 69.

Halpin, A (2006) 'Ideology and Law' 11 *Journal of Political Ideologies* 153.

—— (2013) 'Language, Truth and Law' in M Freeman and F Smith (eds), 15 *Current Legal Issues: Law and Language* (Oxford: Oxford University Press).

Hayward, T (2013) 'On Prepositional Duties' 123 *Ethics* 264.

Hohfeld, W (1913) 'Some Fundamental Legal Conceptions as Applied in Judicial Reasoning' 23 *Yale Law Journal* 16.

—— (1917) 'Fundamental Legal Conceptions as Applied in Judicial Reasoning' 26 *Yale Law Journal* 710.

—— (1919) *Fundamental Legal Conceptions as Applied in Judicial Reasoning*, edited with an introduction by Walter Wheeler Cook (New Haven, CT: Yale University Press).

Hull, N (1997) *Roscoe Pound and Karl Llewellyn: Searching for an American Jurisprudence* (Chicago: University of Chicago Press).

Lehavi, A (2013) *The Construction of Property: Norms, Institutions, Challenges* (Cambridge: Cambridge University Press).

Merrill, T (2012) 'Property as Modularity' 125 *Harvard Law Review Forum* 151.

Merrill, T and Smith, H (2000) 'Optimal Standardization in the Law of Property: The *Numerus Clausus* Principle' 110 *Yale Law Journal* 1.

—— (2001) 'What Happened to Property in Law and Economics?' 111 *Yale Law Journal* 357.

Michelon, C (2014) 'Virtuous Circularity: Positive Law and Particular Justice' 27 *Ratio Juris* 271.

Penner, J and Smith, H (2013) 'Introduction' in J Penner and H Smith (eds), *Philosophical Foundations of Property Law* (Oxford: Oxford University Press).

Postema, G (2011) *Legal Philosophy in the Twentieth Century: The Common Law World* (Dordrecht: Springer).

Singer, J (2009) 'Democratic Estates: Property Law in a Free and Democratic Society' 94 *Cornell Law Review* 1009.
Smith, H (2012a) 'Property as the Law of Things' 125 *Harvard Law Review* 1691.
—— (2012b) 'On the Economy of Concepts in Property' 160 *University of Pennsylvania Law Review* 2097.
Sparkes, P (2012) 'Certainty of Property: *Numerus Clausus* or the Rule with No Name?' 20 *European Review of Private Law* 769.
Stewart, H (2012) 'The Definition of a Right' 3 *Jurisprudence* 319.
Twining, W (2012) *Karl Llewellyn and the Realist Movement*, 2nd edn (Cambridge: Cambridge University Press).
Van der Walt, A (2009) *Property in the Margins* (Oxford: Hart Publishing).
Wenar, L (2005) 'The Nature of Rights' 33 *Philosophy & Public Affairs* 223.

2

Legal Competence and Legal Power

VISA AJ KURKI[1]

I. Preliminaries

This essay is focused on the notions of legal power and legal competence. Even though Wesley Newcomb Hohfeld's definition of power (1913) has been very influential, many theorists have deemed the Hohfeldian power be too wide-ranging. I argue that Hohfeld's original definition of powers has its uses; it shouldn't be replaced but rather amplified by a notion of competence that only includes certain types of powers.

As is well known, Hohfeld introduced eight fundamental legal conceptions, four of which concern the permissibility or obligatoriness of a given type of conduct, and the other four how legal relations can be changed. *X*'s having a Hohfeldian legal power with respect to *Y* and *Z* means that *X* can, through volitional conduct, effect a change in a legal relation that currently obtains between *Y* and *Z*. *X* does not actually have to intend to cause the legal change in question as long as *X*'s volitional conduct causes the change. The Hohfeldian power is consequently quite wide-ranging, given that hitting somebody constitutes an exercise of a power because legal relations have been changed through the performance a volitional action. Thus, a homeless person could commit a crime in order to spend the night in jail, and this would constitute an exercise of a legal power according to Hohfeld's account. For many theorists, this constitutes a counterexample to the Hohfeldian conception. Another well-known putative counterexample is moving house, which is an intentional action that has legal consequences, but should, according to many theorists, not constitute the exercise of a legal power, even though this is often merely stipulated.[2] The Hohfeldian power is also broader than

[1] PhD Candidate, University of Cambridge. I would like to thank Matthew Kramer, Andrew Halpin and Timothy Liau for their useful comments on a draft of this paper. Special thanks go to Mark McBride for inviting me to contribute to this volume, as well as for his generous help in finalising the essay. I am grateful to the Kone Foundation whose generous scholarship has allowed me to pursue doctoral studies in Cambridge.

[2] Joseph Raz, for instance, simply stipulates that moving house does not amount to the exercise of a legal power: 'There are many other acts which effect a legal change but are not the exercise of legal powers. By changing my residence from one town to another, or from one country to another, I change my rights and duties, but I do not have a legal power to effect these changes by such action' (1972: 80).

the type of power that HLA Hart was referring to when laying out the notion of power-conferring rules in *The Concept of Law* (1964: 27–28): rules that criminalise an act, such that the doing of the act is the exercise of a Hohfeldian power, are not Hartian power-conferring rules. Finally, even though will theorists often identify right-holding as one's Hohfeldian power to enforce and extinguish others' duties, they, too, are primarily interested in a certain subgroup of Hohfeldian powers to the exclusion of, for example, delicts.

For reasons just mentioned, theorists such as Joseph Raz (1972), Neil MacCormick (1981), Andrew Halpin (1996) and Jaap Hage (2009), have propounded more limited conceptions of legal powers that would exclude the capacity to change one's legal position through committing crimes, but include the capacity to contract. In section II, I point out certain problems in their theories and offer an improved definition of the same concept; however I will call the concept 'competence' rather than 'power'. I will here build especially on the accounts of Halpin and Hage. The necessary and sufficient conditions of legal competence that these two theorists have been seeking to formulate can be explicated rigorously in terms of *minimal sufficiency*.

The subsequent section—section III—propounds a distinction between *dependent* and *independent* competences. This distinction is central to the explanation of how the legal status of minors differs from that of individuals who are *sui iuris*, as competences held by minors are very often of the dependent type. In the closing section IV, I argue that Hohfeldian powers that are not competences are still a useful category that can be used to make certain important distinctions.

II. Defining and Refining Competence

The term 'act-in-the-law' (also 'legal act', 'legal transaction') is used, especially among continental jurists, to refer to intentional acts that constitute the creation, upholding or termination of entitlements, particularly in the field of private law. 'Competence', on the other hand, has to do with one's ability to perform acts-in-the-law.[3]

The notion of competence has been central in Anglo-American legal philosophy ever since Hart made the famous distinction between power-conferring and duty-imposing rules, though he used the label 'power' instead of 'competence' to refer to the notion. He wrote:

> Legal rules defining the ways in which valid contracts or wills or marriages are made do not require persons to act in certain ways whether they wish to or not. Such laws do not impose duties or obligations. Instead, they provide individuals with facilities for realizing their wishes, by conferring legal powers upon them to create, by certain specified

[3] For a good overview of the English-language, German and Scandinavian discussions of this topic, see Spaak (1994).

procedures and subject to certain conditions, structures of rights and duties within the coercive framework of the law (1964: 27–28).

Hart was not referring to Hohfeld's conception of a legal power, but rather to a more circumscribed notion that corresponds with the continental idea of competence. Indeed, Hart himself recognised the relationship between power-conferring rules and competence (1964: 284).

Most theorists who have been unhappy with the expansive Hohfeldian power have attempted to carve out a narrower conception by making reference to the intentions with which an act is performed (eg, MacCormick and Hage). Joseph Raz, though, is an exception; his account focuses instead on the law's reasons for acknowledging that an act effects a legal change:

> An action is the exercise of a legal power only if one of the law's reasons for acknowledging that it effects a legal change is that it is of a type such that it is reasonable to expect that actions of that type will, if they are recognized to have certain legal consequences, standardly be performed only if the person concerned wants to secure these legal consequences (1972: 81).[4]

Raz's account does, for obvious reasons, rule out the homeless-person scenario, but not really the moving-house scenario: if one moves from one place to another, one standardly wants to secure certain legal consequences, such as the duty of everyone else not to enter the new property without permission. In addition, Raz's account is quite complicated and contains a number of evaluative elements, such as 'the law's reasons', reasonable expectations, and the expression 'standardly'. Could a competence rather be identified in the logical structure of the competence-conferring norm? Many theorists have taken this path. Neil MacCormick's account of normative powers is as follows: 'Power is conferred by a rule when the rule contains a condition that is satisfied only by an act performed with the (actual or imputed) intention of invoking the rule' (1981: 98). Andrew Halpin is rather critical of MacCormick's position, even though some of his criticisms can be questioned. For instance, Halpin claims that 'invoking the rule' would have to 'require the conscious reflection upon the law of contract by every consumer who buys a bar of chocolate—or else a denial that the consumer ignorant of the law of contract has the legal power to make a contract' (1996: 142f). However, MacCormick means something quite different with the invoking of a rule: 'Not only do I intend my act as an act fulfilling a condition set in the rule. I intend that the other party recognise that I intend my act as an act fulfilling a condition set in the rule' (1981: 98). The invoking of a rule does, consequently, require a certain degree of awareness of the relevant legal rule, but to describe this level of awareness as 'conscious reflection upon the law of contract' would be too strong.[5]

[4] 'Wants' are of course embedded in Raz's definition, but only such wants that are reasonable to expect in conjunction with standard performances of the relevant type of act, rather than any actually occurrent wants.

[5] The homeless person, on the other hand, could probably be said to have reflected consciously upon criminal law.

MacCormick's definition does, nevertheless, have problems. His reference to rules leaves out competences that are not conferred by rules, such as competences resulting from contracts. In addition, the account—intended as a general account of normative powers—is unsuited for certain types of (putative) legal competences. For instance, it is not obvious that my buying a soft drink from a vending machine has anything to do with my intending to make anyone 'recognise that I intend my act as an act fulfilling a condition' set in a legal norm. It is possible that no one apart from me will ever know that I bought the drink. I have nevertheless altered my legal position in a similar way as if I had bought the drink from a cashier. Given that these types of partly automated transactions are highly important, and serve similar functions to more traditional transactions, we have to look for a different definition.

Halpin deems the paramount feature of a legal power (ie, what I call a competence) to be the *decision* to effect one or more changes in legal positions. Hence, 'whatever the effect of the exercise of a particular power that effect will be decided upon by the power-holder'. This decision is represented by Halpin as $d(r)$ where d is the decision and r the resulting legal relation.[6] The conditions for when legal power p obtains are provided by Halpin in logical notation:[7]

$$[(\mathrm{c} \Rightarrow \mathrm{r})\ \&\ (\mathrm{c} = \mathrm{d(r)})] \Leftrightarrow \mathrm{p}$$

A legal power obtains if and only if condition c results in legal change r, and c is the decision to bring about r (Halpin 1996: 145). This notation is problematic and also quite likely does not represent Halpin's actual position. The problem here is that legal systems normally do not treat decisions as sufficient conditions for legal changes because decisions are not manifested events. Rather, the legal change is typically brought about by a subsequent act, performed with the intention to bring about a desired legal change. If an individual decides to make changes to his will but dies in a car accident before getting to his lawyer's office to sign the new will, the old will remains valid in spite of the decision. Reporting one's decision may occasionally be sufficient to effect a legal change ('I have decided to sack you'), but that reporting is then the requisite act. It is likely that this—the non-sufficiency of decisions for legal changes—is Halpin's actual position as well, which becomes apparent from another passage:

> The power of the judge to pass a mandatory sentence discussed above is sufficient demonstration of the point that legal power may exist without choice … Yet the judge [is] *still required to express their [sic.] decision* … in order to effect the change in legal position that is wrought by the legal power (1996: 151, emphasis added).

[6] For Halpin, r is actually the resulting legal *position* rather than legal *relation*, but I will use 'relation' here because a change in a legal position must always be accompanied by a change in its correlative, and the two correlatives constitute a legal relation.

[7] I've added the brackets to the notation to make clear that the antecedent of the biconditional is the conjunction of $c \Rightarrow r$ and $c = d(r)$. I would like to thank Matthew Kramer for pointing this out.

Here Halpin requires that the decision be expressed in order for the legal change to take place (see also Halpin 1997: 44). We could now modify Halpin's logical notation to take this into account. However, before doing this, we should address yet another issue.

Halpin has formulated his account in terms of decisions, in contrast to scholars such as MacCormick and Hage who have employed the notion of intentions. Decisions and intentions are of course closely related. However, decisions are in this case a more cumbersome concept because acts are typically performed *with* a certain intention but only *preceded by* the decision to perform the act.[8] If one were to employ decisions in one's account, one would have to consider how the decision to perform act *a* can be cancelled by a later decision to omit *a*. One must also solve problematic cases where, for instance, one decides to effect a given change in legal relations but later becomes indifferent to the matter, and then effects that legal change inadvertently. Consider Professor *X* who decides to buy book *A* online at *T1* but neglects to confirm the order. The offer is never placed but rather remains in *X*'s virtual shopping cart, of which she is blissfully unaware. However, later that day *X* realises that book *A* is actually not necessary for her purposes. She would now not order the book, but neither does she bother to cancel the presumed order. Further along she decides to go to the same website to order book *B*, which is better suited for her purposes, and when ordering book *B* at *T2* she also inadvertently confirms the order of book *A*. Has she exercised a legal competence when ordering book *A* at *T2*? We should first note that Halpin excludes the inadvertent exercises of competences; this is a matter I will return to below. Assuming that competences can only be exercised deliberately, we need to ask whether *X's* earlier decision to buy book *A* still 'counts'. An intention-based account can answer the question quite straightforwardly: *X* did not perform the act at *T2* with the intention to buy book *A*, which is why the purchase does not count as a deliberate exercise of competence. Simplicity thus speaks for an intention-based account. A decision-based account, on the other hand, does not have any obvious benefits—and nor are any provided by Halpin.

We can now refine Halpin's definition to include acts performed with certain intentions:

$$[(c \Rightarrow r) \ \& \ (c = a(X,r))] \Leftrightarrow C(X,r)$$

X holds the competence *C* to bring about the legal relation *r* if and only if *c* is a sufficient condition for *r*, and *c* is the act of *X*, performed in order to bring about *r*. However, the definition remains problematic because it can, in fact, still be said to include cases like that of the vagrant. This pertains to a larger problem that has been addressed by many authors, having to do with the exact logical structure of the competence-conferring norm. For instance, Jaap Hage's definition of legal transactions,

[8] One might also argue that some acts are not preceded by any (conscious) decision to perform the act.

that is, acts-in-the-law, is as follows: 'Legal transactions are acts, performed with the intention to bring about changes in the world of law (legal consequences), to which legal rules attach the intended consequences because they were intended' (2009: 107). Hage's definition is correctly focused on the acts that bring about legal consequences. However, his use of the conjunction 'because' is not clear. What does it mean that 'legal rules attach the intended consequences' to the act 'because they were intended'? Does this refer to the legislator's reasons-for-action, as in Raz's definition, or to the formulation of the rules? Does it mean that act *a*, performed with the intention *i(r)* to bring about the legal result *r*, constitutes a legal transaction only if *i(r)* is a necessary condition for *r*? This would exclude cases where *r* can also come about through other means. For instance, there are at least two ways in which the legal consequences associated with a contract can be brought about: intention and reliance. One can intend to enter into a contract, and then express this intention in a way that constitutes entering into a contract. On the other hand, one can also become bound by a contract despite one's not intending it, if one's behaviour leads someone else to believe justifiably that one has intended to enter into the contract in question.[9] Some odd implications follow from the definition that act *a* constitutes a legal transaction if and only if performing *a* with *i(r)* is a necessary condition for *r*. This definition would entail that my entering a contract in a jurisdiction that includes a doctrine of reliance could never be a legal transaction, because the intention would not be a necessary condition of *r*.

The modified account of Halpin's, presented above, employs sufficiency instead—which is, however, also problematic. First, we should note that legal conditions like *c* cover act-types under a certain description, but they can also include more specific act-types. Thus, the act-type of '*X*'s buying some object *O* from *Y*' (*a1*) includes numerous act-types that cover a smaller range of act-tokens, such as '*X*'s buying *O* from *Y* and paying in cash' (*a2*). Obviously, any act-token falling under *a2* also falls under *a1*, and thus the legal condition *c1*, which attaches legal consequences to *a1*, includes legal condition *c2* which attaches the same consequences to *a2*. Similarly—according to the criminal law doctrines that I am familiar with—the type of intent involved in an *actus reus*, 'guilty act', includes acts performed with the intention to effect a change in one's legal status. *X*'s act of robbing-someone-with-the-intention-to-bring-about-the-officials'-duty-to-jail-*X* falls under the act-type of *X*'s robbing someone, and performing any act of the latter type creates the relevant duty of the officials.[10] Such an action would then constitute an exercise of competence because the robbing, performed by *X* in order to bring about *r*, would be a sufficient condition to bring about *r*. This problem could perhaps be solved by a careful differentiation of the different types

[9] These are mere sketches of the concepts.

[10] I am assuming here that the concept of robbing includes *mens rea* as its necessary component.

of intention involved. One might perchance also be able to distinguish between complete laws and deductions from complete laws, and then stipulate that *c* must be a complete law.[11] (Thus, *c1* above would be a complete law and *c2* a deduction from a complete law.) However, a more straightforward solution is to employ the idea of *minimal sufficiency*.

Minimal sufficiency obtains when a set of facts is jointly sufficient for some state of affairs *S* to obtain, and every element in the set is necessary for the sufficiency of the set. Let us contrast minimal sufficiency with joint sufficiency. If my signing a contract is sufficient in order for me to become bound by that contract, then my signing that contract while wearing a green hat is (ordinarily) also sufficient. The signing and the hat-wearing are thus jointly sufficient for the contractual obligations to obtain. However, these two conditions are jointly not *minimally* sufficient because the hat-wearing is, in fact, completely irrelevant for the legal consequence to obtain. Nor is minimal sufficiency equivalent to the logical structure where certain conditions are individually necessary and jointly sufficient for a state of affairs to obtain, because minimal sufficiency does not presuppose that the individual elements, included in a set that is minimally sufficient for *S*, are necessary conditions for *S* itself.

Matthew Kramer has employed minimal sufficiency in *Bentham's test*, which limits the number of third-party right-holders in Kramer's interest theory of rights. According to the test, when determining whether someone is a right-holder under a contract or another legal norm, one needs to examine the minimally sufficient facts that are needed to conclude that a breach of the norm has taken place:

> If and only if at least one minimally sufficient set of facts includes the undergoing of a detriment by some person Q at the hands of some other person R who bears a duty under the contract or norm, Q holds a right—correlative to that duty—under the contract or norm (Kramer 2010: 36–37).[12]

In other words: there may be different ways of establishing that the duty has been breached. If at least one such way necessarily includes establishing that *Q* has undergone detriment, then *Q* holds a claim-right correlative to the duty.

A similar logical structure as with Bentham's test is pertinent here. The case of the homeless person does not have to do with legal competence because there is no way for him to effect the duty-of-the-officials-to-jail-him that would *necessarily* include his having performed *a* with the intention to bring about that duty. It suffices that he performed the prohibited action intentionally, with *mens rea*.

[11] The phrase 'complete law' is used by Raz (1972: 87–88).

[12] Kramer defines minimal sufficiency as follows: 'A set of facts is minimally sufficient to constitute a violation of a legal mandate if and only if (1) the set is sufficient to constitute such a violation, and (2) every element of the set is necessary for the set's sufficiency' (2010: 38). The phrase 'undergoing of a detriment' should be read as 'undergoing of some development that is typically detrimental for a human being', a group or a non-human animal (2010: 37f).

Using the idea of minimal sufficiency, we can define the concepts of legal competence and act-in-the-law:

Legal competence:

(1) *x* holds the competence *C* to effect the legal consequence *r* if and only if *x* can perform an act-in-the-law to bring about *r*.

Act-in-the-law:

Act *a*, performed by *x*, constitutes an act-in-the-law if and only if

(1) *x* performs *a* with the intention to bring about the legal consequence *r*, and
(2) the fact that *x* has performed *a* in order to bring about *r* is an element of a set of actually occurrent conditions minimally sufficient for *r*.

This definition captures the central difference between acts of contracting as opposed to, say, criminal acts, and the essence of powers in Hart's power-conferring rules. In addition, it relies on fewer evaluative notions than Raz's definition. Let us now look at certain features of competence closer.

Initially, even though acts-in-the-law must be performed with the intention to effect a change in legal relations, one does not need to grasp all the relevant legal consequences. Such a requirement would be far too strong; it is very often not the case that one would be aware of every single legal implication of the act that one is about to perform. For instance, the legal consequences of marrying someone are typically very wide-reaching. In the TV show *The Sopranos*, a character chooses to marry a mafioso in order to claim spousal privilege to avoid testifying against him. However, she misunderstands the rules pertaining to the privilege—a privilege which doesn't in fact apply to the couple. Does this mean that she did not exercise a legal competence when marrying him? Quite pointless is a definition of competence according to which only skilled family lawyers really exercise a competence when getting married. Rather, the threshold must be set considerably lower. In the case of a legal contract, it is sufficient to understand that one is agreeing to perform or omit some action, and that one will face certain legal consequences if one does not follow through on one's agreement.

A related important question is that of whether unintentional contracting should constitute an exercise of competence. Both Hage (2009: 107f) and Halpin (1996: 146–47) maintain that an act where one inadvertently enters a contract should not constitute a legal transaction or an exercise of a legal power, respectively. Raz (1972: 81) and MacCormick (1981: 97), on the other hand, do think such cases should be included. Hage and Halpin do have a point. Contracting by reliance does lack the feature that has now been identified as distinctive of legal competences: the attachment of a legal consequence to an act performed with the intention to effect that legal consequence. Accounting for unintentional contracting might also lead to very cumbersome definitions with numerous evaluative elements. However, I side with Raz and MacCormick here—completely excluding unintentional contracting would leave out a great number of acts that are given the exact same legal recognition as standard acts-in-the-law. In addition, unintentional exercises of competences can in fact be included quite elegantly in the definition:

Legal competence:

(1) *X* holds the competence *C* to effect the legal consequence *r* if and only if *X* can perform an act-in-the-law to bring about *r*.
(2) If *X* holds *C*, any act by *X* that effects *r* is an exercise of *C*.

The inclusion of (2) entails that non-intentional promising and contracting by *X* are now included as exercises of the competence of *X*, even though such acts are not acts-in-the-law. I thus distinguish between acts-in-the-law and exercises of competences. The chosen terminology is somewhat arbitrary, but the distinction itself is important: acts-in the-law have to do with how individuals can use the law as a tool 'for realizing their wishes' (Hart 1964: 67), whereas the possibility of exercising competences unintentionally must be justified on other grounds. I do not intend to offer an exhaustive list of such grounds here, but they include the facilitation of trust in generally accepted forms of communication. The possibility of exercising competences unintentionally might also be justified morally by the notion of *opacity respect*, which 'involves abstaining from looking behind the exteriors people present to us as moral agents' (Carter 2011: 551). By not questioning whether an individual has actually intended the legal consequences his or her act effects, we also abstain from questioning that individual's moral agency.[13]

One of the strengths of the way in which non-intentional promises and contracts are included in (2) is that the formulation does not rely on evaluative elements and is neutral between different doctrines of reliance. As long as a legal system treats a given act by *X* as having the same legal consequence as an act-in-the-law (performed by *X*) would have, the act constitutes an exercise of a competence. My account thus does not need to take sides with regard to (say) whether the reliance involved in contracting is *subjective* or *objective*, that is, whether one should focus on how *Y* actually interpreted *X*'s conduct or rather on how a reasonable person would have interpreted that conduct. This brings us to the topic of objective contracts.

One possible objection to the offered theory of competence would be to claim that the theory completely excludes contracts in jurisdictions that adhere to the so-called *objective theory of contract*—so-called because the parties' actual intentions would (supposedly) in these jurisdictions be completely irrelevant to contract formation. The only relevant question would rather be whether a reasonable person would impute the relevant kind of intention to the party, based on that party's conduct. However, objective theories are primarily applied in the *interpretation* of contracts rather than in *establishing whether a contract has been entered into at all* (Smith 1993: 173–76). Daniel Markovits puts this as follows: '[O]nce a contract is established by specific intent, the law is willing, through any number of

[13] However, the scope of application of opacity respect—as laid out by Carter—is limited and has primarily to do with state–citizen relationships.

doctrines concerning both interpretation and gap-filling, to impute to the parties a general intent that their contracts contain optimal terms' (2015: section 3.1). As I noted above, the intention that is necessary for an act-in-the-law need not encompass every legal consequence that performing the act will have. It would be an impractical definition of acts-in-the-law if an act would only constitute an act-in-the-law if one had intended precisely every legal consequence that performing the act constitutes. Thus, the offered account of competence does encompass contracting even when the details of a contract are settled on an objective rather than on a subjective basis.

One could also object to the offered theory of competence that a court can never have direct access to *X*'s mind, but must rather look at the available evidence when trying to determine whether *X* has intended to enter into a contract. However, such evidentiary issues are involved in *any* determination of someone else's mental states; any such objection would prove too much, and thus this does not entail that an intention could not be a condition for a legal consequence.

A further question bearing on the offered theory of competence is what is meant by a 'legal consequence' or 'legal result'. Raz claims that the legal consequences that can be brought about by an exercise of a competence cannot be reduced to simply Hohfeldian legal positions because 'a legal change may consist in change of status or in the creation or liquidation of a legal person, and Hohfeld was mistaken in thinking that these are no more than bundles of rights and duties' (Raz 1972: 81). It is quite unclear what Raz means by 'status' here, and why it wouldn't be reducible to the Hohfeldian positions.[14] In any case, whether *X* is a legal person is indeed a question of the legal positions held by *X*. Unfortunately, I cannot argue for this position here comprehensively but I will make one relevant point.[15]

Legal personality is often defined as the capacity to hold rights and duties. Such a definition can be understood in a multitude of ways—as the capacity to hold claim-rights or will-theory rights, or even as the capacity to hold any Hohfeldian positions. However, no one can have the legal power to grant someone or something the *capacity* to hold any of these positions. Either *X can hold* claim-rights—in which case the legislator *may endow X* with claim-rights—or *X cannot hold* claim-rights—in which case the legislator *may not* do so. There is one relevant exception, however: typically, only legal persons can hold legally enforceable *special rights*, which 'arise out of special transactions between individuals or out of some special relationship in which they stand to each other' and where 'the persons who have the right and those who have the corresponding obligation are limited to the parties to the special transaction or relationship' (Hart 1955: 183). Here we need to distinguish the *conceptual* and the *legal* capacity to hold special rights. Rocks lack the *conceptual* capacity to hold special rights because they cannot hold any legal positions, and there is nothing the legislator can do about that. Slaves, on the other

[14] By 'rights and duties', I take Raz to mean all the Hohfeldian positions.

[15] The whole of my doctoral dissertation, entitled 'A Theory of Legal Personality', addresses this topic.

hand, lacked the *legal* capacity to hold such rights because the legal system did not, for instance, enforce their agreements. But, contrastingly, the legislator can do—indeed, should have done—something about that. And the legal capacity-to-be-endowed-with-a-special-right can be explained in terms of Hohfeldian powers and liabilities. The same applies, *mutatis mutandis*, to exercises of competence that result in the creation of a corporation.

Let us, then, focus on the most central type of corporation, that is, organised human collectivities with a specific legal status.[16] There are two main ways of understanding such collectivities. Some theorists maintain that collectivities can be legal actors in their own right and hence irreducible to their individual members (eg, List and Pettit 2011; Kramer 1998). Such an understanding of collectivities often comes with the inclination to think that corporations can hold legal positions that are irreducible to positions held by the individual members. On the other hand, one can also think that all collectivities are reducible to their individual members. Theorists sympathetic to such a position would understand any talk of the rights and duties of corporations as a shorthand for a complex of legal positions held by the shareholders, the executive board and so on. However, regardless of which position is correct, surely the legislator cannot change this: the ontological status of groups cannot be changed by legal decisions. The legislator may perhaps create a legal framework that facilitates group cohesion, but not more than that. Either the collectivities addressed here are conceptually capable of holding various legal positions, such as claim-rights—in which case they can be endowed with claim-rights and with the powers and liabilities to hold special rights—or they cannot hold these legal positions—in which case they cannot be so endowed. I happen to think that collectivities are capable of holding such positions, but if I were wrong, their legal personality should be understood in terms of a complex of legal positions held by the shareholders, the executive board and so on. Hohfeld's original account of legal consequences is thus unproblematic (on either view).

Competence and legal personality share other connections as well. Legal minors are often understood as not being legal persons in the fullest sense, and one of the hallmarks of legal minority is that minors do not hold as many competences as individuals who are *sui iuris*. For instance, according to the historical Finnish–Swedish doctrine of guardianship (*edusmiehyys* in Finnish, *målsmanskap* in Swedish), a woman could own property in her own name, but it could only be administered by her husband or some other man. The relevant competences were thus held by the male. Historians often associate the steps taken towards women's independence in this regard as steps towards their full recognition as legal persons (see Pylkkänen 2009).

The fact that minors hold fewer competences than majors has been recognised by legal theorists. However, a more neglected topic is the fact that minors' competences are often also qualitatively different. This is an issue I will address next.

[16] Other types of corporations include shell corporations and one-person corporations.

III. Dependent and Independent Competences

Let us at first note two reasons why certain beings' possibilities to exercise competences are limited.

There are some beings (such as infants and non-human animals) that are simply unable to form intentions that pertain to the legal system. I'll use a somewhat silly example: think of a jurisdiction where the staff of any zoo is statutorily required to feed the animals in their zoo whenever the creatures signal that they want to be fed. Would the statute endow the animals with competences? The animals could very well signal their need with the intention-to-be-provided-with-food, but they could not perform this act with the intention-to-impose-a-legal-duty-on-the-laboratory-employees-to-provide-them-with-food. It would hence be conceptually impossible for the legislator to endow these beings with competences. Infants are relevantly similar in this regard: they lack the conceptual apparatus to be able to intend to effect legal consequences, even if they may signal certain needs.

However, there also cases where one's capacity to hold or exercise competences is limited for other than conceptual reasons. Historically, slaves and women have held a very limited number of competences. Depriving them of these competences has often been justified with paternalistic reasoning: limiting these people's legal capacity was putatively for their own good, due to their lacking the requisite mental capacities.[17] Depriving certain groups of people categorically of their capacity to perform acts-in-the-law is increasingly rare, but it does still happen: young children and people with severe mental deficiencies can be completely, or almost completely, unable to exercise competences.

The number of competences held by an ordinary human individual typically increases gradually until the age of majority. Babies hold no competences and bear no duties, but as they grow, the legal system normally grants them an increasing number of legal competences. They will also be held increasingly accountable for how they choose to exercise those competences.[18] This is generally recognised by theorists. However, a much more neglected topic is the fact that minors are typically *dependent* in how they are able to exercise these competences until they reach the age of majority and become *sui iuris*. Whereas adults of sound mind typically have the final say in their choices, a minor's competences are subject to oversight by a parent or a legally appointed guardian who can, say, retroactively cancel a transaction the minor has performed. Even minors can, however, have a 'sphere of independence' within which the guardian cannot interfere with how they choose

[17] The paternalistic justification of slavery in the United States is a major theme in Eugene Genovese's work (1976). Slaves in ancient Rome, however, were not considered inferior in this sense. As Alan Watson puts it, '[s]lavery was a misfortune that could happen to anyone. However lowly the economic and social position of a slave might be, the slave was not necessarily and in all ways regarded as inferior as a human being simply because he was a slave' (1988: 3). This was reflected in the fact that slaves could enter into contracts on their masters' behalf and perform some other acts-in-the-law.

[18] Not all legal responsibilities have to do with the exercise of legal competences, of course.

to exercise their competences. For instance, minors are, according to Finnish law, freely able to dispose of any money they have earned through their own labour.[19]

When children and mentally disabled individuals hold competences, they are in most cases of the dependent type. However, it is important to keep in mind that the justification for these limitations is in most cases moral rather than conceptual. I see no conceptual hinder that would prevent most minors or mentally disabled individuals from being able to exercise competences wholly independently. Acts-in-the-law include as their necessary component the intention to effect a legal consequence. Such intentions presuppose some kind of grasp of institutional reality and of how one can manipulate this reality through the use of symbols. Even though infants and animals do not possess such understanding, relatively young children do already begin to have a rudimentary grasp of these issues, and most disabled people do—to my knowledge—possess such comprehension.

Eilionóir Flynn and Anna Arstein-Kerslake have argued for a model of supported decision-making which would endow a disabled individual with the capacity to exercise competences independently. In their model, one 'chooses a number of trusted individuals to assist in the decision-making process'. However, 'support can only be offered to an individual, and she should be free to accept or reject the support—ie, supported decision-making should never be imposed on an individual against her will' (Flynn and Arstein-Kerslake 2014: 95). Given that the disabled individual would have the final say in any exercise of a competence, these competences would be of the independent type. There are nevertheless most likely some disabled individuals whose decision-making capabilities are so limited that the support model would not be suitable, as Flynn and Arstein-Kerslake recognise—albeit hesitantly (2014: 94).

IV. On Hohfeldian Powers

A definition of legal competences has now been outlined. However, the offered notion of competence is not intended as a replacement of the Hohfeldian conception of power. Competences are a subgroup—a proper subset—of powers, but powers that are not competences are also a useful category in our conceptual toolbox.

When addressing legal powers, Hohfeld made his oft-cited distinction between changes in legal relations that result 'from some superadded fact or group of facts which are under the volitional control of one or more human beings' and other types of changes (1913: 44). The volitional control referred to in the first category endows its possessor with a legal power. This account clearly includes cases not covered by the notion of competence, such as committing suicide, which is

[19] Guardianship Services Act (*Holhoustoimilaki*, 442/1999) s 25.

a volitional act that effects numerous changes in legal relations. Hohfeld might, however, have been envisaging a more limited conception than his account encompasses. He was in general sceptical of the idea that one could define the fundamental jural conceptions precisely and relied heavily on examples in his exposition. When introducing his notion of powers, he wrote that '[t]oo close an analysis' of 'this constantly employed and very important term of legal discourse' could 'seem metaphysical rather than useful'. His presentation was thus 'intended only as an approximate explanation sufficient for all practical purposes' (1913: 44). All the examples provided thenceforth were instances of competence: abandonment, contracting, conveyance and so on (1913: 45).

Regardless of what Hohfeld actually intended to include in his conception of legal powers, his original definition is still useful. Raz notes that legal theorists introduced the technical concept of power 'because they saw the need for a general concept to draw attention to important similarities between otherwise heterogeneous phenomena' (1972: 79). The Hohfeldian power does exactly this.

We should first note that some 'abilities' to change legal relations are neither powers nor competences.[20] A flood that extinguishes property rights has not 'exercised' any powers but rather 'quasi-powers'.[21] All three concepts can be expressed in 'if-then' terms: if *c*, then change *r* in legal relations occurs.[22] However, as regards powers and competences, *c* either includes or is brought about by the volitional conduct of an agent, whereas this is not the case with quasi-powers. This difference between powers and competences on one hand, and quasi-powers on the other, is salient and reflects the central philosophical distinction between actions and occurrences, that is, between something being done and something merely happening. Insights from the philosophy of action are straightforwardly relevant for the notions of power and competence, and quite irrelevant with regard to quasi-powers. Relatedly, our *predictive strategy* is different when explaining the behaviour of volitional agents as opposed to that of non-agents. As Daniel Dennett (1987) has pointed out, we employ the *physical stance* when trying to predict the behaviour of an object based purely on its physical qualities, whereas using the *intentional stance* involves making reference to the entity's motivational states.

A clear example of where Hohfeldian powers are useful is that of modelling the legal consequences of wrongdoing. A duty is in most cases accompanied by a power-to-subject-oneself-to-legal-sanctions-through-acting-in-breach-of-the-duty, and a corresponding liability, as with the vagrant case above. These three positions (duty, power and liability) cannot be combined into one without sacrificing the *sui generis* nature of the Hohfeldian elements. In addition, treating the duty and the power as indistinguishable would make the Hohfeldian system unable to distinguish between genuine and nominal duties and their corresponding claim-rights (see Kramer 1998: 9). Only a breach of genuine duties gives rise

[20] Even though all competences are powers, I talk about 'powers and competences' for clarity's sake.

[21] The term 'quasi-power' has been proposed by Kramer in private correspondence.

[22] This has been recognised by Halpin, among others (Halpin 1996: 141).

to legal sanctions. Thus, a genuine duty is accompanied by the kinds of powers and liabilities just outlined, whereas a nominal duty is not. One could of course make the argument that nominal duties are not legal duties at all, but a theoretical system should in any case not rule out their existence outright.

One might also raise the objection that talking of lawbreakers' powers-to-subject-themselves-to-legal-sanctions does not adhere to any established linguistic usage of 'power'. We should first ask whether this ought to concern us. The theorists writing on this topic have in general not sought to elucidate the ordinary meanings of words. However, neither have they been completely oblivious to the ordinary meaning of words; it is *ceteris paribus* a virtue of jurisprudential terminology to reflect ordinary usage. Indeed, this is why Hohfeld picked words such as 'privilege' and 'liability' as labels for his concepts rather than, say, 'alpha' and 'beta'. When choosing a label for power, Hohfeld likely had in mind examples that are covered by the concept of competence. But 'power' is not a completely outlandish term even when used in the broader sense, given that it always has to do with changing legal relations through a volitional action. For instance, it is perhaps unusual, but certainly not preposterous, to say that the homeless person who commits a crime in order to spend the night in a warm cell is exercising a legal power: he is availing himself of a possibility to manipulate the normative reality in a way beneficial to him. Describing the homeless person's criminal action as a 'mere condition' for the criminal consequence, as Halpin's account would imply, does not, in any case, conform to ordinary usage any better.[23] The same can be said of the moving-house example. Think of an authoritarian regime *R1* that restricts its citizens' freedom of movement. The regime could either forbid its citizens from moving or simply refuse to recognise de jure a citizen's decision to move from place *A* to place *B*. In the latter case, any citizen would consequently have to go back to place *A* to get married or to use the public health services etc. In this instantiation of *R1*, the legal system would be less responsive to its citizens' choices than jurisdiction *R2*, which is otherwise similar to *R1*, but has no similar restrictions pertaining to freedom of movement. It would, again, not constitute an abuse of language to say that the citizens of *R2* hold legal powers that the citizens of *R1* do not.[24]

Though I take the proposed labels of 'competence' and 'power' to be the most appropriate, I should note that these terms are not politically and morally pregnant in the way 'right' and 'freedom' are. One could also label the narrower concept 'power', as Raz and Halpin have done, even if one would then have to introduce a new label for the original Hohfeldian power. The labelling I propose, on the other hand, is compatible with the established terminology of many of the relevant debates. For instance, will theorists can still talk of the powers of enforcement and waiver, though they can also use the more precise term 'competence'.

[23] Halpin only allows for two categories in his scheme concerning how legal relations can be changed: the exercise of powers and the fulfilment of 'mere conditions'. As Halpin's powers are what I call competences, the vagrant's petty crime must fall in the latter category, together with purely natural events such as lightning strikes and floods.

[24] The relevant powers would be of the type 'power-to-acquire-the-competence-to-marry-in-place-*B*'.

I should finally mention that even though infants and non-human animals are unable to hold competences, they do—can—hold legal powers. Hohfeld did of course, in his definition of power, refer to 'the volitional control of one or more *human beings*' but this does not imply that restricting the domain of powers to human beings would be the only alternative. It is possible, for instance, that Hohfeld believed animals to be incapable of volition. Animals only figured in Hohfeld's texts as 'tangible objects'. His animal of choice was the horse, which was bought, sold and wrongfully possessed in his examples (1917: 733, 738). Whatever his reasons were for excluding non-human animals from his definition of power, science has since then shown that many animals are clearly capable of having intentions and performing volitional actions.[25] Many animals perform actions which effectuate legal changes. If a dog attacks a human being, this typically has all sorts of legal consequences, such as giving that individual the power to sue the owner of the dog.

V. Finally

The main aims of this essay have been twofold: first, to refine the theories of legal powers propounded by theorists such as MacCormick, Raz, Halpin and Hage; and second, to establish that the 'original' Hohfeldian power is a useful concept as well.

Legal competence can be defined compactly and elegantly in terms of minimal sufficiency. The central way of exercising legal competences is through the performance of acts-in-the-law, but legal systems also allow for the unintentional exercise of competences. The proposed theory manages to account for the unintentional exercises of competence without having to rely on evaluative terms.

Even though legal competences have their distinct logical form, they are nevertheless a subgroup of legal powers which have to do with how individuals manipulate the legal realm through the performance of intentional actions. This wider conception of legal power is useful for various purposes, of which numerous examples have been provided. Hohfeld's original account of legal consequences is also unproblematic, both for the purposes of powers and competences.

Topics such as contracting by reliance have received much attention from jurisprudents, whereas the distinction between dependent and independent competences has been relatively neglected. This essay has merely touched upon that bifurcation, but further theoretical work on the topic could shed light on issues of legal majority and minority, as well as possibly that of agency and representation.

[25] See for instance The Cambridge Declaration on Consciousness, according to which '[c]onvergent evidence indicates that non-human animals have the neuroanatomical, neurochemical, and neurophysiological substrates of conscious states along with the capacity to exhibit intentional behaviors', available at *fcmconference.org/img/CambridgeDeclarationOnConsciousness.pdf*.

References

Carter, I (2011) 'Respect and the Basis of Equality' 121(3) *Ethics* 538.

—— (2015) 'Value-freeness and Value-neutrality in the Analysis of Political Concepts' in D Sobel, P Vallentyne and S Wall (eds), *Oxford Studies in Political Philosophy, Volume 1* (Oxford: Oxford University Press).

Dennett, D (1987) *The Intentional Stance* (Cambridge, MA: MIT Press).

Flynn, E and Arstein-Kerslake, A (2014) 'Legislating Personhood: Realising the Right to Support in Exercising Legal Capacity' 10(1) *International Journal of Law in Context* 81.

Genovese, E (1976) *Roll, Jordan, Roll: The World the Slaves Made* (New York: Random House USA, Inc).

Hage, J (2009) 'What is a Legal Transaction?' in M Del Mar and Z Bankowski (eds), *Law as Institutional Normative Order* (Surrey: Ashgate).

Halpin, A (1996) 'The Concept of a Legal Power' 16(1) *Oxford Journal of Legal Studies* 129.

—— (1997) *Rights and Law, Analysis and Theory* (Oxford: Hart Publishing).

Hart, HLA (1955) 'Are There Any Natural Rights?' 64 *Philosophical Review* 175.

—— (1964) *The Concept of Law* (Oxford: Clarendon Press).

Hohfeld, WN (1913) 'Some Fundamental Legal Conceptions as Applied in Legal Reasoning' 23 *Yale Law Journal* 16.

—— (1917) 'Fundamental Legal Conceptions as Applied in Judicial Reasoning' 26 *Yale Law Journal* 710.

Kramer, MH (1998) 'Rights Without Trimmings' in MH Kramer, NE Simmonds and H Steiner, *A Debate Over Rights. Philosophical Enquiries* (Oxford: Oxford University Press).

—— (2010) 'Refining the Interest Theory of Rights' 55 *The American Journal of Jurisprudence* 31.

List, C and Pettit, P (2011) *Group Agency: The Possibility, Design, and Status of Corporate Agents* (Oxford: Oxford University Press).

MacCormick, N (1981) *HLA Hart* (Stanford, CA: Stanford University Press).

Markovits, D (2015) 'Theories of the Common Law of Contracts' in *Stanford Encyclopedia of Philosophy*.

Pylkkänen, A (2009) *Trapped in Equality: Women as Legal Persons in the Modernisation of Finnish Law* (Helsinki: Suomalaisen Kirjallisuuden Seura/Finnish Literature Society).

Raz, J (1972) 'Voluntary Obligations and Normative Powers' 46 *Proceedings of the Aristotelian Society* 79.

Smith, SA (1993) *Contract Theory* (Oxford: Oxford University Press).

Spaak, T (1994) *The Concept of Legal Competence. An Essay in Conceptual Analysis* (Aldershot: Dartmouth).

Watson, A (1988) *Roman Slave Law* (Baltimore, MD: The Johns Hopkins University Press).

3

In Defence of the Interest Theory of Right-Holding: Rejoinders to Leif Wenar on Rights

MATTHEW H KRAMER

In two quite recent essays, Leif Wenar (2008; 2013) has impugned my version of the Interest Theory of right-holding and has proposed a theory which he commends as an alternative to mine. In this essay I will rebut Wenar's objections to my version of the Interest Theory, and I will contest his view that his own theory is a promising alternative to mine.

I. Kramer's Version of the Interest Theory of Right-Holding

Although the Interest Theory in its sundry incarnations is typically characterised as a theory of rights—and although I myself usually characterise it in that manner—my version of it is better designated as a theory of right-holding. It presents a criterion that enables us to identify the holder of a legal right that correlates with a particular legal duty. That criterion is encapsulated in the following two theses:

> (IT-1) Necessary though insufficient for the holding of a legal right by *X* is that the duty correlative to the right, when actual, normatively protects some aspect of *X*'s situation that on balance is typically beneficial for a being like *X* (namely, a human individual or a collectivity or a non-human animal).[1]

> (IT-2) Neither necessary nor sufficient for the holding of some specified legal right by *X* is that *X* is competent and authorised to demand or waive the enforcement of the duty that is correlative to the right.

[1] I have argued at length elsewhere, on ethical grounds, for the restriction of the class of potential right-holders to human individuals and collectivities and non-human animals. See Kramer (2001). However, the first tenet of the Interest Theory could be formulated more expansively by someone who believes that legal rights can correctly be ascribed to certain insentient entities such as trees or rivers.

My previous writings on rights and right-holding have amplified and elucidated these two theses in a number of ways (Kramer 1998; 2001; 2008; 2010; 2013; Kramer and Steiner 2007). For the moment, I will highlight only two points. First, unlike some other versions of the Interest Theory—most notably Joseph Raz's version (1986: ch 7)—my account of right-holding does not focus on the justifications for the duties that are correlative to rights. Without knowing the justificatory basis for some existent duty D, anyone guided by my account can ascertain the identity of the holder of a right that is correlative to D. The holder of the right is the person or collectivity or animal to whom D is owed. It need not be the case, though it can be the case, that the interests of the right-holder are the justificatory basis for the existence of D.

Second, like other versions of the Interest Theory, my version is opposed to the rival Will Theory. That latter doctrine is encapsulated in the following thesis:

> (WT) Both necessary and sufficient for the holding of some specified legal right by *X* is that *X* is competent and authorised to demand/waive the enforcement of the duty that is correlative to the right.

II. Ordinary Usage and Armchairs

In each of the two essays that are under scrutiny here, but especially in the 2008 essay, Wenar again and again insists that the definitive touchstone for selecting among theories of right-holding is the extent to which the implications of each such theory tally with the conclusions that are generated by ordinary usage of the language of 'rights'. If some implications do not coincide with the ordinary-language conclusions, the theory that carries those implications is *pro tanto* defective in his eyes. Wenar asserts that

> [t]he 'data' of ordinary understanding are … significantly less contentious than the 'data' of what rights there really are, and focusing on ordinary understanding allows debates over the nature of rights to refer to a common set of facts to be explained (2008: 252).

He insists that

> both sides [of the debates between Interest Theorists and Will Theorists] take extensional fit with ordinary usage as a primary standard of success—that is, both aim to present theories that capture all and only rights-assertions that make sense to competent users of the language. This standard of success is accepted here (2013: 202–03).

He similarly contends that

> [t]heorists of rights have, in the main, taken an ordinary understanding of rights to set the phenomena to be explained. For example, a rights theorist will reject any theory that ascribes rights to tomato plants, or to ant colonies, because such a theory is incompatible with an ordinary understanding of rights (2008: 252).

This methodological position staked out by Wenar, which takes ordinary usage to be a decisive lodestar, is vulnerable to a number of criticisms.

A. A Misunderstanding of Appeals to Ordinary Understandings

Wenar in his 2013 article does not offer any citations to back up his claim that Interest Theorists and Will Theorists are determined to arrive at conclusions that match those of ordinary speakers, nor does he there address the passages in which they disavow any such methodological stricture. By contrast, his 2008 essay does endeavour to deal with those points. Here and elsewhere, I will respond to him chiefly with reference to my own version of the Interest Theory rather than with reference to the Interest Theory and Will Theory more broadly.

Wenar acknowledges that I do not in fact regard ordinary linguistic usage as some sort of template with which any tenable theory of rights must fit very closely. As I have emphasised since my earliest publications on rights and right-holding, ordinary usage is marked by too much imprecision and inconsistency to be serviceable as such a template. Moreover, even if everyday usage were much more rigorous than it is, it would scarcely be an unchallengeable point of reference. As I have argued elsewhere at length (2001: 29–57), some aspects of my Interest Theory of right-holding are straightforwardly oriented towards ethics rather than towards patterns of linguistic usage. Hence, some supplementation and regimentation of ordinary usage are inevitable in any satisfactory theory of right-holding.

Wenar alleges that I 'attempt to cast enough aspersions on ordinary "rights-talk" that there will appear to be no option but to shift from an ordinary to a technical explanandum' (2008: 264), and he submits that there is a tension if not a downright inconsistency between those aspersions and my appeals to ordinary understandings in some of my criticisms of the Will Theory. He condemns me along with other theorists of right-holding:

> They ... insist that ordinary rights-talk is vague and inconsistent in order to attempt to shift attention toward their favoured technical recharacterisations of the term 'rights'. Yet when attention is so shifted, they once again attempt to embrace an ordinary understanding of rights as the guarantor of their theory's superiority. This position holds the ordinary understanding of rights to be so irremediably vague and inconsistent as to be useless as the object of theoretical explanation, but not so corrupt as to be useless in mediating between artificially constructed definitions of 'rights' (2008: 264).

Wenar has misunderstood the point of the invocations of ordinary understandings which he reports. There is no tension whatsoever between (1) insisting that some regimentation of ordinary linguistic usage is unavoidable in any coherent philosophical theory of right-holding and (2) commending one's theory of right-holding for capturing far more of ordinary usage than does the main alternative theory. Moreover, and relatedly, nobody has ever denied that ordinary understandings are an important anchor for one's theorising about rights and right-holding. As I stated two decades ago in my first main essay on the topic (1998: 22–23), one's theorising about rights would be unintelligible if its key terms did not have any rooting in ordinary discourse. Wesley Hohfeld's disambiguation of the notion of rights into claims, liberties, powers and immunities is apt in this respect as in many other respects; the terms with which Hohfeld labelled the four disentangled entitlements are all salutarily rooted in ordinary discourse.[2] Without any inconsistency, one can commend this aspect of Hohfeld's analytical framework while also insisting that ordinary discourse is too loose and multifarious to be reproduced fully by that framework or by any coherent philosophical account of rights.

Also worth noting here is that the philosophers who call for some regimentation of ordinary usage are doing so only in relation to philosophical and juristic discourse. Nobody has been suggesting that everyday discussions of these matters should be similarly regimented. Any suggestion along those lines would be risibly futile.

B. *Tu Quoque*

As Wenar remarks, the chief way in which I seek to refine the language of 'rights' for philosophical theorising is to confine it to Hohfeldian claims (accompanied by Hohfeldian immunities against the cancellation of the claims). He states: 'Interest theorists ... stipulate that their theories are not meant to account for rights as commonly understood, but only for "rights" defined as Hohfeldian claim-rights' (2008: 262). Wenar takes exception to this mode of regimentation: 'Kramer wishes to work within a sphere of discourse in which the referent of "rights" is claim-rights ... Kramer faces the difficulty that ordinary discourse does not line up with his technical definition' (2008: 263). Apart from the fact that Wenar ignores my arguments in support of restricting the language of 'rights' to Hohfeldian claims, the main peculiarity of his criticism of such a restriction is that it leaves him vulnerable to an obvious '*tu quoque*' retort. His 2013 article begins with the following sentence: 'This is a new analysis of rights, particularly of the paradigm: the claim-right' (2013: 202). The rest of the article is very much in keeping with that opening sentence, as Wenar focuses his analysis on claim-rights throughout. Having upbraided Hohfeld and me for contending that the term 'rights' is applicable in its strictest sense to claim-rights (2008: 263–64), Wenar himself now declares that that term is applicable in its paradigmatic sense to claim-rights. At one juncture he accuses his opponents of resembling a person who suffers from a mental illness that leads her to embrace and repudiate something simultaneously (2008: 264–65), but he should perhaps have applied that misdirected allegation to himself.

[2] For an exposition of Hohfeld's analysis of legal entitlements and their correlates, see Kramer (1998: 7–60). Hohfeld himself usually employed the term 'privilege' to denote the entitlement which most Hohfeldians (including me) generally designate as a 'liberty'. Most Hohfeldians prefer the latter designation precisely because it corresponds better to ordinary usage. Strangely, given the emphasis placed by Wenar on conformity to ordinary usage, he himself generally follows Hohfeld in employing the term 'privilege'.

C. The View from an Armchair

Wenar's sundry assertions about ordinary usage of the language of 'rights' are of course empirical contentions. Many of them are sufficiently clear-cut to be in no need of empirical substantiation, but some of them are less straightforward. Consider, for example, the following statement: 'Few thoughtful laymen would insist that it is a conceptual impossibility, for example, for the comatose to have rights against bodily mutilation' (Wenar 2008, 255). Though the adjective 'thoughtful' might be taken to indicate that this statement is not really an empirical contention but is instead a partial explication of the ethical property of thoughtfulness, Wenar cannot rely on such an interpretation. The sentence which leads into the quoted statement makes clear that he takes himself to be recounting an element of the 'ordinary understanding of rights' (2008: 255). Hence, he is indeed advancing an empirical hypothesis here. He marshals no evidence whatsoever in support of that empirical hypothesis, yet evidence is sorely needed—for the correctness of his hypothesis is by no means obvious when judged *in abstracto*. On a question as complicated as the question whether participants in everyday discourse accept that comatose people can hold legal rights, surmises are inadequate.

D. More from Wenar's Armchair

Wenar asserts that philosophers of rights have not established that quotidian understandings of rights are in need of regimentation, and he contends from his armchair that those understandings are often if not always precise and unconfused. He writes as follows:

> [T]echnical rights theorists have not in fact established that ordinary discourse is frequently vague and contradictory, instead of being a discourse that systematically assigns different meanings to the same word in different contexts. Such systematic variation in meaning is familiar in common speech. For example there is nothing vague or contradictory in the statement that 'in a free market one is free to lend money interest-free'. 'Free' in this statement takes three different but determinate meanings, the meaning of each occurrence being determined by the context. Similarly in ordinary discourse one often hears the word 'right' used to refer variously to privilege-rights, claim-rights, power-rights, and immunity-rights, with the intended referent made clear by the context. Interpretations of ordinary speech that find vagueness or inconsistency instead of precise and determinate variation in usage are often just poor interpretations of ordinary speech (2008: 265).

Short of conducting a full-scale empirical study, the only way to support claims about paralogisms and inconsistencies in ordinary discourse is to adduce examples of such paralogisms and inconsistencies. Contrary to the impression conveyed here by Wenar, Hohfeld adduced a plethora of such examples involving both jurists and legal theorists. In my 1998 essay 'Rights without Trimmings', I have marshalled a number of more recent examples involving legal philosophers.

Such examples hardly amount to a systematic survey, but they do reveal that instances of confusion and inconsistency are not outlandishly uncommon even among very sophisticated people.

By contrast, Wenar does not supply any evidence whatsoever to support his empirical claims about the precision and unconfusedness of ordinary usage. He simply states that he often hears precise and consistent invocations of the language of 'rights'. No examples are provided. Of course, I do not doubt that he could have come up with some examples if he had endeavoured to do so; nobody has ever suggested that everyday discourse is *always* confused and inconsistent. My point is that he has not taken even a single step towards substantiating his broad empirical contentions. Pronouncements from his armchair do not constitute such a step.

III. A Preposterous Methodological Demand

Wenar tries to saddle me with the following methodological demand:

> A full treatment of Kramer's interest theory must wait until Kramer has had the opportunity to present a complete statement of his revised theory, by explaining what he believes are the necessary and sufficient conditions for the ascription of a right and by offering some systematic account of how one can tell whether these conditions have been met' (2008: 258, fn 9).

Each of the two strands in this methodological demand is misconceived.

First, in my formulations of my version of the Interest Theory, I have always deliberately forborne from specifying the sufficient conditions for the holding of a legal right. My caution on that point is due to the fact that those conditions include the existence of a correlative legal duty—which means that a full specification of those conditions would include the conditions that are sufficient for the existence of a legal duty. Accordingly, a full specification would have to draw upon a theory of the nature of law and upon an account of legal interpretation. Because no exposition of the nature of right-holding should carry so many jurisprudential commitments, there are solid grounds for my disinclination to recount sufficient conditions for the holding of a legal right.

Second, Wenar has again left himself open to a '*tu quoque*' rejoinder when he declares (in the statement quoted above) that I should be 'offering some systematic account of how one can tell whether these conditions [for the holding of a legal right] have been met'. In his presentation of his own theory of right-holding in his 2013 article, Wenar repeatedly commends his approach for its inability in some important cases to determine whether the conditions specified by his theory have been met or not. He asserts that 'tracking uncertainty is not a failure in a conceptual analysis so much as an advertisement for it', and he proclaims that his 'theory mirrors uncertainty on one side of the biconditional with uncertainty on the other, as a good conceptual analysis should' (2013: 222–23). These assertions are unexceptionable in themselves, but they reveal the extravagance of Wenar's demand that I must offer an algorithmic account that will enable us to ascertain whether the Interest Theory's conditions for the holding of a right are fulfilled or not in every particular situation.

IV. The Misplacing of a Quantifier

Wenar misunderstands or misrepresents my version of the Interest Theory of right-holding by incorrectly locating the plurative quantifier that is operative in its first thesis, IT-1 above. He submits that

> interest theorists have framed their theories around weak generalizations, which only attempt to explain some but not all rights … Kramer presents his theory in terms of what is '*generally* beneficial for any *typical* human being or collectivity or non-human creature' … The qualifications … 'generally' and 'typical' limit the domain of rights that [Kramer's theory] will attempt to explain to a domain with certain rights (specifically, the counterexamples) removed.

Wenar adds:

> Weak generalizations are unsatisfying because of their lack of comprehensiveness. A linguist studying English will not rest content with the rule that *in all normal circumstances, 'i' comes before 'e'*. Nor will a toxicologist be satisfied with the thesis that *mushrooms are generally harmless when eaten*. It is unlikely that the best theory of rights takes the form: 'All rights have feature F (except for those that lack feature F)'.[3]

Wenar repeats his misunderstanding or misrepresentation in his later essay (2013: 204–05), but I will concentrate here on the statements just quoted. One preliminary point to be noted is that the wording of IT-1 as it has stood since 2013 is not quite the same as the wording which Wenar quotes from my 2007 article.[4] However, the differences are inconsequential in the present context; I will therefore ignore them and concentrate on IT-1 as it has stood since 2013.

Wenar has incorrectly placed the plurative quantifier—the quantifier rendered in my formulation of IT-1 as 'typically'—in his interpretation of IT-1. He construes that tenet of my theory as if it were worded as follows:

> Typically the holding of a legal right by *X* is such that the duty correlative to the right, when actual, protects some aspect of *X*'s situation that on balance is beneficial for a being like *X* (namely, a human individual or a collectivity or a nonhuman animal).

[3] Wenar (2008: 257). The quotation within the quotation is from Kramer and Steiner (2007: 290), emphasis added by Wenar.

[4] I modified IT-1 in 2013 in response to a suggestion from Henry Richardson. My modification of it had nothing to do with anything written by Wenar. I have refined IT-1 several times since first propounding it in 1998.

Were IT-1 formulated in that fashion, Wenar's remarks would be accurate. However, given that it is formulated as it is, his dismissive remarks are ill judged. Contrary to what Wenar contends, IT-1 ascribes a property to every instance of right-holding rather than only to certain such instances. The main quantifier in that thesis, an implicit quantifier, is universal rather than plurative. There is of course a plurative quantifier in IT-1, but it governs the content of the ascribed property—the property of being beneficial on balance for someone like *X*—rather than the whole ascription. (Wenar persists in his mistaken understanding when he writes as follows in a footnote:

> It is of course possible to try to recapture universal application by specifying some property specially rigged for the purpose, for example 'all rights share the property of belonging to a set whose members generally have feature F'. But the weak spot in the generalization will always remain (2008: 257, fn 8).

In this rigged formulation as well as in his other pronouncements on this matter, Wenar incorrectly has the plurative quantifier governing the ascription of F rather than governing the content of F.)

Though my version of the Interest Theory is not vulnerable to Wenar's rather disparaging comments about weak generalisations, his own theory of right-holding is. Once again Wenar has left himself exposed to a '*tu quoque*' riposte. When he unfurls his theory of right-holding in his 2013 article, he formulates its third tenet as follows: 'Enforcement of this duty [namely, the duty correlative to the right that is held] is appropriate, ceteris paribus' (2013: 209, 219). Wenar nowhere tells us how to determine whether the '*ceteris paribus*' qualification is satisfied, and indeed he makes no effort whatsoever to elucidate that qualification. His theory therefore takes the form which he fleers in the passage that I have quoted in the antepenultimate paragraph above: 'All rights have feature F (except for those that lack feature F)'.

V. A Theory Not Focused on Justification

As has been emphasised in the first main section of this essay, one major difference between my version of the Interest Theory of right-holding and Raz's version is that my account is not focused on the justifications for legal duties and their correlative rights. In particular my account does not maintain that, whenever a legal duty is correlative to a legal right, the duty is justified by the ethical weightiness of the right-holder's interests. Wenar is acquainted with this feature of my theory of right-holding, but he often obscures it or forgets about it in his criticisms of me—especially when he is engaging with an expansive variant of my theory, which covers not only claim-rights but also each instance of the other Hohfeldian entitlements that is pertinently classified as a right.

A. A First Instance

Wenar asks his readers to

> consider the fact that a judge's power to sentence criminals is properly classified as a right. It would sound odd to say that this fact is explained by the fact that the possession of this power is generally beneficial for the judge. Similarly with the fact that a policeman's liberty to detain a suspect is properly classified as a right. One might not think that this fact is explained by the fact that the possession of such a liberty is generally beneficial for the policeman (2008: 259).

Strictly speaking, Wenar characterises the *explanandum* accurately in each of his two examples. In the first example, what is to be explained is not the fact that the judge is endowed with a legal power to sentence criminals, but instead the fact that the judge's power is correctly classifiable as a right. In the second example, what is to be explained is not the fact that the policeman is legally at liberty to detain a suspect, but instead the fact that the policeman's liberty is correctly classifiable as a right. However, although Wenar has stated each *explanandum* accurately, the persuasiveness of his queries about the capacious variant of the Interest Theory in application to each of his examples is dependent on his readers' misidentifying the actual *explanandum*.

If we ask whether it would be odd to say that the reason for the vesting of a judge with the legal power to sentence criminals is that her being so vested is generally beneficial for her, the answer to that question is obviously affirmative. If we instead ask whether it would be odd to say that the reason for classifying a judge's legal power to sentence criminals as a legal right held by the judge is that the possession of such an entitlement is generally beneficial for someone who bears the legal responsibilities of a judicial office, the answer to this second question is negative. If Wenar thinks otherwise, he will have to present arguments—or perhaps empirical evidence about the responses of ordinary people to this second question—rather than sheer assertions. Given the absence of any arguments or evidence in his terse objection to the capacious variant of the Interest Theory, he appears to be relying on his readers to mistake the second question for the first.

Much the same can be said about his other example. If we ask whether it would be odd to say that the reason for endowing a policeman with the legal liberty to detain a suspect is that his being so at liberty is generally beneficial for him, the answer to that question is obviously affirmative. If we instead ask whether it would be odd to say that the reason for classifying a policeman's legal liberty to detain a suspect as a legal right is that the possession of such an entitlement is generally beneficial for someone who bears the responsibilities of a policeman, the answer is negative. Again, if Wenar thinks otherwise, he will have to adduce arguments or perhaps empirical evidence to substantiate his position. Sheer assertions are scarcely sufficient. He once again appears to be relying on his readers to mistake the second of these two questions for the first.

B. Another Instance

While continuing to focus on the examples of the judge and the policeman, Wenar contends that my 'line of reasoning [about the judge's power and the policeman's liberty] simultaneously relies upon and misunderstands the norms that are roles'. He elaborates as follows (2008: 260, footnote omitted):

> It is not as though there is a coherent role described as 'judge who has the responsibility to sentence but no power to sentence'—and then we make a separate determination that the life of someone filling that role would go better if they gained the power to sentence. The original description makes no sense: a role that assigns a responsibility to φ but with no normative ability to φ is not a role that fits into any recognizable human practice. Similarly with the patrolman. There is no intelligible job that is 'policeman who has the duty not to detain suspects whenever he has the duty to detain suspects'. Such a job could be imagined only at the edges of a fantasy, if there; speculation about the interests of such a job-holder is moot. In reality, offices such as 'judge' and 'policeman' always pair the responsibilities of office with the normative abilities appropriate for carrying out these responsibilities. 'Rights of office' are not optional add-ons that help a person do a job; rather, rights of office are an integral part of every job's description.

Nothing in this passage has any bearing on the ways in which the capacious variant of my version of the Interest Theory applies to the examples of the judge and the policeman. Wenar's remarks would have such a bearing if the relevant *explananda* were the fact that the judge has legal powers of sentencing and the fact that the policeman has legal liberties to detain suspects. If I were trying to explain those facts, my explanations which advert to the interests of the office-holders would be ludicrous for the reasons indicated in this passage. However, once again, those facts are not the relevant *explananda*. Rather, the capacious variant of my version of the Interest Theory is aiming to explain why the legal powers of the judge are properly classifiable as legal rights and why the legal liberties of the policeman are properly classifiable as legal rights. I am addressing not a question concerning why the judge and the policeman hold certain entitlements, but instead a question concerning the status of those entitlements as rights. Wenar's observations do not bear on that latter question nor on my answer to it.

C. A Further Instance

Wenar's inadvertent or deliberate conflation of the irrelevant *explananda* with the relevant *explananda* is epitomised in a slightly later pair of sentences:

> An interest-theoretical approach such as [the capacious variant of Kramer's theory] cannot be the path toward understanding the rights of offices and positions. Rights of office cannot be explained by the interests of the individuals who occupy the office as currently defined (2008: 262).

These sentences are tantalisingly ambiguous between the two sets of *explananda*. To any reader of those sentences who is not unusually vigilant, Wenar will almost certainly appear to be indicating that I have sought to explain why some office-holders are vested with the entitlements which they possess. Whether Wenar has deliberately sought to create such an impression or has instead simply neglected to avert it, the misdirectedness of his rejoinders to the capacious variant of the Interest Theory will very likely go undiscerned by any reader who is not exceptionally vigilant against being misled.

D. Snippet Quotations Out of Context

Wenar submits that I have displayed inconsistency by 'appeal[ing] to the purpose[s] of legal norms to make sense of [certain] cases …, where a few pages earlier [Kramer] had said that purposes had no "determinative bearing" and were "quite immaterial" in his theory' (2008: 259, fn 11). In fact, there is no inconsistency whatsoever between the two passages (in Kramer and Steiner 2007: 289–90, 293–94) to which Wenar refers. In the earlier passage, from which he takes his snippet quotations, I deny that a *necessary* condition for the conferral of a legal right upon some person *X* by a legal norm is that the underlying purpose of the norm is to benefit *X* or people like *X*; the existence of such an underlying purpose is not a *necessary* condition for the conferral of a right upon *X*. By contrast, in the later passage that appeals to the purpose of a law *L*, I maintain that that purpose can combine with the terms and the predictable effects of *L* to constitute a *sufficient* condition for the holding of a right by *X* thereunder. In circumstances where the terms and the predictable effects of *L* are not themselves enough to form such a condition, they can be supplemented to that end by *L*'s purpose. In short, contrary to the impression conveyed by Wenar with his snippet quotations, the passages to which he adverts are perfectly compatible.

E. A Related Error

Wenar asserts that the capacious variant of my version of the Interest Theory cannot 'account for the fact that … discretionary liberties are rights' (2008: 261). He focuses on an example of a parent who is legally at liberty to punish her child and legally at liberty not to punish the child. As he observes, I have discussed that example in my 2007 article on right-holding. More specifically, I have there sought to explain why a capacious variant of my version of the Interest Theory would classify the legal liberty-to-punish as a legal right (Kramer and Steiner 2007: 291–92). Wenar purports to summarise the gist of my analysis:

> Imagine a world in which a parent has no liberty to punish her child (ie, she has a duty not to punish), but in which she retains the liberty not to punish her child. In such a

> world, Kramer says, the parent would be better off if she gained the liberty to punish her child because then she would no longer be liable to penalties whenever she did punish.

He retorts:

> In Kramer's imagined world parents are prohibited from punishing their children. In this world parents also have no duty to punish their children. Why in this world would a parent be better off if she gained a liberty to punish her child? She will be better off gaining a liberty to punish her child only if she has some reason to punish her child. Yet there is no reason that Kramer can depend upon here (2008: 261).

Wenar's retort is misguided in more than one respect.

In the first place, Wenar errs in stating that a parent 'will be better off gaining a liberty to punish her child only if she has some reason to punish her child'. Indeed, such a statement ignores the chief point in my analysis of the situation. Even if *mirabile dictu* a parent has no reason to punish her child, she might punish her child—perhaps because she mistakenly believes that she has a reason to do so. If she is legally at liberty to punish her child, she will not be liable to legal sanctions for having done what she is at liberty to do. Contrariwise, if she is not legally at liberty to punish her child, she will be liable to legal sanctions for having done what she is legally obligated not to do. In that crucial respect, her situation is on balance better if she possesses the legal liberty in question than if she lacks it.

Moreover, Wenar displays a paucity of imagination when he asserts that there are no reasons which I can attribute to the parent in this example. A parent might gain some peace and quiet by punishing her child for being unruly, or her infliction of a punishment might help to administer a moral education to the child both for his sake and for the parent's own sake. These considerations and other considerations that commonly militate in favor of punishing a child would not disappear if acts of punishing were to be legally proscribed. Given that such considerations will frequently be operative, the benefits to the parent from her being legally at liberty to punish her child are especially obvious. Decidedly peculiar is Wenar's apparent assumption that the existence of reasons for a parent to punish her child is dependent on her being under a legal duty to punish her child.

F. A Related Error Continued

Wenar continues his discussion of the example of the parent with the following rejoinder to my analysis of the situation:

> Kramer appears to suggest that in his imagined world a parent would have a *role-based* reason to punish her child, and so would be better off with the liberty to punish. He says that with this liberty she would 'not have to worry about being penalized for taking steps which she reasonably deems necessary for the effective performance of her role as a parent'. Yet within this imagined world parents are prohibited from punishing their children, so their role is quite different than in our world. In this imagined world, the role of parent could at best be described as 'raising one's children well, so far as one can do so without

> punishing them'. Punishing one's child could not be a step reasonably deemed necessary for the effective performance of *that* role. In the imagined world, discipline is no part of a parent's job description. So Kramer has no role-based reason available to explain an interest in gaining the liberty to punish.[5]

Contrary to what is suggested by Wenar in this passage and in the other quoted passages about the example of the parent, I do not invoke the language of counterfactual worlds in my ruminations on that example. My focus in coming to grips with that example has always lain preponderantly on the actual world. Of course, my analysis does have a counterfactual dimension—because I am pondering why the possession of the liberty-to-punish is generally beneficial for a parent, and because I therefore need to contemplate what the absence of that liberty would involve. However, given that my focus is on the actual world, the counterfactual world that serves as the point of comparison should differ as little as possible from actuality. In other words, the only difference should be the presence of a prohibition on punishing one's children in the counterfactual world, versus the absence of such a prohibition in the actual world. I am not asking whether the possession of the liberty-to-punish is generally beneficial for a parent in comparison with a situation in which that liberty is absent and in which the role of a parent is very different. Rather, I am asking whether the possession of such a liberty is generally beneficial for a parent in comparison with a situation in which that liberty is absent and in which the role of a parent is otherwise unchanged.[6] When the comparison is posed correctly in that fashion, my conclusion about the generally beneficial character of the specified liberty for a parent straightforwardly follows. Wenar's effort to block that conclusion by postulating additional contrasts between the actual world and the germane counterfactual world is baseless.

G. A Related Error Still Further

Wenar concludes his meditations on the example of the parent as follows (2008: 261–62, footnote omitted, emphasis in original):

> Kramer might instead venture that a parent in his imagined world would have some *non-role-based* reason to discipline her child. Yet this depends entirely on how we imagine

[5] Wenar (2008: 261), citation omitted, emphasis in original. The quotation within the quotation is from Kramer and Steiner (2007: 292).

[6] Perhaps Wenar is assuming that one's legal liberty to punish one's offspring is an essential constituent of one's role as a parent, such that any person who lacks a liberty of that kind is not performing the role of a parent even if she solicitously attends to her offspring exactly as a parent would. Let us leave aside the fact that Wenar does not offer any hint of an argument in support of such a bold and implausible assumption (an assumption which he might not be making). Even so, I could easily reformulate my argument here to grant that implausible assumption *arguendo*. Instead of comparing the situation of a parent who possesses the legal liberty-to-punish and the situation of a parent who does not possess such a liberty, I would compare the situation of a parent who possesses such a liberty and the situation of a quasi-parent whose conduct and legal entitlements and responsibilities are the same as those of a parent except that the quasi-parent lacks a legal liberty-to-punish.

> this world to be. For example, in this imagined world where parents have no duty to discipline their children and indeed are prohibited from doing so, the responsibility for disciplining children might well be (indeed likely would be) assigned to someone else. Were we to posit that parents have an interest in punishing their children even when someone else is effectively doing so, we would seem to be making parents out to be simply cruel. Or again: parents in Kramer's imagined world might be just as glad, all things considered, to be legally prohibited from punishing their children. They might think that gaining the liberty to punish would result in their having endless headaches (familiar from our world) that they would just as soon avoid.

Until the final two sentences of this latest passage, Wenar simply repeats some errors which I have already exposed as such. He again fails to recognise that the key question is not whether a parent typically has an interest in punishing her child, but instead whether a parent typically has an interest in not being subject to legal penalties for punishing her child. And he again is unimaginative as he fails to come up with any of the reasons which a parent might plausibly have for punishing her child even though she is not under a legal duty to punish.

Having committed those errors afresh, Wenar introduces a new line of thought in the closing two sentences of this passage. He suggests there that a parent legally prohibited from punishing her child might on balance benefit from the prohibition, because she will no longer have to decide whether to punish her child in any given situation. The problem for such a line of thought is that a parent will indeed continue to face decisions whether to punish her child or not in sundry circumstances, only now with the added complication that she might be subjected to legal penalties if she does elect to go ahead in any of those circumstances. After all, a mode of conduct prohibited is not a mode of conduct precluded; a parent will still be able to punish even if she is not legally permitted to punish, and she will therefore have to choose whether to exert that ability or not. Moreover, even in the extremely unlikely event that the legal prohibition disinclines a parent ever to consider whether to punish her child, she will now confront all the difficulties that ensue from the non-subjection of her child to discipline (or from her needing to rely on the clumsy device of having someone else punish her child, in the improbable event that other people are legally permitted to punish children while parents are not). Wenar has done nothing to make credible the notion that a parent in a scenario of this kind will typically benefit on balance from being deprived of the legal liberty to punish her child. On the contrary, that notion is outlandish.

H. A Coda to the Related Error

In a footnote, Wenar asserts that

> reflection on paternalistic legislation gives further reason to doubt Kramer's [position]. Paternalistic legislation is just an attempt to make people better off by instituting a legal prohibition that disinclines them from doing something risky or difficult that they would otherwise do. For Kramer to establish that it is extremely rare for a legal prohibition to

further the interests of those restricted by it, he would need to show that it is extremely rare for paternalistic legislation to achieve its aims (2008: 262, fn 16).

Unlike the example of the parent, the example of paternalistic legislation may indeed point to some Hohfeldian liberties that are not generally beneficial on balance for the people who hold them. However, the example is not as clear-cut as Wenar suggests, and in any event he draws an invalid conclusion from it.

i. Inconclusiveness

For several reasons, the example is not as clear-cut as Wenar suggests. Let us designate a paternalistically prohibited activity as 'Z'. Wenar appears to presume that the relevant contrast is between (1) a situation in which Z is legally prohibited and in which very few people do Z and (2) a situation in which Z is legally unprohibited and in which many people do Z. He also appears to presume that, if doing Z is on balance detrimental for most people and if the removal of the Hohfeldian liberty-to-do-Z will incline all or nearly all people against doing Z, the removal of the Hohfeldian liberty-to-do-Z is on balance beneficial for most people.

Now, there are multiple ways in which a paternalistic prohibition can be detrimental on balance for most people. For one thing, legislators might err in thinking that doing Z would on balance be detrimental for people who are inclined to do it. For another thing, the contrast which Wenar poses may be inapposite. Z might be an activity which hardly anyone is disposed to undertake even in the absence of a legal ban, or it might be an activity which most people are disposed to undertake even in the presence of a legal ban.

Furthermore, even if the legislators are correct in thinking that doing Z is on balance detrimental for anyone who does it, and even if the legal proscription of Z will incline nearly everyone against pursuing that activity which nearly everyone would otherwise have pursued, the proscription might be detrimental on balance for most people. After all, the germane contrast is not simply between doing Z and abstaining from doing Z. Rather, the germane contrast is also between being legally free to do Z and being legally unfree to do Z. Because the state of being legally unfree to do Z is imposed for paternalistic reasons, it involves indignity for the person whose freedom has been removed (especially if the paternalism is hard rather than soft—something which Wenar does not specify). Even somebody who does not regard paternalism as always morally impermissible can recognise that the indignity of being subjected to a paternalistic restriction is almost always an ethical reason against the imposition of the restriction.[7] That reason may surpass the importance of any considerations that favour the restriction.

Moreover, as Ian Carter has argued persuasively—in Carter (1999: ch 2)—freedom is possessed of content-independent value. (Carter focuses his arguments chiefly on physical freedom as abilities rather than on legal freedom as permissions.

[7] See, eg, Quong (2011: ch 3).

However, the factors that he invokes can be extended *mutatis mutandis* to freedom of the latter type.) The inherent value and constitutive value and instrumental value attributed by Carter to freedom will be at stake when paternalistic prohibitions are being contemplated. Someone who adverts only to the contrast between doing Z and not doing Z is overlooking much that is lost when the legal liberty-to-do-Z is removed.

Finally, if the paternalism underlying a legal ban is hard rather than soft, it runs afoul of the arguments which I have advanced elsewhere in favour of the proposition that such paternalism is always morally wrong (Kramer 2017: ch 6). Adopting a predominantly government-focused perspective rather than a predominantly citizen-focused perspective, I have argued that hard-paternalist mandates bespeak a quidnunc mentality that undermines the moral legitimacy of those mandates. Someone who concentrates solely on the differences for citizens between doing Z and not doing Z will have neglected this government-focused consideration altogether.

Of course, this laconic listing of queries about the ethical bearings of paternalistic prohibitions is not decisive. Some of the queries are inconclusive *in abstracto*, and none of them is sufficient to disallow all soft-paternalist measures. Besides, I have here merely outlined the queries instead of adducing any sustained arguments in support of them. Hence, this subsection has simply aimed to show that the question of the moral legitimacy or illegitimacy of paternalistic prohibitions is an even more difficult question than Wenar implies.

ii. An Invalid Conclusion

Wenar presumes that, if any paternalistic legal bans are morally legitimate, the legal liberties eliminated by those bans are counterexamples to an expansive variant of my version of the Interest Theory of right-holding. Such an inference is invalid. The legal liberties in question are counterexamples to the proposition that every legal liberty is typically beneficial on balance for anyone who holds it, but that proposition is not entailed or presupposed by the expansive variant of my version of the Interest Theory. Rather, as has already been indicated, the expansive variant of my version of the Interest Theory maintains that every legal liberty *pertinently classifiable as a legal right* is typically beneficial on balance for anyone who holds it. Hence, fully consistent with the expansive variant of my version of the Interest Theory is the existence of some paternalistic legal bans that are morally legitimate. Someone upholding that expansive variant should conclude that the legal liberties eliminated by those bans are not pertinently classifiable as legal rights.

I. An Application of Wenar's Own Theory

After Wenar has moved on from his criticism of me and is expounding his own account of right-holding, he purports to have solved 'a problem that has vexed rights theory for decades' (2013: 219). As will be seen, he rests this bold claim on his insistence that the perceived justifications for various duties are keys to identifying the holders of the claim-rights that are correlative to those duties. He prompts his readers to envision a livestock ranch where the cowhands are forbidden to abuse the animals, and he then asks whether the prohibition on abuse has vested each animal with a right not to be abused. His answer to that question ascribes a pivotal role to the perceived justification that underlies the prohibition:

> [W]hether the rules of the ranch ascribe the animals a right will depend on how those applying the norm regard them. If the cowhands have a duty not to abuse the animals as livestock—as creatures raised for profit—then the rule does not ascribe a right to the animals. Livestock are not seen as having reasons at all; they are just commodities with hoofs. However, if the cowhands have a duty not to abuse the animals as animals—that is, as sensate beings who have reason to want not to be abused—then the rule does ascribe a right to the animals. The contents of the cowhands' duty may be identical under the two descriptions of 'animals'. Whether the animals have a right corresponding to this duty depends entirely on what kind of thing they are seen, on the ranch, as being (2013: 219–20).

Wenar's analysis would obviously apply also to human beings. For example, if slaves in some jurisdiction J are legally protected in various ways because they are (regarded as) valuable items of property belonging to their owners, then the slaves in J do not hold any legal rights. Even if the legal protections are very extensive, and even if the legal officials in J often refer to those protections as legal rights held by the slaves, Wenar will conclude that the officials are mistaken and that the slaves are not in fact holders of legal rights in J.

Likewise, Wenar's analysis will apply to inanimate entities. Suppose that everyone in some country K is legally obligated not to damage any of the country's grand stone formations, and suppose that the legal-governmental officials in K rather oddly believe that the stone formations are worthy of legal protection because they are sentient creatures of ultimate value. In that event, Wenar will conclude that the stone formations are holders of legal rights in K. Each stone formation there has a legal right not to be disfigured, according to Wenar.

In its deference to the justificatory beliefs of legal-governmental officials, Wenar's approach to the holding of legal rights does differ from my version of the Interest Theory. Under my theory, the status of individuals or collectivities or creatures as potential holders of legal rights is an objective ethical matter rather than something that depends on the justificatory beliefs of legal-governmental officials in any particular jurisdiction. Slaves and cattle are potential holders of legal rights in every jurisdiction, while stone formations are not potential holders of legal rights in any jurisdiction. Wenar does not even begin to explain why his position on this matter is preferable to mine. Instead, he simply professes to have solved a problem that has supposedly bedevilled other theorists of rights for decades. (In fact, the problem addressed by his example of the livestock ranch—the problem of pinning down the status of beings as potential holders of legal rights—is handled quite straightforwardly by my version of the Interest Theory. My 2001 essay 'Getting Rights Right' deals sustainedly with that very matter.)

Nor does Wenar even begin to explain how we are to ascertain the perceived justifications of legal requirements. Having myself written elsewhere on that topic at some length—in Kramer (2015: 13–24)—I readily accept that enquiries into the perceived justifications of laws are manageable. However, a crucial point to be noted here is that any such enquiry is partly ethical (even if its upshot is the conclusion that a law has been justified by officials on self-interested or otherwise immoral grounds). Hence, if Wenar thinks that his approach to the matter of delimiting the class of potential holders of legal rights is preferable to my approach because he does not have to rely on ethical judgements whereas I do, he is quite mistaken.

VI. Form and Substance

Wenar declares that typically Interest Theorists and Will Theorists have advanced their doctrines 'not as an independent exercise in conceptual analysis, but as a prelude to introducing a substantive theory of what rights there really are' (2008: 270–71). He observes that Hillel Steiner has propounded a version of the Will Theory as a component of a left-libertarian account of justice and that Raz has propounded a version of the Interest Theory as a component of a perfectionist account of autonomy and governance. Wenar believes that he has detected a surreptitious strategy in these philosophers' writings:

> The strategy here is to use a monistic analysis of an ordinary understanding of rights to relieve some of the justificatory burden from the substantive theory that will follow. On this strategy, if Steiner is accused of putting forward a substantive account of rights within which animals have no rights, he can reply that on the best analysis of an ordinary understanding of rights it is impossible for animals to have rights. If Raz is confronted by the objection that his political theory quite controversially rests the justification of rights on the interests (instead of, say, on the intrinsic dignity) of the right-holder, he can reply that on the best analysis of an ordinary understanding of rights the function of rights is to further the interest of the right-holder.

Wenar concludes:

> Within moral and political theory, the will theory has been used to support Kantian normative theories (which emphasize autonomy), while the interest theory has been used to support welfarist normative theories (which emphasize individual well-being). 'Fit with the theorist's preferred substantive theory' has in this way been a suppressed desideratum in presenting theories to account for an ordinary understanding of the nature of rights (2008: 271).

Whatever the pertinence of Wenar's remarks in application to Steiner,[8] they are wholly misguided in application to me and in application to some other theorists

[8] Wenar's remarks in application to Raz are grossly unfair, for Raz states explicitly in the opening chapter of *The Morality of Freedom* that his explications of concepts are in the service of his principles of political morality. See Raz (1986: 14–16).

of right-holding such as John Finnis. As is evident especially from my most recent books (2009; 2011; 2014; 2017), my moral outlook is that of a Stoical deontologist. Far from seeking to support welfarism furtively through my espousal of the Interest Theory of right-holding, I have assailed welfarism unremittingly insofar as it involves any contraventions of deontological constraints. Likewise, Finnis, who espouses a variant of the Interest Theory (1980: 205), is a Thomist deontologist. He too has assailed welfarism sustainedly (1980: 111–18; 1983: chs 4–5). In short, Wenar's effort to portray the Interest/Will debates as a proxy for debates between welfarists and Kantians is highly simplistic at best. In application to me and to some others such as Finnis, Wenar's portrayal is downright inaccurate. At least within legal philosophy, the Interest/Will debates have a distinctive dynamic that is not reducible to—or a surrogate for—the dynamic of any other philosophical disputation.

VII. Putative Counterexamples

In his 2013 essay, Wenar purports to deliver some telling blows against my version of the Interest Theory by coming up with some counterexamples to its theses. Without indicating as much, he in fact appears to be engaging mainly with the expansive variant of my version of the Interest Theory. At any rate, let us probe his ostensible counterexamples.

A. Strange Instances

Wenar begins his onslaught with some decidedly peculiar examples: 'We get warnings of trouble in cases like the right of the bomb squadder to disarm bombs, the right of the kamikaze to his allocation of fuel, and so on' (2013: 205). It is quite unclear what Wenar has in mind when he refers to the right of a soldier in a bomb squad to disarm bombs. Perhaps he has in mind the legal liberty of the soldier to disarm bombs, or perhaps he has in mind the soldier's claim-right against interference with the task of disarming bombs, or perhaps he has in mind both the legal liberty and the legal claim-right. However we are supposed to construe the example, it is completely unavailing as an objection to my version of the Interest Theory or to the expansive variant of my version. A soldier in a bomb squad is under a legal duty to proceed with the task of disarming bombs. If he is not legally at liberty to proceed with that task, he will be liable to undergo legal sanctions for doing what he is legally duty-bound to do. Hence, his being vested with that legal liberty will affect his situation in a way that is typically beneficial on balance for someone like him.

If Wenar instead has in mind a claim-right against interference with the task of disarming bombs, then he again is broaching an entitlement that will affect the soldier's situation in a way that is typically beneficial on balance for someone like the soldier. After all, as I have remarked in the preceding paragraph, the soldier is under a legal duty to disarm the bombs. If he does not hold any claim-right against interference with his performance of that task, then he will be legally unprotected against the thwarting of his efforts to fulfil his legal duty. A legal claim-right against his being thwarted will protect those efforts and will thus affect his situation in a way that is typically beneficial on balance for someone like him. (Of course, the government or the relevant branch of the military will also hold a claim-right correlative to any duty of non-interference.)

Wenar might retort by maintaining that the soldier on balance will be better off if he lacks a claim-right against interference, because he will then be spared from the dangerous task of disarming bombs. Any such retort would be problematic in several respects. First, whether actions of interference will spare the soldier from dangers is something that depends heavily on the nature of the interference. Many such actions will increase rather than diminish the hazardousness of his situation. Second, even if other people are legally at liberty to interfere with the soldier's endeavours, there might be an extremely low likelihood that anyone will exercise such a liberty. If so, then the soldier will not be spared from any perils by interference with his efforts. Third, any diversion of the soldier from his task will involve his contravening his legal duty to carry out that task. Unless he can raise a legal excuse that will shield him from sanctions for his non-fulfilment of his responsibilities, he will be liable to undergo such sanctions. Quite dubious is the proposition that the diversion will on balance have made the soldier better off; the dishonour of his failure to fulfil his responsibilities and the possible sanctions for that failure might well surpass the benefit of being spared (temporarily) from a dangerous mission. Fourth, even if the three foregoing points are put aside, and thus even if we assume *arguendo* that interference will occur and that it will affect the situation of the soldier in a way that is on balance typically beneficial for someone like him, the example of the soldier is consistent with my version of the Interest Theory. After all, the example will then involve duties of non-interference that do not correlate with any claim-rights held by the soldier.[9] My version of the Interest Theory will hence generate the conclusion that those duties correlate solely with claim-rights held by the government or by the relevant branch of the military. In other words, if all the assumptions that underlie Wenar's example are accepted *arguendo*, my version of the Interest Theory will generate the conclusion that Wenar has misattributed the claim-rights that are correlative with the aforementioned duties. Those duties are owed exclusively to the government or to the relevant branch of the military rather than to the soldier.

A full analysis of the example of the kamikaze pilot would be closely similar to my analysis of the example of the soldier in the bomb squad. Hence, I will confine

[9] Wenar's ascription of a legal right to the soldier presupposes that at least one other person is under a legal duty to abstain from interference with the soldier's task. Because such a duty is almost certainly owed by everyone else, I refer in the text to multiple duties that correlate with multiple rights.

myself here to the chief difference between the two examples. Whereas the full success of the task of disarming bombs does not involve the death of the person who undertakes that task, the full success of a kamikaze mission does involve the death of the person who undertakes it. Hence, the third of my four points in the preceding paragraph might seem to be inapplicable to the example of the kamikaze pilot. However, anyone who draws that conclusion is ignoring what I have elsewhere said about the relevant evaluations. Although the germane evaluative stance for applying my version of the Interest Theory is predominantly objective, it allows that 'one of the interests of a typical person resides in being [able] to satisfy his or her strongly felt desires'.[10] Anyone who is disposed to fly a kamikaze mission will very likely be fanatically devoted to the cause for which he is prepared to die, and he would thus regard the dishonour of a thwarted mission as worse than the loss of his life. Given as much, and given the importance of one's being able to satisfy one's strongly felt desires, the ascription of a legal right of non-interference to the kamikaze pilot will be apposite; the fulfilment of the duty correlative to the right will affect the pilot's situation in a way that is generally beneficial for someone like the pilot.

B. Rights to Arrange Marriages

In his scattershot objections to my version of the Interest Theory, Wenar next adverts to the existence of legal rights to arrange marriages (2008: 205):

> In some societies, parents have a legal right to arrange marriages. That statement is clearly true, and remains true, even if it is also true that the human beings who are parents will normally be better off when parents have no legal right to arrange marriages (perhaps this is stressful or fuels resentment).

Wenar is here again taking aim at the expansive variant of my version of the Interest Theory, since the legal entitlements principally involved are powers and liberties. If the parents are not under any legal duties to exercise those legal powers and liberties, then the possession of the powers and liberties will affect the situation of the parents in a way that is typically beneficial for people like them. In such circumstances, after all, they are legally at liberty to exercise their powers and legally at liberty not to exercise their powers. If they sense that exercising those powers would be stressful or resentment-inducing, they can exercise their liberties not to exercise those powers.

By contrast, if the parents are under legal duties to exercise their powers and liberties to arrange marriages, they are legally required to proceed even if they sense that their doing so will be stressful or resentment-inducing. However, what are burdensome for the parents in such circumstances are not the liberties and

[10] Kramer (2003: 435–36). The strength of desires is a property that pertains both to their intensity and to their tenacity. A desire is strong in the sense of being tenacious if it would continue to be harboured after the elimination of any misconceptions or ignorance relating to the physical and psychological facts that bear on the fulfilment of the desire.

powers but instead the duties. As for the liberties and powers themselves, they are pertinently classifiable as rights unless the stress-producing or resentment-eliciting situations are typical rather than exceptional. In the unlikely event that such situations are indeed typical, those Hohfeldian liberties and powers are not properly classifiable as rights.

C. Rights to Choose Marriage Partners

Wenar adduces a further putative counterexample to the expansive variant of my version of the Interest Theory (2013: 205): '[I]n some societies, adults have a legal right to choose their own marriage partners. Yet it could be that adults would normally be better off were marriages arranged by parents (perhaps parents choose better partners)'. As can be inferred from much of what I have said in section V.H.i, Wenar's parenthetical comment on the factors at stake in this example is glib. Even in the rather improbable event that parents would typically choose better marriage partners for their offspring than would the offspring themselves, the vesting of the offspring with liberties and powers to choose their own partners will uphold their dignity and will lessen the control which their parents are able to exert over them. Moreover, if somebody wishes to abide by her parents' choice of a partner for her, she will almost always be at liberty to do so. Hence, decidedly far-fetched are the societies in which young adults will not typically be better off on balance as a result of being vested with the liberties and powers that are at issue in this example. If there are any such societies, those Hohfeldian liberties and powers are not properly classifiable as rights therein.

D. The Message to be Gathered

Wenar sums up the message which he has attempted to convey through his onslaughts against the expansive variant of my version of the Interest Theory: 'What legal rights there are does not depend on what makes a human life go well, so we cannot make the analysis of the former turn on the truth about the latter' (2013: 205). If this pronouncement is an affirmation of the legal-positivist insistence on the separability of law and morality, then it is correct—but, as an admonition, it is superfluous. I am already well acquainted with the strengths of legal positivism. If the pronouncement is instead an assertion that the holders of legal rights can be identified without any evaluations of the sort required under my version of the Interest Theory, it is an *ipse dixit* whose only 'support' stems from the aforementioned onslaughts.

Wenar tries to provide further support in a footnote by invoking Rousseau and Marx and Jesus:

> Or consider the legal rights of property owners. Both Rousseau and Marx insist that it is bad for humans to own private property, because of the antagonistic relations and

antisocial attitudes this brings. Jesus adds the thesis that it is worse to be rich than poor. These claims may be true or false, but no analysis of rights should make the existence of property rights within, say, the Swiss legal system turn on the truth or falsity of humanist critiques of capitalism, or on the truth or falsity of the thesis that the rich man shall hardly enter into the kingdom of heaven (2013: 205, fn 9).

i. Rousseau and Marx

Let us begin with Rousseau and Marx. One important distinction blurred by Wenar here is the difference between the overarching institution of private property and particular instances of the rights that can be acquired under that institution, and another important distinction obfuscated here by Wenar is the difference between what is generally beneficial or detrimental for humanity and what is generally beneficial or detrimental for a particular owner of property. Although Rousseau and Marx regarded the institution of private property as detrimental for humanity, each of them could recognise that there is a straightforward sense in which a particular owner of assets is typically better off by dint of her ownership than she would be in the absence of that status. This point becomes clear when we note that the relevant evaluative judgements—the judgements concerning whether the owner O is better off or not—are to be reached through a contrast with a nearby possible world rather than through a contrast with a preposterously remote world (a world that might not even be possible). That is, we need to draw a contrast between a state of affairs in which O possesses some rights of ownership and an otherwise similar state of affairs in which O lacks those rights. Although O may be worse off in each of those states of affairs than she would be in some socialist utopia, people like O in the actual world and in any proximate worlds are typically better off with some rights of ownership than without any. Even someone who regrets the inexistence of the aforementioned utopia can recognise as much.

ii. Jesus

Jesus, in his responses to the rich young ruler and in a number of his other pronouncements, contended that people are decisively worse off by dint of being vested with abundant rights of ownership. That is, by laying up treasures on earth, they are failing to lay up treasures in heaven. Thus, Jesus and his followers might appear to be committed to the proposition that legal rights of ownership are generally on balance detrimental for the people who hold them. Notwithstanding, Jesus and his followers could recognise that such legal rights are indeed legal rights. Or so Wenar has apparently reasoned.

Now, given that Jesus emphasised that his kingdom is not of this world and that his followers should render to Caesar what is Caesar's, he could readily accept that the nature of legal rights is to be ascertained by reference to the concerns and practices of this earthly vale of tears. After all, legal rights are decidedly earthly entities. At any rate, whatever Jesus might have thought about the matter, any philosophers of legal rights should recognise that they are exploring a worldly phenomenon whose nature is to be elucidated by reference to worldly values rather than by reference to the eschatological preoccupations of Jesus. Accordingly, in the evaluative judgements through which we determine whether legal rights of ownership are typically detrimental or typically beneficial for the people who hold them, we should be prescinding from supramundane considerations and should be concentrating instead on terrestrial matters. When our evaluative judgements are so focused, we shall conclude that legal rights of ownership are typically beneficial for the people who hold them.

VIII. The Roles of Right-Holders

Building on a passing remark by Raz (1986: 180), Wenar thinks that he has come up with a novel insight into the connections between rights and roles. He asserts that '[m]any problems in the analysis of rights can be solved when we start with the idea that rights attach not to individuals, but to roles' (2013: 206). Now, even if we leave aside the fact that not all rights are role-based—as Wenar eventually acknowledges—the dichotomy posed in this formulation is untenable. Role-based rights attach to individuals by dint of their occupying the roles which they occupy. From January 1993 to January 2001, the rights of the Presidency of the United States attached to Bill Clinton because he occupied that office. Of course, it is true that the general rights appurtenant to such an office persist after any occupant of the office has vacated it. However, it is also true that those rights are instantiated as rights held by each individual who occupies the Presidency; the instantiations of the general rights are held by each such individual during his or her period of office.

More sensibly, Wenar suggests that the role-based character of numerous rights should lead us to focus on the interests of role-occupants when we bring to bear the Interest Theory on a situation that involves such rights: 'We should consider the interests not of Michael, the human being who has accepted a promise … We should consider the interests of Michael qua promisee' (2013: 206). Though Wenar has in mind Raz's version of the Interest Theory at this juncture in his article, these quoted sentences are pertinent in application to my version. Indeed, the problem for Wenar is that the insight encapsulated in those sentences is not unique to his theory. As is apparent in IT-1 in section I above, that insight figures in my version of the Interest Theory of right-holding. In IT-1, the interests to be considered when we apply my version of the Interest Theory are those of 'a being like *X*'. That deliberately flexible wording leaves room for context-specific factors to determine the relevant class of beings in each case. In myriads of cases, the relevant classes of beings comprise the holders of roles.

IX. Applications of Wenar's Theory

Wenar brings to bear his role-focused theory of right-holding on two scenarios, each of which—so he presumes—involves a legal duty to which no legal claim-right is correlative (2013: 211). In the first of these scenarios, an inmate of a prison is under a legal duty to abstain from trying to escape. According to Wenar, the warden of the prison does not have any legal right to the inmate's forbearance. Using a first-person plural pronoun in lieu of any effort to substantiate an empirical claim about the way in which most people would view the situation, Wenar asserts that 'we do not say that a warden has a right that a prisoner stay in his prison' (2013: 211). Having attributed such a view of the matter to some unspecified class of people denoted by the first-person plural pronoun, Wenar tries to vindicate that view with some a priori assertions about the contents or formulations of legal norms that pertain to prisons. He tells us that 'legal norms do not support statements that bring the warden into the specification of a prisoner's duty' (2013: 211). He nowhere tells us which legal norms he has in mind or even which jurisdiction he has in mind.

At any rate, I am clearly not within the extension of Wenar's first-person plural pronoun, because my version of the Interest Theory will lead to conclusions markedly different from his. Correlative to the prisoner's duty are (1) a claim-right held by the state or by the relevant organ of the state and (2) a claim-right held by the warden. An affirmation of the existence of those claim-rights is readily inferable from IT-1 and IT-2, when IT-1 and IT-2 are applied to the circumstances of the aforementioned parties and are conjoined with my arguments elsewhere about the reality of collectively held rights (Kramer 1998: 49–60).

In his other scenario, involving a capital convict, Wenar does tell us which jurisdiction he has in mind. He puzzlingly submits that the members of a firing squad in Oklahoma are legally obligated to shoot a capital convict whose execution by firing squad has been duly scheduled. Perhaps Wenar is referring to Oklahoma in some counterfactual world, because—as he himself obliquely acknowledges in a footnote (2013: 211, fn 19)—the sole method of execution used in Oklahoma in the actual world for more than a quarter of a century has been that of lethal injection. At any rate, let us for present purposes assume that there is a legal obligation of the sort which Wenar posits. He opines that 'Oklahomans would not of course say that capital criminals have a right to be shot' (2013: 211). Though this quoted statement is another armchair empirical conjecture, it is safe enough. No elaborate survey is needed to confirm it. Moreover, in denying that a capital convict has a claim-right to be shot, Wenar arrives at the same conclusion that follows straightforwardly from my version of the Interest Theory. However, he draws an inapt inference from that conclusion. That is, he infers that the duty of the members of the firing squad does not correlate with any claim-right. Such an inference is incorrect, for the claim-right correlative to that duty is held by the state or by the relevant organ of the state.

X. Further Applications of Wenar's Theory

Wenar goes on to present two further sets of examples to which he applies his role-focused account of right-holding. Let us take those sets of examples in turn.

A. Third Parties

In his first set of examples, Wenar unexceptionably contends that a third party to whom a contract pertains might not be a right-holder under the terms of the contract (2013: 213). Such a contention is obviously correct and is obviously in accordance with my version of the Interest Theory. For example, suppose that a company enters into a contract with a prison to keep every high-security inmate securely incarcerated. It is not the case that each such inmate has a claim-right to be securely incarcerated under the terms of the contract.

Wenar proceeds to the matter of third-party beneficiaries. (He invokes the doctrine of *jus tertii*, but his discussion and citation make clear that he instead has in mind the somewhat different problem of third-party-beneficiary contracts.) He declares that, if 'the relevant legal norm [in some jurisdiction] affirm[s] a duty relating the promisor and … a third-party beneficiary', then any third-party-beneficiary contract governed by such a norm in that jurisdiction vests the beneficiary with a legal right to the promisor's performance (2013: 213). Though Wenar does not explicitly indicate to his readers how they are supposed to tell whether any legal norm in some jurisdiction does provide for duties owed to third-party beneficiaries, his citation of the UK Contracts (Rights of Third Parties) Act of 1999 reveals that he is largely aligning himself with the Will Theory on this issue. That is, he believes that a third-party beneficiary is a right-holder under the terms of some contract if and only if the beneficiary is legally empowered through any relevant norm(s) of the jurisdiction to demand enforcement of a duty imposed by that contract. Note that such a position does not fully align Wenar with the Will Theory on this issue, since he appears to presume that the status of a beneficiary as a beneficiary is a necessary condition for her status as a right-holder under the terms of the contract. Still, his position largely aligns him with the Will Theory on this matter, and it thus confronts him with the difficulties which beset that theory.

Indeed, the difficulties afflicting the Will Theory are compounded by Wenar's explanation of his stance. Wenar declares that a legal system LS which empowers third-party beneficiaries to demand enforcement of contractual duties is thereby sending out a message about such beneficiaries: 'Beneficiaries, these legal systems hold, want benefits' (2013: 213). Because such a message can be attributed to LS, Wenar contends, third-party beneficiaries are holders of rights under the terms of the contracts that make them beneficiaries. Yet suppose that some other legal system LX empowers a state agency to pursue enforcement proceedings on behalf of third-party beneficiaries. Suppose that the legislators or jurists in LX who introduce such an arrangement expressly affirm that they have done so because a state agency can bear the costs of enforcement proceedings more efficiently than can individual beneficiaries; hence, the arrangement will more effectively secure the conferral of contractually specified benefits on those to whom the benefits are due. Should we conclude that LX is not conveying the message that third-party beneficiaries want benefits? If Wenar answers this question affirmatively, his position is not credible. If he instead answers the question negatively, he is in effect conceding that the only necessary condition for right-holding which he has managed to ferret out is the status of a third-party beneficiary as a beneficiary. His position in that respect does not differ from my version of the Interest Theory.

Unlike my version of the Interest Theory, however, Wenar's position on this matter is heir to all the shortcomings of a Will-Theory approach. Even if we leave aside for now the strange desiderative focus of his role-centred account of right-holding, his account will run afoul of those shortcomings. For example, suppose that the third-party beneficiary under the terms of some contract is an infant or animal, and suppose that the relevant law of the jurisdiction empowers a guardian to demand enforcement of the contract on behalf of the third-party beneficiary. Is the infant or animal a right-holder under the terms of the contract? If Wenar answers affirmatively—in accordance with what he says later in his article (2013: 219–20)—then his dalliance with the Will Theory is at an end. If he instead answers negatively, then he is exposing himself to the very criticisms of the Will Theory which he rehearses.

Wenar's remarks on the example of the third-party beneficiary are uninformatively laconic, but perhaps they are meant to hint at a more complex account of right-holding. Perhaps Wenar thinks that such a beneficiary is a right-holder under the terms of the relevant contract if and only if the law of the jurisdiction either (1) empowers third-party beneficiaries themselves to enforce the duties owed to them or (2) establishes that such duties can be enforced by individuals or organisations who act as guardians of the third-party beneficiaries. If Wenar does have this disjunctive test in mind for his approach to the matter of third-party beneficiaries, then he has not formed a dalliance with the Will Theory on the matter—contrary to what his stark discussion appears to imply. Still, such an approach would be vulnerable to some major objections.

First, even in a jurisdiction where the doctrine of privity of contract has not been displaced by anything like the UK Contracts (Rights of Third Parties) Act of 1999, quite a few third-party beneficiaries will be classifiable as right-holders under Wenar's disjunctive test—since quite a few contracts involving such beneficiaries are formed by parties who act as guardians of them. For instance, suppose that a prison service enters into a contract with a caterer for the provision of nutritionally balanced meals to the prison service's inmates. According to the disjunctive test, the inmates are right-holders under the terms of the contract; the prison service empowered to enforce the contract is not only a direct party to the contract but is also a guardian of the inmates with fiduciary duties to look after their basic well-being. Of course, I agree with this implication of the disjunctive test, for it concurs with the conclusion that would be generated by my version of the Interest Theory. However, as I shall remark in a moment, Wenar has proclaimed that his approach to the matter of third-party beneficiaries is an alternative to the Interest Theory rather than a version thereof.

Second, the rationale for the restrictiveness of Wenar's disjunctive test is quite unclear. That is, why should we not classify third-party beneficiaries as right-holders even in a legal system where the disjunctive test is not satisfied? Wenar's answer appears to be that the 'beneficiaries want benefits' message is conveyed by the law of a jurisdiction in which the disjunctive test is satisfied but not by the law of a jurisdiction in which that test is unsatisfied. Nowhere does Wenar try to furnish any explication or defence of the theory of legal interpretation that leads him to such a curious conclusion.

At any rate, the main source of bemusement in Wenar's discussion of this issue is his contention that his role-centred approach to the matter of third-party beneficiaries is 'a simple solution to a problem that has bedeviled the Interest Theory' (2013: 213). If somebody question-beggingly assumes that my thesis IT-2 is incorrect, then of course he or she will further believe that the problem of third-party beneficiaries is nettlesome for my theory. However, from the perspective of someone who does not beg the question in that fashion, the matter of third-party beneficiaries is not nettlesome at all. Far from amounting to a crux that bedevils my version of the Interest Theory, that matter is straightforwardly handled by the combination of IT-1 and IT-2.

Is there any non-question-begging consideration that might be invoked in favour of Wenar's contention that the matter of third-party beneficiaries is problematic for the Interest Theory? A legal power of enforcement, vested in each party to a contract—and vested in a third-party beneficiary in a jurisdiction where the doctrine of privity of contract has been circumscribed—is quite often designated in English-speaking countries as a 'right of action'. Wenar makes no mention of that fact, but he might have invoked it in support of his contention. Any such invocation would have been futile, however. Wenar raises the matter of third-party beneficiaries in an article focused on claim-rights, and my version of the Interest Theory is likewise focused on claim-rights (accompanied by arrays of immunities). Yet the term 'right' in 'right of action' is not being used to denote a claim-right; rather, it is manifestly being used to denote a power-right. A capacious variant of my version of the Interest Theory can explain why that power of enforcement is aptly classified as a right—in the expansive or generic sense of 'right'—but my point here is simply that its being so classified does not cast any doubt whatsoever on my account of the holding of claim-rights.

B. The Meter Attendant and the Army Captain

Wenar introduces a further pair of examples to illustrate the virtues of his role-centred theory of right-holding. He first envisages a meter attendant who issues a parking ticket that directs a motorist to pay a fine, and he then envisages an army captain who orders a soldier to peel some potatoes. With another evidence-free use of a first-person plural pronoun, Wenar asserts: 'We are ordinarily inclined to say that a meter attendant does not have a right that the car owner pays his ticket, while the captain does have a right that the corporal do what she ordered' (2013: 213–14). The conclusions ascribed by Wenar from his armchair to ordinary users of the English language are correct, and they are fully in accordance with my version of the Interest Theory. Because the meter attendant as described by Wenar does not bear any responsibility to ensure that the duty imposed through her issuance of the ticket is fulfilled, the existence of that duty does not normatively protect any aspect of her situation that is normally beneficial for someone like her. Because the captain's fulfilment of his own responsibilities depends on the general compliance of the soldiers with the commands that have been issued to them, the duty imposed on the corporal does normatively protect an aspect of the situation of the captain that is normally beneficial for someone like him. Insofar as Wenar's theory also leads to these conclusions, it does not differ one whit—at least extensionally—from my version of the Interest Theory.

XI. Enforceability

As we have seen in section IV above, the third tenet of Wenar's role-centred account of right-holding is as follows: 'Enforcement of this duty [namely, the duty correlative to the right that is held] is appropriate, ceteris paribus' (2013: 209). I have already queried the unelucidated and undefended inclusion of the *ceteris paribus* qualification in this tenet of Wenar's theory. Let us now glance at his terse exposition of the tenet as a whole:

> [The third tenet of the role-centered theory] requires that claim-rights correlate with enforceable duties: duties that (absent countervailing considerations) are appropriately enforced, either by coercing performance or by penalizing nonperformance. Here the analysis is detecting a feature of rights persisting from their origins in the law. [The first and second tenets of the role-centered theory] alone may be fulfilled within affective relationships. For instance, a friend may have a duty to try to repair the damage from the terrible gaffe he made, and his buddy may have reason to want him to try. But enforcement of duties is rarely appropriate within such relations, so we are wary of speaking of rights here (2013: 214).

One point to be noted here is that the *ceteris paribus* clause and the 'absent countervailing considerations' qualification are at odds with Wenar's later assertion that '[a]ll claim-rights are enforceable' (2013: 226). Now, although I have criticised Wenar for including a *ceteris paribus* clause after his derision of me for invoking a somewhat similar qualification in IT-1—a qualification which Wenar incorrectly locates, as I have already argued—the inclusion of such a clause somewhere in his third tenet is salutary as a corrective to the excessive sweepingness of his later assertion about all claim-rights. Not only are some moral claim-rights unenforceable, but so too are some legal claim-rights. To be sure, unenforceable legal claim-rights are decidedly atypical, and their unenforceability warrants their being labelled as 'nominal'. Nonetheless, as I have argued elsewhere, unenforceable legal claim-rights can be meaningful in certain respects.[11]

Still, although a qualification is needed in the third tenet of the role-centred theory of right-holding, the quoted passage—unlike the formulation of the third tenet itself—reveals that Wenar has positioned the qualification inappositely. Were we to be guided by the formulation of the third tenet itself, we might naturally presume that Wenar is advancing the following thesis:

> *Typical Enforceability Thesis*: All duties correlate with claim-rights, and duties are typically enforceable.

As is made clear by the final sentence in the passage quoted above, however, Wenar is instead advancing the following thesis:

> *Typical Correlation Thesis:* Duties typically correlate with claim-rights, and correlated duties are enforceable.

Wenar adheres to the latter thesis rather than to the former, for he contends that duties are not correlated with claim-rights when the enforcement of the duties would be inappropriate. His only attempt to justify the Typical Correlation Thesis, in the final sentence of the quoted passage, is another unsubstantiated use of a first-person plural pronoun to propound an empirical claim about ordinary discourse. That ersatz justification is patently unsatisfactory, for the Typical Enforceability Thesis rather than the Typical Correlation Thesis is the apt corrective to Wenar's later universally quantified assertion about the enforceability of claim-rights.

Furthermore, Wenar is mistaken in thinking that the moral duty which he recounts is not enforceable. Should the blundering friend not suitably fulfil his moral duty of repair by apologising and taking any other requisite measures, the offended friend can enforce the duty by terminating or suspending or attenuating the friendship. If Wenar does not think that such a response by the offended friend would be properly classifiable as an instance of enforcement, he has done nothing to explain why it would not be.

XII. Interests Versus Desires

Towards the end of his 2013 article, Wenar seeks to establish that his focus on desires in his role-centred account and kind-centred account of right-holding is

[11] See Kramer (2001: 74–78). Note that I am here talking about unenforceable legal duties rather than about legal duties that are enforceable but unenforced. In contrast with legal duties that are unenforceable, unenforced legal duties are commonplace.

superior to the focus on interests in the Interest Theory. As a prelude to my final set of engagements with his work, which will concentrate on this concluding strand of his argumentation, we should recall some points made in earlier portions of this essay. First, my version of the Interest Theory is not justificatory in its orientation. It adverts to the interests of a right-holder not in order to ascertain whether those interests are sufficiently important ethically to justify the existence of some duty D, but instead in order to ascertain who holds the right that correlates with D. Second, nothing in my version of the Interest Theory smacks of welfarism. My version of that theory is not propping up any variety of consequentialism, and the conception of interests that imbues it is predominantly objective.

Moreover, as is emphasised in my earliest essay on rights (1998: 91), my conception of interests is deliberately thin in the sense of being unspecific. Under my conception, some state of affairs or some event is in the interest of a holder of legal rights RH if and only if the actuality of that state of affairs or the occurrence of that event would on balance bring about an improvement in RH's situation or avert a worsening therein. The abstract notions in this conception can be filled in with the correct set of evaluative judgements that will address any of the circumstances with which my version of the Interest Theory may be confronted.

A. An Unfounded Characterisation of Interests

Wenar submits that Interest Theorists associate the notion of interests with well-being, welfare, or quality of life. He then adverts to two rival accounts of such properties: a hedonic account and an objective-list account. According to the former, the goodness of a person's life increases in direct proportion to the degree of pleasure which the person experiences, and in inverse proportion to the degree of pain which she experiences. Nothing else has any bearing on how good her life is. According to the objective-list conception of well-being, 'pleasure is not the only thing that makes a life go better … [Also on] the list [are] values such as knowledge, the awareness of beauty, and the experience of mutual love' (2013: 227). Wenar purports here to be drawing upon Derek Parfit's famous discussion of what makes a life go better, but he curiously misrepresents Parfit's exposition of the objective-list approach. Parfit nowhere intimates that pleasure as such is on the objective list of good things, and indeed he suggests that two types of pleasure—sadistic pleasure, and aesthetic pleasure in what is in fact ugly—are objectively bad (Parfit 1984: 499). His exclusion of pleasure as such from the objective list of good things is wise, for its inclusion would imply that someone can lead an unalloyedly good life while being permanently connected to the experience machine broached by Robert Nozick (1974: 42–45).

Wenar's misrepresentation of Parfit on the content of the objective list is odd, but it appears to be connected to his insistence that proponents of the Interest Theory are advancing their accounts of right-holding in the service of some underlying welfarist doctrines. Let it be emphasised again, then, that I am not a devotee of welfarism. Yet, in one significant respect, my conception of interests does depart from a list of what is objectively conducive to the goodness of a person's life.[12] As has already been remarked, my conception of interests is predominantly but not exclusively objective. It allows that the fulfilment of strongly held desires is good for a person, and it does not exclude any desires on ethical grounds. Were I offering a list of what is objectively conducive to the goodness of a person's life, I would have to place ethical constraints on the strongly held desires whose fulfilment is to be classified as good. I agree with Parfit about the objective badness of sadistic pleasure for the person who experiences the pleasure. However, for the purposes of expounding and applying my version of the Interest Theory of right-holding—and also for the purposes of expounding and applying my separately developed theory of freedom (Kramer 2003: 435–36)—my conception of interests is pre-ethical. That conception takes account not only of the things which a person should desire, but also of the things which a person does (strongly) desire. The things which a person should desire are contained in the objective component of my conception, whereas the things which a person does strongly desire are contained in the subjective component. Of course, for any typical person, many desiderata will be comprehended within both components; but the immoral ends of any person's strongly held immoral desires are located only within the subjective component. Because my conception of interests comprises both components, it is not an ethical conception of a good life along the lines of the objective list broached by Parfit. It is instead a pre-ethical account of the things that are advantageous for any potential right-holder *X*, given what *X*'s character is. If some *X* is depravedly enamoured of certain wicked pursuits, his being legally protected against interference with his engaging in those pursuits is advantageous for him in this pre-ethical sense.

B. Some Examples Redux

In the final pages of his 2013 article, Wenar returns to a few of the examples which he has invoked earlier in the article. In so doing, he draws upon what he has in the interim said about his opponents' understanding of interests. He writes:

> The interests (say, the pleasures) of parents cannot explain their legal rights to receive child support, or to arrange marriages; nor do the pleasures of soccer goalies explain their right not to be obstructed. Similarly, the rights of members of the bomb squad will not likely turn on their pleasures, awareness of beauty, or experience of mutual love (2013: 228).

Let us here leave aside the fact that pleasure is not an item on the objective list which Parfit outlines. In connection with my version of the Interest Theory, what

[12] I concentrate here on the interests of persons. My remarks could be amplified to cover the interests of other potential holders of legal rights, but such an amplification would involve complexities that are beside the point of my present discussion.

is chiefly objectionable about this latest passage is that Wenar is plainly focusing on justificatory versions of the Interest Theory. He is impugning any versions that are centred on the justifications for rights and their correlative duties. Since my version of the Interest Theory is not concerned with such justifications, it is wholly untouched by everything that Wenar says here.

Wenar goes on to maintain that the failings in the versions of the Interest Theory which he assails are overcome by his role-focused account of right-holding with its attributions of role-based desires to the occupants of roles. He contends:

> Desires are conceptually prior in such contexts; 'interest' derives its meaning from desires. And, as we have seen, role-based desires themselves often derive from role-based duties. Parents want to receive child support because this helps them do their duty as parents; goalies want not to be obstructed because this helps them support their team (2013: 228).

Far from clear is what impels Wenar to think that attributions of desires to the occupants of roles are crucial and salutary for an understanding of the status of the occupants as right-holders. The interests of a goalie in being able to fulfil the responsibilities of his role are the key factor that enables my version of the Interest Theory to identify him as the holder of a claim-right that correlates with the duty of every other player to abstain from interference with his performance of that role. Likewise, the interests of a parent in being able to fulfil her legal and moral responsibilities are the key factor that enables my version of the Interest Theory to identify her as the holder of a claim-right that correlates with the duty of the government to make child-support payments. Wenar repeatedly asserts (as in this latest quotation) that '[d]esires are conceptually prior in such contexts', but the reiteration of that assertion does not shed any light upon it or render it true. We do not need to attribute desires to role-occupants, when we can instead simply point to the responsibilities of a role and observe that the situation of someone who occupies that role will typically be better if she is legally protected against interference with her fulfilment of those responsibilities—or if she is legally entitled to be assisted in her fulfilment of those responsibilities. Such an observation does not per se explain why or whether the existence of a legal duty of non-interference (or a legal duty of assistance) is justified, but it does enable us to identify the holder of the claim-right which correlates with that legal duty.

XIII. Conclusion

This essay has aimed to defend my version of the Interest Theory of right-holding against Wenar's broadsides. Because those broadsides do not form a single line of argument, I have had to pursue a number of distinct lines of argument in response. Still, quite a few of my rejoinders overlap, and they are all aimed at showing that Wenar's criticisms of my version of the Interest Theory are otiose. Having pursued that endeavour, I have said hardly anything herein about Wenar's remarks on the

Razian version of the Interest Theory or about his remarks on the Will Theory. With some of his objections to those theories I am in agreement. However, on the decisive question whether Wenar's role-centred/kind-centred alternative to my version of the Interest Theory is a promising and much-needed path, this essay dissents from his contentions. His presentation of his alternative theory badly underestimates the resourcefulness of my version of the Interest Theory, and some aspects of his alternative are exceedingly dubious.[13]

References

Carter, I (1999) *A Measure of Freedom* (Oxford: Oxford University Press).

Finnis, J (1980) *Natural Law and Natural Rights* (Oxford: Oxford University Press).

—— (1983) *Fundamentals of Ethics* (Washington, DC: Georgetown University Press).

Kramer, MH (1998) 'Rights Without Trimmings' in MH Kramer, NE Simmonds and H Steiner, *A Debate over Rights. Philosophical Enquiries* (Oxford: Oxford University Press).

—— (2001) 'Getting Rights Right' in MH Kramer (ed), *Rights, Wrongs and Responsibilities* (Basingstoke: Palgrave Macmillan).

—— (2003) *The Quality of Freedom* (Oxford: Oxford University Press).

—— (2008) 'Rights in Legal and Political Philosophy' in K Whittington, D Kelemen and G Caldeira (eds), *The Oxford Handbook of Law and Politics* (Oxford: Oxford University Press).

—— (2009) *Moral Realism as a Moral Doctrine* (Oxford: Wiley-Blackwell).

—— (2010) 'Refining the Interest Theory of Rights' 55 *The American Journal of Jurisprudence* 31.

—— (2011) *The Ethics of Capital Punishment* (Oxford: Oxford University Press).

—— (2013) 'Some Doubts about Alternatives to the Interest Theory of Rights' 123 *Ethics* 245.

—— (2014) *Torture and Moral Integrity* (Oxford: Oxford University Press).

—— (2015) 'Paternalism, Perfectionism, and Public Goods' 60 *The American Journal of Jurisprudence* 1.

—— (2017) *Liberalism with Excellence* (Oxford: Oxford University Press).

Kramer, MH and Steiner, H (2007) 'Theories of Rights: Is There a Third Way?' 27 *Oxford Journal of Legal Studies* 281.

Nozick, R (1974) *Anarchy, State, and Utopia* (New York, NY: Basic Books).

Parfit, D (1984) *Reasons and Persons* (Oxford: Oxford University Press).

[13] An earlier version of this essay was written for a conference at the National University of Singapore in May 2016. I am extremely grateful to the following participants for their valuable comments and queries: Rowan Cuft, Mike Grainger, Andrew Halpin, Mark McBride, Diego Mejia-Lemos, James Penner and Gopal Sreenivasan.

Quong, J (2011) *Liberalism Without Perfection* (Oxford: Oxford University Press).
Raz, J (1986) *The Morality of Freedom* (Oxford: Oxford University Press).
Wenar, L (2008) 'The Analysis of Rights' in MH Kramer et al (eds), *The Legacy of HLA Hart: Legal, Political, and Moral Philosophy* (Oxford: Oxford University Press).
—— (2013) 'The Nature of Claim-Rights' 123 *Ethics* 202.

4

Desires, Interests and Claim-Rights

SIMON CĂBULEA MAY*

An individual's claim-right is her right that another agent fulfil a duty to act in some way.[1] The agent owes this duty to the individual and would wrong her by violating it. The two parties accordingly stand in a special relationship, one that is not shared with third parties. An analysis of the concept must specify criteria for the ascription of a claim-right to an individual. The analysis should satisfy two conditions: it ought to be both extensionally adequate and capable of underpinning an explanation of the significance of claim-rights in social life.

Leif Wenar's (2013) kind-desire theory states that an individual holds a claim-right against an agent only because she has reason to desire, as a member of a particular social or natural kind, that the agent fulfil his duty. He argues that the kind-desire theory is superior to the interest theory of claim-rights, which states that an individual holds a claim-right against an agent only because his duty is in some manner beneficial to her (Kramer 2002; Raz 1986). The fundamental difference between the two approaches is therefore whether it is an individual's desires or her interests that ground her claim-rights.

In this essay, I compare the merits of the kind-desire theory and a particular type of interest theory. The justificatory interest theory states that an individual holds a claim-right against an agent only because her interests serve to justify his duty. I argue that the kind-desire theory does not satisfy either condition for a satisfactory analysis of claim-rights as well as a version of this justificatory interest theory. Since my thesis is strictly comparative, I do not also defend the justificatory interest theory as correct, all things considered.

In the first section, I set out and illustrate the kind-desire theory. In the second section, I discuss and respond to Wenar's claim that the interest theory is extensionally inadequate. In the third section, I argue that it is instead the

* Earlier versions of this essay were presented at the Bled Philosophical Conference, the University of Pavia, and the University of Miami in 2016. I am grateful to the participants for their comments in discussion. I am especially grateful to Rowan Cruft, Mark McBride and Leif Wenar for their written comments on an earlier draft.

[1] In the Hohfeldian analytical framework, claim-rights are distinguished from liberty-rights, powers and immunities (Hohfeld 1919).

kind-desire theory that is extensionally inadequate. In the final section, I argue that the justificatory interest theory better explains why an individual's claim-rights are important for her status within a practice. Since this is an essential aspect of the significance of claim-rights in social life, the justificatory interest theory also fares better on the second condition for a satisfactory account.

I. The Kind-Desire Theory

Wenar (2013: 219) formally states his theory as follows:

> Consider a system of norms *S* that refers to entities under descriptions that are kinds, *D* and *R*. If and only if, in circumstances *C*, a norm of *S* supports statements of the form:
>
> 1. Some *D* (*qua D*) has a duty to *phi* some *R* (*qua R*); where '*phi*' is a verb phrase specifying an action …
> 2. *R*'s (*qua R*'s) want such duties to be fulfilled; and
> 3. Enforcement of this duty is appropriate, *ceteris paribus*;
>
> Then: the *R* has a claim-right in *S* that the *D* fulfill this duty in circumstances *C*.

This formalisation can be explained in five points:

Domain: The kind-desire theory applies to all normative domains, whether law, morality, or social practices and conventions. The analysis it offers is uniform across all systems of norms that contain claim-rights: goalkeepers hold rights against opposing players under the rules of soccer in the same way that factory workers holds rights against their employers under labour law. Whether this uniformity is necessary for an analysis of claim-rights or merely a desideratum is not a matter I take up here.

Kinds: The theory asserts that an individual has claim-rights only insofar as she is regarded as a member of some or other kind. Wenar's central example of a kind is a social role. For instance, the law might recognise a person as a property owner, office-holder, contracting party, citizen, or spouse. Many of the person's legal rights and duties depend on how the law comprehends her under one such role description or another. Not all relevant kinds are social roles. Wenar expands the theory from social roles to other types of social and natural kinds. A person has legal rights simply as a human being, but being human is not a role one plays.

Content: The first criterion of the biconditional is that a norm of the system must specify a duty of one party to perform an action with regard to another party, where both parties are considered as members of kinds. It is essential to the kind-desire theory that each party appear in the statement of the duty. In Wenar's (2013: 211) example, a prison warden has no claim-right that her prisoners do not escape from the prison because she does not appear in the content of their duty not to escape. Duties can always be re-described, interpreted, or elaborated in ways that do not mention the correlative right-holder. For instance, suppose that Rita has a claim-right against Dudley that he not harm her, and that he can avoid harming her only if he stops running. Other things being equal, Rita therefore has a claim-right against Dudley that he stop running. This latter claim makes no mention of Rita in the content of Dudley's duty. But this is consistent with the kind-desire theory, since the operative norm is the principle that one should not harm others, not any principle governing the duration of one's run as such. I set aside here whether there are examples of claim-rights in which the right-holder does not appear in the content of the duty as it is expressed by the operative norm.

Desires: The second criterion requires that the individual desire that the agent perform his duty. The attribution of this desire to the individual does not record a psychological fact about her (Wenar 2013: 215). Whether or not someone has a certain claim-right does not typically depend on her actual desires—we can often confidently ascribe rights to people without knowing very much about their psychological states. Instead, Wenar's point is that individuals have, as members of various kinds, reason to want particular things, whether or not they in fact do. Such kind-based desires can sometimes be inferred from claims about the interests that people have as members of the kind in question (Wenar: 2013: 227). For instance, children *qua* children want to be looked after by caring and responsible adults because this is what is good for them. If human flourishing consists in living in a community of equals, then this is what humans, as such, can be presumed to want.

When desires are attributed to the individuals on the basis of their interests as members of a kind, the difference between the two theories may seem academic. But some role-based desires are not grounded in prior claims about interests. Wenar identifies two ways that a desire can be attributed to the bearer of a social role. First, the desire may be derived from a duty or responsibility. Someone who has a job to do can be presumed to want to do her job: surgeons want to operate successfully on their patients; bus drivers want to transport passengers safely; concierges want to assist hotel guests efficiently, and so on. Second, the desire may be based on a normative stipulation or assumption about the role. Chess players have no duty to checkmate their opponents but the nature of chess as a competitive game presupposes that this is what each player tries to do. It may be that winning the game is in a player's interests—she might enjoy the thrill of victory—but considered simply as a player she needs no such motivation.

Enforcement: The third criterion is that enforcement of the duties correlative to claim-rights must be appropriate, other things being equal, although not necessarily by the right-holder herself. Wenar (2013: 214) suggests that the first two criteria capture the idea of a directed duty—a duty that is owed to an individual—whereas the third transforms this directed duty into a claim-right. In his example, a host might be owed a duty of gratitude but would not have a correlative claim-right against the guests insofar as this duty cannot be demanded of them. I do not take up this issue here and grant the plausibility of Wenar's suggestion for present purposes.

To see how the five elements of the kind-desire theory work together, consider two examples. First, suppose Dudley happens to be running along the lane next to Rita's farm. As a member of the public, Dudley has a legal duty not to trespass on Rita's property. This duty makes essential reference to Rita as the owner of the farm—Dudley has no relevant legal duties governing his spatial location as such. Moreover, the duty is enforceable—Rita could call the police to have Dudley removed if he should jump the fence. As the owner of the property, Rita can be presumed to want Dudley to stay off her land. The law supposes that if property owners want guests then they will invite them in, and Rita has done no such thing. Consequently, the kind-desire theory implies that Rita holds a legal claim-right against Dudley that he not trespass on her farm.

Second, suppose that Dudley has promised Rita not to trample the wild flowers alongside the lane. Dudley has this moral duty, not as a member of the public, but as a promisor. Perhaps other people might destroy the flowers with abandon, but Dudley owes Rita a duty to keep his promises to her. This duty is enforceable insofar as Rita can sanction Dudley if he should break his promise. (She might justifiably rescind her promise to take him fishing.) Moreover, as a promisee, Rita can be presumed to want Dudley to keep his word. If she did not care whether the promise was kept, then she either would not have accepted it or could have waived it. The kind-desire theory therefore implies that Rita holds a moral claim-right against Dudley that he keeps his promise to her by not trampling the flowers.

II. Extensional Adequacy: The Interest Theory

The interest theory asserts that an individual holds a claim-right against an agent only because his duty promotes her interests in some way.[2] This requirement is compatible with four of the five elements of the kind-desire theory. The interest theory can be advanced as an analysis of claim-rights across all normative domains; it can focus on the interests that individuals have as members of kinds; it can require that the operative norm refer to the right-holder in the content of the agent's duty; and it can assert that the duty must be enforceable. Moreover, the interest theory agrees with the kind-desire theory in many cases. Rita has interests in not being physically harmed by Dudley as he runs, in not having unwanted guests on her property, and in having promises made to her kept. This overlap is unsurprising insofar as the kind-desire theory allows that the relevant desires of the right-holder can sometimes be inferred from her interests.

[2] Both Raz (1986) and Kramer (2002) advance their versions of the interest theory as accounts of rights in general, not just of claim-rights. I set this issue aside here.

Despite the overlap between the two accounts, Wenar argues that the interest theory is extensionally inadequate in that it incorrectly excludes at least some claim-rights, rights that the kind-desire theory includes. There are two versions of this criticism.

A. Detrimental Claim-Rights

The first version asserts that some claim-rights do not, or at least need not, further the interests of the right-holder. Consider three of his examples:

i. Kamikaze pilots have a right to their allocation of fuel, but would be better off if they were not able to depart on their missions.
ii. A bomb disposal specialist has the right to disarm bombs although this endangers him.
iii. In some legal systems, parents have the right to arrange their children's marriages even if it would be less stressful for them to lack this authority.

The kind-desire theory can plausibly accommodate the three cases by invoking the norms governing each role. But there are two reasons why they do not provide compelling counterexamples to the interest theory. First, the cases do not present unambiguous examples of claim-rights since no specification is made of any correlative duty on the part of other agents.[3] The kamikaze pilot holds no right against his commanding officer that his plane be prepared for flight; the bomb disposal specialist would not be wronged if a mortar crew had first shelled the affected area, rendering his presence unnecessary; and the right of the matchmaking parents need not be violated if their offspring refused to accept the latest suitor. Once plausible correlative duties are identified, however, the right-holder's interests start to reappear. For instance, suppose that nearby troops have a duty not to interfere with the bomb disposal specialist as he completes his task. If so, he may hold a claim-right against them to this effect. But it is also clearly to his benefit that they leave him alone since their interference could distract his attention at precisely the wrong moment (Kramer: this volume). Similarly, foreign NGO workers may have a legal duty not to encourage the matchmakers' child to elope with her paramour against their wishes. But the parents can be presumed to have an interest in outsiders not meddling in their family affairs.

Second, the interest theory need not assert that the agent's duty must be in the right-holder's interests all things considered.[4] Instead, she can hold the claim-right in virtue of the fact that the agent's duty is in some relevant respect beneficial to her. Rita might be better off, considered as a biological human being, if Dudley

[3] Kramer in this volume also advances this objection to Wenar's examples.

[4] Kramer (2002) requires only that the duty be typically advantageous to the right-holder. As Wenar (2013: 205–06) notes, Raz (1986: 180) identifies the interests of individuals as bearers of particular roles.

purloined the packet of cigarettes she bought in a moment of weakness, since this would forestall her relapse into nicotine addiction. Nevertheless, she holds a claim-right against him that he not steal the cigarettes insofar as she has an interest in keeping her possessions. Similarly, the kamikaze pilot's life might go better, on the whole, if he does not fly off to die in an enormous fireball. But he may well have a right under the norms of the Imperial Japanese military that his ground crew fuel his aircraft insofar as any hint of cowardice or dereliction of duty would dishonour him. No plausible version of the interest theory should assert that the ascription of rights turns on a comprehensive assessment of each person's wellbeing.[5]

B. The Insufficiency Problem

The second version of Wenar's criticism targets the justificatory interest theory in particular. Although every version of the interest theory asserts that the right-holder must benefit in some way from a duty, not just any beneficiary has a right to its performance. For instance, Rita's neighbour has no moral right that Dudley not disturb the wild flowers, even if they make his life more pleasant. The justificatory approach excludes third parties whose benefit plays no role in justifying the duty. In Joseph Raz's (1986: 166) formulation of the approach, a person has a right just when some aspect of her wellbeing is a sufficient reason to hold another person to be under a duty. Wenar uses two examples to illustrate an insufficiency problem for Raz's view:

i. Journalists have a right that public prosecutors not force them to reveal their sources.
ii. Parents have a right to receive child support payments from the state's child welfare agency.

In each case, the interests of people other than the right-holders play an essential role in the justification of the duty. Journalists enjoy special entitlements only because this serves the public interest in a free press and parents are entitled to child support only because this benefits their children. But a justificatory interest theory need not suppose that only the right-holder's interests play a role in justifying the duty.[6] What is essential to the approach is that the interests of the right-holder

[5] Wenar claims that an interest theory cannot go to the opposite extreme and allow just any respect in which a duty might promote a person's interests. Such an approach would risk proliferating claim-rights excessively 'since nearly every state of affairs, however awful, is normally beneficial to humans in some tightly specified way or other' (Wenar 2013: 205). A full statement of the interest theory should therefore advance constraints on the interests that ground claim-rights in each normative domain.

[6] In his discussion of the problem, Raz (1986: 247–56) allows that benefits to third parties can figure in the duty's justification when they are promoted by benefiting the right-holder—the journalist's interests are sufficient to justify the public prosecutor's duty when the consequences of promoting them are taken into account. I criticise this particular proposal in May (2012).

play a *special* justificatory role—one that distinguishes her from third-party beneficiaries—even if they are not always sufficient to justify the duty by themselves. In particular, if the right in question can be derived from an antecedent right that is justified by the right-holder's interests alone, then her interests could play a sufficiently distinctive role. Consider the following justificatory schema:[7]

1. R holds a claim-right against D that D ϕ,
2. D can only ϕ if D ψs,
3. R holds a claim-right against D that D ψ, and
4. Propositions 1 and 2 justify, *ceteris paribus*, proposition 3.[8]

To illustrate, recall that Rita holds a claim-right against Dudley that he not harm her. Since he can only avoid harming her if he stops running, it follows, *ceteris paribus*, that Rita holds a claim-right against Dudley that he stop running. In this example, the second proposition conveys a purely empirical claim. But there is nothing in the schema that prevents the proposition reflecting a normative claim, one that is justified, for example, by appeal to the interests of people other than the right-holder. This opens a way to solve the insufficiency problem illustrated by the two examples Wenar mentions.

First, a citizen holds a claim-right against public officials that she not be subjected to onerous legal burdens that are not plausibly warranted by the public interest. For instance, police officers have a duty not to arrest someone without probable cause or a valid warrant—such wrongful arrest violates the individual's rights. But requiring journalists to reveal their sources is also, *ex hypothesi*, unwarranted by the public interest—in most such cases, the public interest in the efficient administration of justice is outweighed by the public interest in a free press. Thus, *ceteris paribus*, citizens who work as journalists hold a claim-right against prosecutors that they not be required to reveal their sources or risk being held in contempt (May 2012: 127–28).

Second, a citizen holds a claim-right against state agencies that she not be expected to bear onerous financial burdens that it is the responsibility of those state agencies to bear. For instance, it is the responsibility of the criminal justice system to ensure that each defendant has a competent attorney—refusing to appoint an attorney for a defendant who cannot afford private legal counsel would violate her rights. But it is also, *ex hypothesi*, the responsibility of the state's child welfare agency to ensure that children have an adequate standard of living. If the agency refused to pay child support benefits to a parent who meets the relevant criteria for financial need, it would impose an onerous burden on her—she would be expected to carry the full cost of ensuring her children's standard of living.

[7] I advance a version of this schema in May (2012).

[8] The fourth proposition is required since the first two propositions do not always imply the third, even *ceteris paribus*. This implication occurs when ψ is a condition for both the fulfilment of R's claim-right that D ϕ and for its existence.

Thus, *ceteris paribus*, the parent holds a claim-right against the state's child welfare agency to receive child support benefits.[9]

In these interpretations of the two examples, protecting the interests of the right-holder serves as a fundamental or non-instrumental reason why the public official must perform an action, even if only in combination with consideration of the interests of others. Unless there are claim-rights in which the interests of the right-holder play no such special justificatory role whatsoever, the insufficiency problem does not present a compelling reason to abandon the justificatory interest theory.

III. Extensional Adequacy: The Kind-Desire Theory

I have argued against Wenar's claim that the interest theory is extensionally inadequate. In this section, I reverse the criticism. I argue that there are some cases in which the kind-desire theory incorrectly ascribes claim-rights. The argument for this conclusion assumes two generic claims about the role-based desires of the participants in a rule-governed social practice or institution:

i. The bearer of a role in a social practice wants to perform the functions of her position, as the rules of the practice require of her.
ii. The bearer of a role in a social practice wants other participants to cooperate with her, as the rules of the practice require of them, in the performance of her functions.

The first claim restates Wenar's point that people with jobs to do have a duty-derived desire to do their jobs. But claim-rights are rights to the actions of other agents and this desire concerns the role-bearer's own actions. The second claim extends the first as directly as possible to other agents. If the duty-derived desires of the first claim can be attributed to the role-bearers in a social practice, then so too can the cooperation-oriented desires of the second. For example, if a surgeon wants to operate successfully on her patients, then she also wants other members of the surgical team to cooperate with her as required of them: she wants the scrub nurse to pass the scalpel when needed, the anaesthetist to monitor the patient's breathing, the hospital security personnel to prevent lost visitors from wandering

[9] Suppose, instead, that the child welfare system paid benefits to grandparents rather than parents, on the assumption that they could be relied upon to use the money for the children's needs equally efficiently. (I owe this suggestion to Leif Wenar.) In this case, no financial burden would be placed on the parents themselves. But it is also unclear whether such a system would violate any parental claim-right to the subsidy, especially in societies that lack norms of exclusive parental authority within the nuclear family.

into the operating theatre, and so on. It would make little sense for the surgeon to have a desire to operate successfully on her patients but be indifferent to whether other members of the team cooperated with her towards this end.

Many instances of role-based cooperation-oriented desires fit with the kind-desire theory's analysis. The scrub nurse has a duty to pass the scalpel to the surgeon when she needs it and the surgeon might plausibly be said to hold a claim-right against him to this effect. In Wenar's own example, an army captain has a claim-right that a corporal carry out her order—the corporal has a duty to obey her commands and the captain certainly desires his cooperation in the matter (2013: 213–14). But some instances of cooperation-oriented desires generate false positives. Consider two examples of parties with subordinate roles and two examples of agents with roles as neutral parties:

Princess: Suppose a traditional monarchy places great importance on the continuity of the royal lineage. According to the conservative mores of this society, the crown prince has a duty to marry and produce a legitimate heir with his wife. The duty is enforceable insofar as the prince would be passed over in the line of succession and stripped of various honours and titles if the couple were to remain childless. The primary duty of the crown princess is to assist her husband in the fulfilment of this task. She therefore has a duty-derived desire to become pregnant with the prince's child and a cooperation-oriented desire that the prince impregnate her. But she holds no claim-right against the prince, within the society's patriarchal norms, that he do so. For all that has been said, she would not be wronged if the prince insisted on always using contraceptives or secretly had a vasectomy to spite his family.

Counsel: Assume a political system in which the president has the power to grant pardons to convicted criminals but has a legal duty to confer with her legal counsel about each case before making a decision. Suppose also that this duty is enforceable in various ways: the courts can quash procedurally irregular executive orders and the legislature can impeach the president for granting pardons without proper consultation. The president's legal counsel has a duty-derived desire to assist the president in her decision-making on such matters and a legal duty to request a meeting when the occasion arises. In submitting this formal request, the counsel expresses a cooperation-oriented desire that the president consult with him so that he can provide her with his considered legal opinion. But he holds no legal claim-right against the president that she do so.

Umpire: The laws of cricket require that a bowler who wishes to change the mode of his delivery, say by bowling around rather than over the wicket, must first inform the umpire, who must then inform the batsman on strike.[10] If the bowler does not comply with this rule, the umpire will penalise the bowling side by

[10] Law 24 (No Ball) 1. Mode of Delivery. A right-handed bowler bowls around the wicket when he bowls from the right side of the stumps at the bowling end, and over the wicket when he bowls from the left side.

declaring a no-ball.[11] The umpire has a duty-derived desire to conduct the match in accordance with the laws of the game, and accordingly desires that the players cooperate with her in this regard. (We can imagine she regards it as part of her duties to express this desire to the players before the match starts.) She therefore wants the bowler to inform her if he intends to start bowling around the wicket. But the umpire does not hold a claim-right against the bowler to this effect. It is the batsman on strike, not the umpire, who would most plausibly be wronged if the bowler tried to take him by surprise unfairly.

Mediator: Suppose the law requires parents in a child custody dispute to attempt resolution of the matter through mediation. Failure to attend the scheduled mediation sessions can result in the imposition of penalties and the forfeiture of custodial rights. The parents accordingly have a legal duty to meet with each other and the court-appointed mediator at the scheduled times. The mediator has a duty-derived desire to discuss the dispute with the parents so as to facilitate an equitable resolution. She accordingly desires that they cooperate with her in pursuit of this goal by, inter alia, attending the sessions (as she expresses in the appointment notification she sends to them). But the mediator does not herself hold a legal claim-right against the parties that they comply with this requirement.

In all four examples, the three requirements of the kind-desire theory are satisfied: the operative norm in question specifies a duty that makes reference both to the agent and to another individual under their role-descriptions; this individual has a role-based desire that the agent performs his duty; and the duty is enforceable. But the individuals do not hold any correlative claim-rights of their own. The kind-desire theory is therefore extensionally inadequate.

A response to the argument objects that it is possible to interpret the four examples so that the individuals in question actually do have claim-rights. For instance, the princess could have a right that the prince cooperate with her in conceiving a child if the shame she would otherwise suffer is taken into account. The president's counsel might have a right to be consulted if his reputation as a lawyer would otherwise be seriously damaged. If the purpose of cricket's mode of delivery law is, in part, to protect the umpire's authority over the players, and not merely to ensure that the batsman is not taken by surprise, then the law may give her a right to be informed. The mediator would no doubt be inconvenienced if one of the parents failed to show for the session, and perhaps this would be sufficient to vest her with a right to their attendance. I do not believe that these interpretations are especially plausible, but that is beside the point. All four appeals conceive of the individuals as parties whose interests matter in their own right—that is, as independent interested parties—whereas the kind-desire theory denies that interests are necessary for claim-rights. A successful demonstration of the essential role of the right-holder's desires must provide interpretations of the examples that avoid all such appeals to interests.

11 A no-ball adds a run to the batting side's total.

IV. The Significance of Claim-Rights

I have argued that the kind-desire theory incorrectly implies claim-rights where none exist. This is not a problem that stems from the particular formulation of the theory that Wenar advances—one that could perhaps be avoided with a few more qualifications. Instead, it stems from the fundamental difference between the two theories: the claim that it is the right-holder's desires rather than her interests that ground her claim-rights. In this section, I argue that grounding claim-rights in desires alone cannot explain the significance of these rights. It is this underlying inability that generates the counterexamples to the kind-desire theory.

Since claim-rights correlate with duties that people want to see fulfilled, they are very useful things to have. But these rights are also important for the recognition of an individual's status. A person who holds claim-rights is not just someone who might be satisfied or benefited by the fulfilment of duties. In addition, she is a person who matters non-instrumentally within a social practice, that is, someone who warrants respect as an end. The paradigm of an individual without rights is the slave: in the eyes of the law she is just a tool for the use of her owner. To deny a person any rights is not simply to disappoint or harm her, therefore, it is also to diminish her status and to conceive of her as if she were akin to a slave. A satisfactory analysis should help explain this dimension of the significance of claim-rights.[12] Consider each theory in turn:

A. Kind-Desires and Counterfeit Rights

I have argued that if duty-derived desires can be attributed to role-bearers, then cooperation-oriented desires can too. These desires are inherent in any social practice in which the role-bearers must cooperate with each other to fulfil their responsibilities, including those practices in which some role-bearers are not regarded as persons who matter non-instrumentally. Since slaves have tasks that require the cooperation of others, they too have cooperation-oriented desires. This means that the kind-desire theory would ascribe claim-rights to slaves if ever their desires happened to align in the required way with the enforceable duties of other agents. But the fact of this alignment could do nothing in itself to change the status of the slaves. The rights the kind-desire theory would ascribe to them are counterfeit.

To illustrate, suppose that a Sparta-like society entrusts the welfare of a select class of aristocratic infants to a cohort of helots. Each of these helots has a duty

[12] Feinberg (1970) sets out the seminal statement of the essential link between rights and respect. Cruft (2013) advances a similar respect-based argument against the kind-desire theory but agrees with Wenar that his theory is extensionally adequate and the interest theory inadequate.

to act as a guardian for her bevy of children until they reach a certain age.[13] Since the helots have no property or income of their own, the state provides them with a monthly allowance to cover the children's upkeep. Each helot has a role-based desire to care for her assigned infants and a cooperation-oriented desire that the public treasurer fulfil his duty to disburse her allowance—she needs the money to do her job. As far as this description of the role goes, the helot is in just the same position as the parent entitled to receive child welfare benefits from the state. The pivotal difference between the two examples is that helots have no antecedent right not to be subjected to onerous financial burdens that it is the responsibility of the state to bear.

The problem of counterfeit rights cannot be avoided by simply stipulating that the kind-desire theory applies only to beings who are treated as ends within a social practice (or to collectives of such beings). Recall the example of the crown princess. She may have many claim-rights within the patriarchal norms of the monarchy. For instance, she may have the right not to be assaulted by a guard or insulted by a courtier. But with respect to the crown prince's duty to sire a legitimate heir, she is just a means for the continuation of the royal line. In that particular regard, she matters only instrumentally. The same point holds for the president's counsel. He has many claim-rights under the law—as a government employee, for instance, he may be entitled to certain state pension benefits. But with respect to the president's duty of consultation, he is relevant only as a subordinate and not as an independent party in his own right.

B. Interests and the Redundancy Argument

Wenar (2013: 227–28) claims that the concept of interests is redundant in the analysis of claim-rights:

> The meaning of 'interest', like butter, is semisolid. When Interest theorists are rigorous and freeze the concept into hedonist or objective-list meaning, the concept then becomes unsuitable for analyzing rights outside those of a limited … set of natural-kind right-holders like humans, children, and animals. But 'interest' can also be smeared across roles by deriving its meaning from role-based desires. When this is done, it is natural and correct to say that claim-rights are conceptually tied to the right-holder's 'interests'. However, in this usage, the term 'interest' gets its sense from the prior concept of desire. 'Interests' as an independent concept grounds only a minority of claim-rights. Conceptual analysis centered on desires captures all rights-assertions.

I do not think this argument is compelling. Wenar presents something of a false dichotomy. The interest theory does not need to either use a single conception of

[13] Wenar (2013: 219–20) claims that if the cattle on a ranch must be treated well, but only *qua* valuable livestock, then they lack correlative claim-rights. The helots differ from the cattle in this example because they have a duty to care for the children, and hence they are not regarded as mere beasts of burden that lack reasons of their own.

interests for all normative systems or else collapse interests into desires. What matters is that within each system there is some relatively coherent understanding of what makes someone better off. There is no reason why the conception of a pilot's interests within the Imperial Japanese military should be the same as those of a journalist within a liberal state or of a goalkeeper in soccer. Claim-rights exist in different legal systems and moral codes that use quite different assumptions about what benefits a person. The concept is flexible, but not therefore otiose.

Even when a system of norms infers an interest from a desire, it does not follow that the desire acts as the criterion for the ascription of a claim-right. Interests are sometimes inferred from desires and desires are sometimes inferred from interests, just as Wenar claims they are also sometimes inferred from role-based duties and norms. The relationship of relative priority between desires and interests is orthogonal to the grounding relationship between one or other of these elements and claim-rights.

The primary reason why Wenar's redundancy argument fails is that the concept of interests helps avoid the problem of counterfeit rights. Identifying the role played by the right-holder's interests adds something crucial that a focus on desires by itself cannot. The justificatory interest theory can capture the non-instrumental importance of a right-holder insofar as the protection of her interests serves as a fundamental reason why an agent must perform some action. The officials at the child welfare agency must disburse child welfare benefits in part for the sake of the parents, who would otherwise be expected to bear the financial burden of a public responsibility. In contrast, it is not true that the public treasurer in the Sparta-like society must disburse monthly allowances for the sake of the helot guardians. Similarly, it is not true that the crown prince must impregnate his wife, the president consult her counsel, the bowler inform the umpire, or the child custody disputants confer with the mediator, for the sake of these four individuals. In these cases, an ascription of claim-rights would be quite superfluous to their role in expressing the status of the person as an end.

My conclusion is that the justificatory interest theory provides a better explanation of the significance of claim-rights than does the kind-desire theory and that this difference explains why the kind-desire theory is vulnerable to the four counterexamples that I have advanced. To have a claim-right in a system of norms is to be recognised in some respect as an independent interested party and not just as a party whose desires align with the duties of other agents.

References

Cruft, R (2013) 'Why is it Disrespectful to Violate Rights?' 113 *Proceedings of the Aristotelian Society* 201.

Feinberg, J (1970) 'The Nature and Value of Rights' 4 *Journal of Value Inquiry* 243.

Hohfeld, WN (1919) *Fundamental Legal Conceptions as Applied in Judicial Reasoning* (New Haven, CT: Yale University Press).
Kramer, MH (2002) 'Rights Without Trimmings' in MH Kramer, NE Simmonds and H Steiner, *A Debate over Rights. Philosophical Enquiries* (Oxford: Oxford University Press).
May, SC (2012) 'Moral Status and the Direction of Duties' 123 *Ethics* 113.
Raz, J (1986) *The Morality of Freedom* (Oxford: Clarendon Press).
Wenar, L (2013) 'The Nature of Claim-Rights' 123 *Ethics* 202.

5

Legal Powers and the Will and Interest Theories of Rights

JAMES PENNER*

I. Introduction

Whether office-holders such as judges hold the powers of their office *as rights* has been raised by Leif Wenar as a significant issue for the debate between the Will and Interest theories of rights (hereafter WT and IT).[1] According to Wenar, IT cannot account for office-holders' holding their powers *as rights*, for example the power of a judge to sentence criminal offenders. Matthew Kramer disagrees in a reply; for Kramer, IT can fully account for the fact that judges hold the powers of their office as rights. In my view, they are both wrong. I shall argue that judges *do not* hold their powers as rights, neither on WT *nor* IT, once those theories are properly construed and applied. In showing this I shall hope to undermine the apparent intuition that both Kramer and Wenar share that office-holders, such as judges, do hold their powers as rights.

* The research leading to this essay was generously supported by an NUS Research Grant (WBS no. R-241-000-127-133). I am grateful for discussions with, and the comments and suggestions of, Rowan Cruft, David Frydrych, Andrew Halpin, Matthew Kramer, Gopal Sreenivasan, and Leif Wenar. I owe especial thanks to Mark McBride for his precise, sustained and critical attention to every sentence in the text. I am still recovering from his devoted ministrations. Still, neither he nor the others bear any responsibility for any remaining nonsense.

[1] I do not discuss whether the test for right-holding under Gopal Sreenivasan's hybrid theory of rights (Sreenivasan 2005) requires us to say that office-holders like judges hold their powers as rights, because it is not clear to me how the 'matches by design' test would apply. Sreenivasan (in correspondence) suggests that the hybrid theory (at least as elaborated so far) is much less general than some others, including Matthew Kramer's version of the interest theory and Leif Wenar's theory, in so far as it does not cover all rights, just claim-rights (or rather just the correlation between claim-rights and duties). If so, it takes no view of which powers qualify as rights. In addition, it only addresses the central case of individual rights, ie, rights held by individuals in their own right or in their capacity as individuals. It leaves room for an extension to the case of rights held by office-holders, but no hybrid theorist has yet explored that avenue of enquiry, and it would be far beyond the scope of this essay to take it on here.

In getting to this conclusion, I shall be embracing what I understand to be a Razian, if not necessarily Joseph Raz's, version of IT.[2] Furthermore, I shall begin the investigation by looking at legal or moral powers more generally, before treating office-holder's powers specifically. In between those two subjects of discussion I shall revisit the power to enter into contracts and the reasons why third-party beneficiaries of contracts do not have a claim-right against the party whose contractual performance benefits them. The main strategy of making sense of powers will be too look at what interests a power-holder might have in having the power in question per se, such that the power in question is recognised by morality in the case of moral powers, or is justifiably conferred by law in the case of legal powers.

Four preliminary issues:

(1) Like Kramer,[3] the version of IT I shall be operating with is better understood as a theory of 'right-holding' rather than a theory of rights *per se*. This point is especially important in the context of determining whether a power-holder holds her power *as a right*. For the Razian version of IT, the answer to this question is framed in terms of whether the power is conferred by law or is recognised by morality because, according to Raz, it typically serves the interests of the power-holder to have that power. On Kramer's version of IT, the question is whether as a matter of fact it is typically beneficial for the power-holder to have that power. For the purposes of this essay, it will not for the most part be necessary to distinguish between Kramer's and Raz's views on this point. In the interest of brevity, I shall use the 'interest' formulation hereafter unless the need to distinguish the two versions arises.

(2) The version of WT I shall be considering is the one defended by Hillel Steiner.[4] As regards rights, Steiner's WT holds that A has a right vis-à-vis B when B has a duty to ϕ and A is able to waive B's duty. HLA Hart's version of WT was framed somewhat more loosely, in terms of A's having 'some measure of control' over B's duty, including A's having the paired Hohfeldian liberties to enforce or not to enforce B's duty by seeking a remedy when it is breached. If Steiner's version of WT is extended to determine whether a power-holder holds that power as a right, the obvious or natural way to do so is by posing the question 'does that power-holder have a power to waive the correlative liability'.[5] Thus if A has a power to alter B's normative circumstances by exercising the power, then A holds that power as a right if and only if A is able to waive B's liability to the exercise of the power (thus also waiving

[2] See Raz (1984a; 1984b; 1986); see also MacCormick (1977; 1982). I differ from both Raz and MacCormick in rejecting their claim that rights precede duties in the sense that rights 'dynamically' justify the imposition of different duties in different circumstances. See Penner (1997b: 304–11). This difference between us is not, so far as I can tell, material to the present discussion.

[3] Kramer (this volume: p 49).

[4] Steiner (1998).

[5] See also Cruft (2004: 368).

A's power itself, in the same way in the case of right-duty jural relations A's waiving B's duty at the same time amounts to the waiver of A's correlative right.)[6]

(3) The question of whether a person holds a power as a right is determined on the basis of the general or typical interests of someone in the power-holder's position; in the same way that whether or not someone who is the beneficiary of a duty counts as a right-holder turns on whether the person in that position is, typically, interested in the performance of that duty, in the sense that the performance of that duty serves their interests.[7] This is clear in terms of legal rights, for legal norms are, in general, general; they do not track cases where because of idiosyncratic considerations having to do with a particular individual's interests or preferences, a particular right would not, in such a particular case, serve that individual's interest.[8] As I understand it, Cruft,[9] referring to some ugly garden gnomes which he, as owner, has no interest in having, regards the case of the gnomes as a counterexample to IT, at least in so far as the property right in question is a right recognised by morality as opposed to the law. But his intuition needs unpacking, along two dimensions. First, having the right to the gnomes is normally regarded as comprising not only the right to non-interference by others, but that this claim-right both protects and to some extent goes hand in hand with the liberty-right to destroy the gnomes and the powers to transfer them, by way of gift or sale, to someone who does value them. Moreover, it is not uncommon to acknowledge a power to abandon property when it does not serve one's interest.[10] Is Cruft's claim that because his own interest in having the gnomes is non-existent, and so also is any claim-right to them, this entails his absence of a right to destroy them or the power to transfer them away or abandon them? I presume not—he may claim to be focusing upon the claim-right and ignoring any related jural relations which normally go to make up the 'package' of a property right. But if this is right, then it seems to underestimate the resources of IT to deal with the gnomes case. Treating the property right as a package, with both the claim-right and the conventional liberties of destruction and powers to alienate or abandon would seem to reflect the view that

[6] I make no claim as to whether Steiner would approve of such an extension of his theory. As Mark McBride has pointed out to me, if the theory is restricted to claim-rights, then it is obvious that, for example, a judge's powers to sentence are not rights since they are not powers to waive a duty.

[7] Kramer (1998: 61–62); Raz (1986: 166–68); Wenar (2005: 241); Penner (1997b: 300–03).

[8] Cruft (2004: 376) seems to muddle this point; with regard to the right to worthless garden gnomes, the legal right in question is not directed to whether it is in the typical interests of persons to have a right to worthless garden gnomes, but to whether it is typically in the interests of persons to have rights to chattels, ie, tangible personal property. There are no 'worthless garden gnome' laws or 'worthless garden gnome' rights, though of course, being chattels, garden gnomes whether worthless or not fall within the scope of the relevant laws governing the ownership of chattels.

[9] Cruft (2004: 372–76).

[10] Hegel is an example. Hegel (1942: 52, section 65). There is no general power to abandon tangible property, in particular land, at common law.

property rights reflect the typical advantages of having the claim-right to property but are also sensitive to the fact that where the atypical case of the garden gnomes arises, the further norms governing destruction, alienation and abandonment cater to the typical interests of an owner in such circumstances. I suppose Cruft might also say that the power to abandon exists to deal with just such a case, ie, where on IT the individual no longer holds the property right *as a right*. But on the IT reasoning just advanced, this would seem to amount to an endorsement of IT, not a rejection of it, because the rationale for holding a person to have a power to abandon is that it *reflects the typical interests* of the property-holder when her interests are no longer served by having the property in question.[11]

In the second place, as I understand it the underlying intuition here is that morality, unlike law, is not systematic; it does not operate in terms of general norms, but is generally sensitive to the idiosyncratic reading of the interests of morality's subjects. It is not at all clear to me this is right—Kant would certainly deny it—and so it is not clear whether Cruft's intuition about the nature of moral normativity, besides being clearly very controversial, is not also idiosyncratic.

(4) On the reading of IT I endorse, again following Raz, the interests which underlie the analysis are always understood from a perspective, the two most obvious perspectives being that of morality and that of the law of any particular jurisdiction. The law presents its rules as being grounded in morally correct views,[12] but whether the law gets it right morally speaking is of course another question. As I shall be focusing on legal norms, in particular legal powers, I will occasionally take the perspective of common law legal doctrine to illustrate how one particular system of law views the interests of the parties concerned.

II. Moral Powers and their Customary Legal Equivalents

I want now to discuss several moral powers and their customary legal equivalents: (i) the power to license what would otherwise be a trespass to the person or to property; (ii) the power to appropriate property and the powers to share it and transfer it; and (iii) the power to enter into binding agreements (ie, the power to contract).

[11] I note in passing that a power to abandon could not be unrestricted—it also reflects the interests of others. It would surely be in my interest to be able to abandon property in, say, a rabid and vicious dog, but I cannot just abandon that dog so as to impose the problem of dealing with it on others.

[12] Raz (1986: chs 2–4; 1994: ch 9).

From the perspective of morality, Shiffrin explains the interest we have in having a power to allow others to come into physical contact with our bodies, ie, a power to license what would otherwise be a trespass to the person (a battery) or to property, in this way:

> One could imagine a conception of autonomy without consent in which an agent exercises complete sovereignty over her body and other personal spaces, such as the home, but had no ability to share or transfer these powers to others. That is, the agent could not grant consent to others to exercise these powers in lieu of or alongside herself. Such a structure is imaginable but so impoverished as to be utterly implausible. As Joseph Raz has argued, the development and realization of our central autonomous capacities requires a diverse and rich set of meaningful options. Rights of autonomous control that were inalienable to this degree would render (morally) impossible real forms of meaningful human relationships and the full definition and recognition of the self (not to mention making medical and dental care cumbersome, dangerous, and awfully painful). To forge meaningful relationships, embodied human beings must have the ability to interact within the same physical space, to share the use of property, and to touch one another. They must therefore be able to empower particular people. A plausible account of autonomy would have to reject the isolation the constricted model of self-sovereignty would enforce as inconsistent with affording opportunities to lead a decent life and realize one's central capacities. It would have to include the power of consent to share at least some of the powers associated with self-sovereignty.[13]

Shiffrin adapts this analysis to argue for a non-conventional power to enter binding agreeements (to enter into contracts),[14] and I have extended this sort of analysis to the power to appropriate, share and transfer property in a more explicit fashion than that found in Shiffrin's brief reference to powers over property in this passage.[15]

The details of this analysis need not be gone into here, but I take it what this passage reveals is that an IT analysis of powers is more than plausible. It is in the interests of people to have power to interact with others in meaningful ways and so, on IT, these people hold these powers as rights. That is, they hold these *moral* powers as *moral* rights. They are, of course, also legal powers, powers so ancient that they are genuinely customary, not the result of any legislation (although they have been modified both in terms of their detail by common law judges over time, for example in the rise of the doctrine of consideration requirement for legally binding agreements not executed in a deed, and given a statutory footing in other cases, for example, the Sale of Goods Act 1979).

It is also worth noting that it *seems* that the recognition of these powers by morality does not turn on any idiosyncratic features of particular individuals, but on general considerations about people's typical interests in the possibility of meaningfully interacting with others. Be that as it may, it is clear that the law's recognition of such powers *is* general and does not so turn.

[13] Shiffrin (2008: 501–02).
[14] ibid 502–23.
[15] Penner (2013: 264–70).

III. WT and Powers

On a moment's thought, it seems clear that WT cannot account for treating the sorts of moral and legal powers discussed in the last section as rights.

Wenar writes:

> Yet the interest theory is also inadequate to our ordinary understanding of rights. There are many rights the purpose of which is not to further the well-being of the rightholder, even in the general case. This is clearest with rights that define occupational roles. A judge has a (power) right to sentence criminals, but this right is not designed to benefit the judge. Rather, judges are ascribed this right as part of a system of justice that protects the members of the community. A traffic warden has a (power) right to issue parking tickets; but the point of this right is to improve the lives of motorists, not the life of the warden. Similarly, an army captain may have the (power) right to order units, including his own, into battle; yet the specific aim of the rule that confers this right is not to further the captain's well-being. In each of these cases the right is ascribed in order to benefit parties beside the rightholder. The existence of such role-defining rights establishes that the interest theory is implausibly narrow.[16]

And a bit further on Wenar says: '*The will theory captures rights that give discretion to the rightholder without conferring benefits [i.e. judges and traffic wardens]*, but fails to capture rights that confer benefits without giving discretion'.[17] But the statement I have italicised is, it is submitted, clearly false, at least on the extended Steinerian version of WT. To recognise a legal position that X has to be a right, X must, at a minimum, have a power to waive that very legal advantage. But judges and traffic wardens (henceforward in this section I shall ignore the traffic warden case, because the case of the judge is clearer and I must return to it below) have no power to waive the very powers in question. Wenar apparently believes that because *some* judges' powers give judges discretion[18] they *ipso facto* hold (all?) their powers as rights under WT. But the only relevant discretion for the extended Steinerian version of WT is the discretion (the power accompanied by a paired

[16] Wenar (2005: 241–42).

[17] Wenar (2005: 243) my italics; see also Figure 5 at 249.

[18] This not the general case, by the way. As Wenar acknowledges (2005: 231) in the case of many powers, judges have no discretion as to their exercise. A judge has a duty to exercise his powers according the rules of civil procedure in the course of litigation, ordering disclosure of documents for example, and has a duty to exercise his power to render a judgment and issue an order. He has no discretion not to exercise these powers. He is duty bound to do so. Trustees, similarly, have many powers in respect of which they have no discretion as to their exercise. They must exercise them in accordance with the terms of the trust. In the simplest sort of trust, eg, 'on trust for Mary for life and then to her children in equal shares' the trustee has no distributive discretions whatsoever. It is also worth noticing that the use of the term 'discretion' is potentially misleading here. A judge (and the same is true of a trustee) may have to exercise judgement in deciding how to exercise a power, and in this sense is empowered to make a choice between possible (reasonable) alternatives; but once having considered the matter, ie, having exercised her judgement, she has no choice or discretion to act against that judgement; she must exercise her power in the way she judges to best give effect to the power's purpose, to impose a just sentence upon a criminal, for example.

liberty to exercise it or not) to waive the corresponding liability, ie, to extinguish the power-liability jural relation in question. Now Wenar might be advancing a looser, non-Steinerian version of WT, but at the very least the possibility of the extended Steinerian version of WT shows that WT is capable of discriminating between powers which are held as rights, and powers which are not, and that WT in all its forms is not committed to the view that a power-holder holds her power as a right simply because she also holds a paired Hohfeldian liberty either to exercise it or not.

To flesh out this point, let us consider the power to enter into contracts. In general[19] there is no moral or legal duty to enter into any particular contract with any particular content with anyone. So, to use Wenar's term, one has discretion as to the *exercise* of one's power. Another way of saying this is that one has a paired Hohfeldian liberty, to exercise or not exercise the power. But one has no power to waive the power itself. That is what the extended Steinerian WT requires for X to hold his power to enter contracts as a right. And neither the law nor morality gives anyone such a power, because it would not typically be in anyone's interest to have such a power of waiver. To be crystal clear on this, not exercising a power is not the same thing, not the same thing at all, as waiving the power itself. To waive a power is to change one's normative position vis-à-vis the liability-holder at the end of the Hohfeldian jural relation from one of power-liability to one of disability-immunity. Likewise, WT's insistence that a right-holder has a power to waive the correlative duty means that the exercise of the power changes the normative relationship from right/duty to no-right/liberty. Declining to enforce the correlative duty, say by not complaining when Y touches your shoulder, thereby committing a battery, is not the *waiver* of anything. Doing nothing is doing just that, ie, nothing.[20]

Whilst we are on this point, there seems to be a related confusion about the distinction between a liberty to exercise a power of enforcement or not and the power to waive that very power of enforcement. This confusion regarding the enforcement of legal rights originates with Hart but it is shared by both Kramer and Steiner.[21] When D commits a legal wrong against P, it is not the case that D and P come under a power-liability relationship, such that P acquires by operation of law a 'power of enforcement' against D that P could decide to 'waive'. Let me explain.[22]

Hart first raised the issue of 'the power to enforce' a duty in the following famous passage:

> The idea is that of one individual being given by the law exclusive control, more or less extensive, over another person's duty so that in the area of conduct covered by that duty

[19] For exceptions in the moral realm, see Penner (1996: 337). An example would be the duty of parents to enter into agreements so as to determine how they will care for their children.

[20] I therefore disagree with Kramer and Steiner (2007: 286) when they claim that A's failing to bring an action so that the action becomes time-barred by a statute of limitations amounts to a waiver on the part of A. A's action right (not A's power to bring an action) is extinguished by operation of law.

[21] Kramer and Steiner (2007: 285–88); Steiner (1998: 240).

[22] For a fuller treatment of the issues in the remainder of this section, see Penner and Kwek (2016).

> the individual who has the right is a small-scale sovereign to whom the duty is owed. The fullest 'measure of control' comprises three distinguishable elements: (i) the right holder may waive or extinguish the duty or leave it in existence; (ii) after breach or threatened breach of a duty he may leave it 'unenforced' or may 'enforce' it by suing for compensation or, in certain cases, for an injunction or mandatory order to restrain the continued or further breach of the duty; and (iii) he may waive or extinguish the obligation to pay compensation to which the breach gives rise.
>
> ...
>
> These legal *powers* (for such *they are*) over a correlative obligation are of great importance to lawyers[.][23]

Now I suppose that a theorist of either sort, IT or WT, can define what she means by 'a measure of control' any way she wants if it genuinely assists in making sense of her theoretical perspective, but such a definition should not be based on a mistake, in particular an internal equivocation or ambiguity in one of the definition's terms. Just such a mistake, it is submitted, is made in Hart's definition of 'measure of control' in so far as it makes reference to the term 'powers'. It is a shame that HLA Hart, who was once a practising barrister, regards the 'powers' in (ii) and (iii) as genuine legal powers. They are not. Rather, they are paired Hohfeldian legal liberties to exercise the power of bringing a legal action, a power which is not dependent upon any breach of a duty by another person. By contrast, the power in (i) *is* a genuine legal power; if I license you to do what would otherwise be a battery, I change our genuine legal normative relations such that what would otherwise have been a tort is no longer so within the scope of the licence; ie, I change our Hohfeldian jural relations from one of right/duty to one of no-right/liberty. The same is true, for example, of a genuine contractual waiver.

What happens when D breaches a legal duty to P is this: P's substantive right is infringed when the breach occurs. This confers on P a legally recognised *right*, an action right: a right *to* a court order, say an order for damages. The conferral of an action right can be explicated from the legal process: P *will* obtain the ruling and court order if she proves the elements of her cause of action. It is, nevertheless, a *contingent* right; in order to obtain it, P must exercise her power of bringing an action against D. Note, this is not a power against D herself, but a power whose liability-bearer is an institution, the court. Invoking this power will have legal *consequences* for D if the court does its job—rendering D liable to a judgment, rendering D liable to comply with the court's processes, and so on. But here D's liabilities correlate with the power of the court, not any power in P. In other words, P's action rights do not correlate with any duties upon D outside those duties, rights or liabilities that D acquires as a participant in the legal process when P decides to invoke it, such as a duty to disclose, or a right to disclosure from P.[24]

[23] Hart (1982: 183–84) my italics.

[24] Assuming these rights are invokable by P and D themselves, ie, are not merely the obtaining by P or D from the court an order for disclosure.

It is also a mistake to think that D's liability to a court order correlates with P's power to bring an action. As Lord Esher observed:

> A lawsuit may be a suit in equity, or an action at law. In either case the question to be determined by it is—what were the rights of the parties before the suit or action was commenced? The lawsuit does not create the right; it determines what that right was and is. What is called a 'right of action' is not the power of bringing an action. Anybody can bring an action, though he has no right at all.[25]

Another way of putting this point is to say that P's power to bring an action does not depend upon D's actually having committed a wrong against P. If that were so, anyone bringing an action would in principle succeed (so long as they proved their case), ie, all defendants would ipso facto lose.

Now, of course, P may not pursue her action right, in the same way that any other power-holder with a paired Hohfeldian liberty to exercise the power or not may similarly decide not to exercise the power. But that is to do nothing. By doing nothing P's action right is not waived; it doesn't disappear. P can change her mind and bring the action. So a power over the right to enforce which reflects nothing more than P's ability to decide to bring an action or not is *not* in law anything, in particular it is *not a power over P's power to bring an action*. Just as in the case of the power to enter into contracts, a power is something one exercises or not. Failing to exercise a power is not the waiver of a power, as I hope is now clear.

But, you may say, what about the power to settle a claim? Is that not a power to waive one's right of action? No, it is not.

In the first place, the notion of waiver operative for WT is *unilateral*. It cannot turn on the participation of another person. And there is no unilateral power to waive one's right of action. A right to settle a claim is simply an application of the normal power one has to enter into a contract. A contract of settlement imposes a legal obligation on P not to exercise his right of action. It does not extinguish that right of action. It is no different in kind from a contract not to exercise any other power a person has. If I enter into a contract not to compete with another (I 'transfer' to him the 'goodwill' of my business) this doesn't in any way extinguish my right to enter into contracts with others in competition with him. Those contracts are perfectly valid. All that happens in consequence is that I am liable to damages for breach of contract (if my counterparty decides to bring an action against me) because I exercised my continuing power to enter into contracts with others which breached another of my contractual obligations.

By parity of reasoning, simply because the subject matter of my contract in this case is a contract of settlement, that does not mean that the power of contracting is a power to 'waive' the particular right in question, and it is in fact clear in the law that it does not do so. What a contract of settlement does is provide the defendant with a valid defence to the action. But it must be pleaded. If D commits a tort

[25] *Attorney General v Sudeley* (1896) 1 QB 354, 359 (Lord Esher).

against P and then P and D enter into a valid contract of settlement, but P then brings an action for compensation ('damages') anyway and D (or D's incompetent lawyer) fails to plead the contract of settlement, then P's action goes ahead and P will succeed in getting a judgment in his favour and an award of damages. This shows that there is no legal power to waive any right of action that P acquires upon D's initial breach of duty, ie, D's tort.

As to P's 'power' to waive D's duty to compensate (power (iii) from above), again, this could only be by way of a contract not to enforce the award in P's favour, where such enforcement would, for example, involve going back to court upon D's failure to pay the award and getting a ruling authorising execution of the award, ie, empowering a sheriff or bailiff to seize D's goods and sell them to pay the award.[26] There is no more power to waive such a right of enforcement of a damages award than there is a power to waive one's right of action.

Two final points on P's liberties, rights and powers of enforcement. First, I do not deny that there are obvious connections between (i), (ii) and (iii); indeed, the foregoing was an elaboration of those connections. What I do deny is that there are, for example, relations of dependence or consequence between the three in which all are conceived as powers, such that, for example, the exercise of the power in (i) extinguishes the 'power' in (ii).[27] Second, I do not deny that a different legal system might be organised such that (i), (ii) and (iii) could really be framed as powers in the way Hart, Kramer and Steiner envisage them. But I know of no such extant legal system, and my suspicion is that thinking through such a hypothetical legal system in practical terms would reveal why this is so.

IV. Contracts and the Rights of Third-Party Beneficiaries (TPBs)

IT accounts for the fact that power-holders hold their powers as rights because it can show how having those powers are in the interests of their holders whereas, on the extended Steinerian version of WT, WT holds that unless a power-holder can waive the power she holds, she does not hold that power as a right.

So, for example, IT explains why both adults and children hold their powers to enter into contracts as rights, though their powers differ in scope, ie, though adults have full contractual powers minors' powers are more restricted. For example, minors are denied the power to create executory[28] contractual obligations

[26] Unlike contracts of settlement, which are common, I know of no examples of this kind.

[27] See Steiner (1998: 239–47).

[28] Minors, indeed children of a tender age, can, of course, conclude (more or less) 'instantaneous' shop sales and barter transactions. What they cannot do is undertake obligations to fulfil future performances, eg, they cannot undertake debt obligations (except, as mentioned in the text, for the purchase of 'necessaries').

(except for the purchase of 'necessaries'), because the law regards it as not in the interests of minors to have the power, say, to acquire significant debts.

Moreover, IT explains why there is no power to waive one's power to enter into contracts, ie, because it would not be in anyone's typical interest to lack the power to enter into contracts.[29]

So, individuals have a power to make binding agreements with others in both morality and law. It is a facility which serves their interests, because, generally speaking, the ability to make binding voluntary undertakings to others typically serves our interests. But if this is right, my claim is that the facility is one to undertake obligations to specific others if one chooses to do so. It would not be the power that it is if, by promising A to ϕ, B was taken to undertake an obligation to anyone else, irrespective of whether that person would benefit from B's ϕ-ing.[30] If that was what the 'power' did when exercised, it would certainly not, special circumstances aside, generally be in B's interest to have it, and it certainly wouldn't be the power we recognise when we talk about a power to enter into contracts or to make promises.

And this, to my mind, is the correct starting point for analysing the rights of TPBs of contracts. Let me provide the general picture and then deal with two possible rejoinders.

We look first at the power to enter into contracts. Those who would hold that TPBs should, in general, have a claim-right against B—by which I mean a legally significant claim-right that would give a TPB some standing or right to some remedy against B (if the TPB chose to bring his action right to fruition by bringing an action in court) in case B failed to perform his contractual obligation to A—must understand what this means. It would mean that B, despite his own contractual intentions and understanding of what he did when he exercised the power, could, upon exercising the power, have imposed upon him, by *operation of law*, an obligation to the TPB which he himself never intended to undertake. I do not find such a proposition in the least bit attractive, either legally or morally speaking. Now, of course, the law *might* change the normative rules of the game such that B's undertaking a promise to A would expose himself to the stated liability to the TPB, in which case were B to enter into a contract with A he would do so at his peril as regards TPBs. In England and Wales, the Bs of this world are exposed to this peril by virtue of the Contracts (Rights of Third Parties) Act 1999, though the statute explicitly provides that Bs can avoid this consequence.[31]

[29] *Mutatis mutandis* for the power to license others to touch you, to come onto your property, to share a bottle of wine, etc.

[30] The class of TPBs can be restricted to a narrower class of those who benefit under 'Bentham's test' as applied by Kramer. See Kramer (1998: 81–84). However, I agree with Steiner that the invocation of this test to restrict the class of TPBs seems ad hoc, and not in keeping with the motivation of IT as developed by Kramer. See Steiner (1998: 285–86); but nothing in the following turns on which of Kramer or Steiner is right about this.

[31] ss (1), (2). The rule, then, is a default, not a mandatory, rule. My understanding is that, in practice, the power to invoke this section is systematically exercised.

So there is a perfectly sensible IT reading of the case of A, B and the TPB, under which, because of our understanding of the way that the power to enter contracts serves our interests, the TPB is denied a claim-right in relation to B's contract with A, despite the fact that B's contractual undertaking to A benefits the TPB in some way. In those legal systems, like the common law, which deny any contractual rights under A and B's contract to the TPB, this is fully compatible with IT, because in the law's view the interests of A and B in being able to choose to whom they undertake legal obligations is (typically) of more importance than the interests of any TPB in (having control over) receiving the benefit of B's performance.

Now let me explain why, in the sort of TPB case which IT and WT theorists focus on, ie, where B undertakes to A to confer a benefit upon a TPB, it is not, typically, in *the TPB's own interest* to have a claim-right against B for the performance of B's contractual undertaking to A.

Take this example (which is representative of the germane TPB cases). A enters into a contract with B, under which A agrees to pay B, a watch seller, $100 in consideration of B's agreeing to transfer title to a particular model of watch to the TPB. A does this in order to make a birthday gift to the TPB. For my own part, I think the correct analysis of the normative relations in this sort of case turns on understanding A's power to make a gift, and the TPB's right (or Hohfeldian liability) to receive gifts; as well as of B's power to undertake voluntary obligations by way of contract, ie, as we have seen, to choose to whom he makes his voluntary contractual undertakings.

To get the normative picture here one first has to determine A's interest. I take it that having the facility to make gifts is in A's interest. I am not concerned here with any particular theory of gifts, but I take it to be intuitively correct that people's interests are typically served by having such a facility. Let us say that A's interest is 'expressive', ie, that one of the ways A can express his interest in the TPB's interest is by making a gift.[32] It would be a world not our own if people weren't able to share a bottle of wine with others, or to give presents to others, etc.

Moreover, it is analytic of gifts that the recipient has a right (or Hohfeldian 'liability') to receive them, but no (power) right to demand them. A recipient can of course refuse or disclaim a gift, so has that much control over their right or liability to receive, but they cannot require anyone to make gifts to them; ie, the TPB in our example can have no (power) right that A transfer any of A's property to the TPB gratuitously. It is, that is, analytic of gifts that the donor is not under a duty to the donee (contractual or otherwise) to make the gift, and thus analytic of gifts that gifts do not discharge any duty to transfer the property in question to the donee, so the donee has no correlative right to demand the transfer.

None of this reasoning changes when the gift is effected by contract as in the example of the watch. If the TPB were entitled to enforce the contract against B, requiring B to transfer the watch over A's objections, or himself claim damages

[32] For discussion of how gifts can reflect how one person can have an interest in another's interest, ie, an interest in how that other's life goes, see Penner (1997a: 88–90).

against B if B failed to deliver the watch, then the transaction would not amount to a gift. To give the TPB enforcement rights under the contract would erase A's facility to make a gift in this way, which is not in A's interest.

Nor would it be in the TPB's interest to have enforcement rights under the contract, according to this reflection upon the interests that the parties to this transaction (typically) have.[33] For the TPB to have the right to enforce the contract against B, at least in cases where A determines not to enforce the contract against B or, more seriously, positively wishes to waive B's contractual duty,[34] would turn a gift into something else. It would no longer have the character of a gift. The TPB has an interest in receiving the watch *as a gift* and not otherwise. If the TPB could demand the watch from B, at least in the circumstances just adverted to, his receipt would not be gratuitous, ie, not as a gift. The TPB has an interest in having a right/liability to receive property by way of gift—his interest in receiving things is not limited to receipts in discharge of obligations, contractual or otherwise.

That, then, is another application of IT which shows why the TPB has no rights of enforcement against B under the contract.

Now to the rejoinders. A first rejoinder might be that I have smuggled into the concept of a TPB right a WT theory of rights under which right-holders necessarily have a 'power' of enforcement. Thus, why cannot an IT theorist, such as Kramer, hold that on some, in particular his version of IT, a person can have a right though not the 'power' to enforce it? (For reasons given in the last section, I do not think there is a 'power' of enforcement in the way Hart, Kramer and Steiner do, hence the quotation marks around 'power', which I shall henceforward drop.) Kramer offers just such a rejoinder.

Kramer holds that a TPB does have a legal claim-right to the performance of B, but not necessarily any legal standing, ie, no necessary legal action right, to seek a remedy for B's breach of his contractual undertaking. Of a couple who are the third-party beneficiaries of a florist's duty to deliver them flowers, he says:

> The fact that the couple has no power to enforce or waive their claim does not mean that they have no Hohfeldian claim. Indeed, they surely *do* have such a claim, quite as much as the person who ordered the flowers. For the Will Theory, of course, a claim unconjoined with a power of enforcement/waiver in the hands of the claim-holder is a mere claim rather than a right; only for the Interest Theory (and for Hohfeld) is a mere claim a right.[35]

By 'mere claim' Kramer means a claim unconjoined with a power of enforcement. But that does not mean that it is not a genuine right, as opposed to a 'nominal right'—a right with no power of enforcement by anybody.

[33] In a sense the following paragraphs are a development of Sreenivasan's point that under Raz's version of IT the TPB's interests in the transaction are not sufficiently weighty to hold the watch seller to be under a duty towards him; indeed, I argue that the watch seller's having such a duty to the TPB would be contrary to the TPB's interests. See Sreenivasan (2005: 265).

[34] I thank Leif Wenar for helping me to sharpen my thinking on this point.

[35] Kramer (1998: 68) italics original.

On the relationship between genuine rights and enforcement, Kramer says the following:

> A genuine right or claim is enforceable. (Unlike a purely moral claim—which is also enforceable in certain ways—a genuine legal claim is enforceable through the mobilizing of governmental coercion, if necessary.) None the less ... the power to seek enforcement does not necessarily lie within the discretion of the person who has the claim. So long as the claim is duly enforceable, its status as a genuine Hohfeldian claim is unaffected by the precise location of the power to seek enforcement; *that power may be held by the claim-holder, or it may be held by someone acting as a fiduciary on behalf of the claim-holder, or it may be held by a state agency.*[36]

The italicised phrase would seem to state the IT view about the relationship between the question whether X, being the beneficiary of a duty, has a right, and the possibilities of enforcement of that right in an intuitively satisfying fashion. We can ignore enforcement by a state agency here, for that is not in issue with respect to the rights of TPBs. If enforcement by the claim-holder, or by someone acting as a fiduciary on behalf of the claim-holder are the only available options, then clearly the rights of the TPB are not rights even under Kramer's version of IT.

Enforcement by someone acting as a fiduciary on behalf of the claim-holder is conventionally understood to distinguish IT from WT as these theories apply to, for example, the rights of children or the legally incompetent. And it is true that those who bring enforcement actions on behalf of children or the legally incompetent do so in a fiduciary capacity, ie, they must act with only the interests of the claim-right holder in mind. But no fiduciary relationship arises between A and the TPB under the watch-seller contract just in virtue of the contract. A *can* declare a trust over his rights under the contract in favour of the TPB, in which case this relationship would hold, but that is not the case under discussion. It is clear at common law that the couple who are to receive the flowers have no claim-right in the sense that the contract is enforced *on their behalf* in the fiduciary sense when A enforces the contract: A is the one entitled to damages for breach, not the couple.[37] In other words, B is liable only to A, not to the TPB. The doctrine of privity of contract tells us so. So, the question for Kramer is, if the version of IT elaborated above can deliver the right result at law, as I have shown it can, what is the motivation for finding that his version of IT gives a positively wrong result in this, legal, case?

Now Kramer might claim that the options for enforcement set out in the italicised passage above are not exhaustive; there is a special sort of enforcement that operates in the realm of contracts and TPBs. Again, however, given the state of the law in question, what would motivate the hunt for such a special mode of enforcement, non-fiduciary but yet sufficient to treat A's enforcement of the contract as being in some way 'on the TPB's behalf', on the TPB's behalf, that is, in some *legally significant* or *genuine* way?

[36] ibid 9, my italics.

[37] It must be admitted that the courts have at times muddled this. For discussion see Stevens (2009: 188–92).

The relationship between rights and their enforcement is significant in another way. *Ubi ius, ibi remedium* is not just a slogan of justice of the common law; it is reflective of the common law's rationality. Whilst there are legal duties which are not enforceable against the duty-ower,[38] in private law, where contractual rights reside, it makes no sense for the law to impose a right–duty relationship which has no significance for the behaviour of the parties or the resolution of any dispute. In other words, by claiming that TPBs have *legal* Hohfeldian claim-rights to B's performance, but no *legal* action right against B consequent upon B's breach, and no *legal* right to any damages A recovers when A brings an action against B for breach, Kramer is apparently committed to the view that the common law's position is not only arguably unjust, but *irrational*, irrational *under IT*. For on what possible rational basis could the law's perspective vis-à-vis the TPB be that, *in consideration of the TPB's (typical) interests*, the law should confer upon the TPB a *mere* claim-right, ie, a claim-right without an action-right consequent upon its breach? On what possible rational basis is the conferral of a mere claim-right *reflective of the TPB's interest*, which it must be if IT is supposed to be satisfied? With respect, I think Kramer owes us a characterisation of the TPB's interest which shows how the conferral by the law of a mere claim typically operates to benefit TPBs, as opposed to being an essentially legally inert right which it is difficult to see as advancing the TPB's (typical) interest in any way. Or to put this another way, Kramer needs to show why it is in the TPB's interest to have a claim-right whilst at the same time show that it is not in the TPB's interest to have an action right consequent upon its breach; or show, which may amount to the same thing, that it is in the TPB's interest *not* to have an action right consequent upon its breach.

The other rejoinder concerns the possible evaluative commitments of the picture of contractual powers presented above.[39] The idea is that IT and WT make conceptual claims about the nature of rights, and in elaborating my version of IT and how it applies to the interests of people in making contracts and of recipients of receiving gifts *as* gifts and not otherwise, I have smuggled moral evaluative considerations into what it supposed to be a purely conceptual endeavour. But this rejoinder is misguided, or at least it doesn't touch my version of IT. Razian IT says that it is a conceptual feature of rights that they reflect a critical judgement by the right-conferrer (in the case of the law) or the right-recogniser (in the case of morality) that the existence of the right–duty relationship advances a significant interest of the right-bearer, such that the imposition of the duty on the duty-ower is justified. Kramer, by contrast, admits that in certain cases this critical judgement is necessary for determining the scope of a right (what is integral or not

[38] eg, the judge's duty to the litigants to hear the case properly and issue a correct legal ruling and an award if necessary. The disappointed litigants can appeal, but even if (when) the decision of the judge at first instance is overturned, the appellant court doesn't then order the judge at first instance to make the order she ought to have made; rather, the appellant court issues its own order.

[39] Raised to me by Mark McBride.

to determining the way the right works to the benefit of the right-holder)[40] and whether some jural relation bestows a right at all,[41] but in general denies this; in general a right exists where the imposition or recognition of a duty works *in fact* to benefit, in typical circumstances, the right-holder: the intentions or understanding of the right-conferrer or right-recogniser are generally irrelevant. So making reference to a critical understanding of the interests of contracting parties when they exercise their power to enter into contracts, and the interests of recipients of gifts, is not a theoretical solecism on my Razian version of IT, so long as it is understood that the analysis is only as good as the critical understanding set out. I do think that it is in the interests of people to be bound only to those to whom they undertake voluntary obligations, ie, not to anyone else who might benefit from their carrying out that undertaking, and I do think it is good to receive gifts as gifts. But in making these claims I am simply providing what I hope is a plausible analysis of the jural relations in question from the perspective of a Razian IT. But any Razian IT analysis must elaborate these evaluative issues to some extent because it is a conceptual requirement of the Razian concept of rights that *genuine* rights only exist when they are conferred or recognised as a response to a critical appreciation of the right-holder's interests.

V. The Powers of Office-Holders[42]

All of which brings us to the case of office-holders. Both Kramer and Wenar advocate the view that a judge holds the powers of his judicial office as rights. For Kramer, these are rights of his under the capacious version of his IT; for Wenar they are rights which match the judge's 'desires', given the role he undertakes to perform. It is submitted that they are both wrong, and that a proper application of IT tells us why.

Before considering the case of the judge and his powers, it is instructive to consider the case of a classic example of an office-holder in private law, that of a trustee. It is axiomatic that a trustee[43] has no personal interest in his carrying out the terms of the trust. This is reflected in the fact that where the trustee has

[40] Kramer and Steiner (2007: 293–94).

[41] Kramer (1998: 98–101).

[42] I am not, and nor are Kramer and Wenar, concerned here with the claim-rights or powers of office-holders that clearly are claim-rights or powers under IT or WT, eg, the claim-right of a judge to receive his salary, or the claim-right of a trustee to his trustee's fees, or the trustee's indemnity against the trust fund for all expenses properly incurred by the trustee in executing the trust.

[43] Unless he is also a beneficiary: but where a trustee is also one of the beneficiaries of a trust, it is clear that he is interested under the trust *qua* beneficiary, not *qua* trustee, so we can ignore this possibility in our discussion.

to exercise judgement[44] in exercising the powers of his office, whether in terms of administrative powers such as the power to invest the trust property, or in terms of his distributive or 'dispositive' powers, such as the power to pay one beneficiary of the trust more than another (a 'discretionary trust'), he must exercise his judgement with only the interests of the beneficiaries of the trust in mind. In particular, he should not exercise any of his discretions with his own interests in mind and, whether he realises it or not, if he does exercise the power in circumstances where his own interests are at stake—exercises them in 'conflict of interest'—the exercise of the power can be set aside.

In keeping with the way in which we examined the power of individuals to enter into contracts, we should look at the interests of the settlor in creating a trust. Is it typically in the settlor's interest to have a power to confer powers upon a trustee by giving him title to the trust property, and require the trustee not to use any of his powers of title to serve his own interests? Of course it is. The whole rationale of the legal device of the trust is to enable a person to give an office-holder, a trustee, powers so that the settlor can confer the benefits of the property on the beneficiaries, not on the trustee himself.

This point is confirmed if we consider whether the trustee has a power to waive or release the powers he has under the trust, which for identical reasons as those raised regarding Wenar's misapplication of WT to powers generally, shows that, for WT, a trustee does not hold his powers as rights.

Trustees are never entitled to waive the powers they have under a trust, for the simple reason that they hold those powers for the benefit of the beneficiaries, not for their own benefit.[45] However, a third-party holder of a power, under a trust that is conferred for that third-party power-holder's own benefit, *is* able to waive the power, although the term that is generally employed is that of a 'release' of a power. Consider the following two simple examples of trusts:

> All the rest and residue of my estate to my trustees ON TRUST for my beloved wife Mary for life, and then to my three sons, Jacob, Jasper and Jeremy in equal shares, with power to my wife Mary to appoint up to half the capital during her lifetime to such of my sons and in such amounts as she shall in her absolute discretion think fit.

[44] It is common in the case law and the academic literature to use the word 'discretion' in describing the context in which a fiduciary acts for his principal; it is commonly said that a fiduciary is one who must exercise a 'discretion' in exercising his legal powers for his principal. But 'discretion' suggests that the fiduciary has some sort of freedom, to choose one way over another. But this is misconceived: the fiduciary doesn't really have a choice in the matter. The fiduciary *must* follow the course of action which, in his judgement, best advances his principal's interests. Different fiduciaries might in good faith judge differently—that's just an artefact of human judgement—but no individual fiduciary can choose to follow any course of action but the one which he judges to be best for the principal.

[45] Beneficiaries can together vary the terms of the trust, in which case they might take away some of the powers of the trustee, but the trustee has no say in their decision to do so, although a trustee may propose a variation in the terms of the trust when it would be in the beneficiaries' interests to effect such a variation.

> All the rest and residue of my estate to my trustees ON TRUST for my beloved wife Mary for life, and then to my three sons, Jacob, Jasper and Jeremy in equal shares, with power to my wife Mary to appoint up to ten per cent of the capital during her lifetime to such of my wife's brothers and sisters and nieces and nephews in such amounts as she shall in her absolute discretion think fit.

Whilst this is a matter of the construction of these two trusts, in the first case Mary is generally regarded as having a 'power in the nature of a trust', which is to say that she does not hold the power for her own benefit, but as a kind of 'one-off' trustee. The conferral of the power on her in this way construes the settlor's intentions as being to benefit *his sons, not Mary*, by the grant of this power. Mary might be a long-lived old thing, and she might have more than enough income from the trust; why not give her the power to give some of the capital (up to half) to the boys during their lives (they might all be married with children and be able to use the money) rather than making them wait until she drops off her perch? A similar power could be given to the trustee, but presumably the settlor believed Mary would be a better judge of her sons' circumstances than the trustee himself. Holding the power for the benefit of her sons, she would have to consider from time to time exercising it in their favour, and she cannot release the power.

In the second case, it is likely the settlor gave Mary this power for her own benefit, to help her relations out if she chooses, not because the settlor had any particular affection for these people. If Mary decided she no longer cared for these relations, she would be able release the power, ie, waive it, fully and forever. In such a case, on IT and WT, she would hold the power *as a right*: on WT because she has the power of waiver; on IT because it is conferred for her own benefit, ie, it is in her interest that it is conferred, and she has the power to release the power because those in her position typically have an interest in being able to decide whether or not any exercise of the power is likely to serve her interests or not, and therefore she has an interest in being able to release it, ie, unburden herself of it.

Whilst I have elaborated the idea of having powers not to be exercised in one's own interest in relation to the law of trusts, the same point applies across the board to fiduciary relations in private law, for example to agency law. Companies, for example, must act through their agents; it is only by the exercise of those agents' powers that a company can act. The company, as the contractual counterparty, is entitled to determine how the powers and duties that are incidental to the agent/manager's office, benefit sundry third parties. These incidents, to the extent they confer powers or rights on the agent/manager, are created to advance the company's own interests, not those of the agent/manager.

We can now turn our attention to the case of the judge. Kramer and Wenar frame their thoughts in terms of the power of a judge in a criminal case to sentence the defendant upon conviction. I am going to tweak the example by making the judge a civil law judge, ie, a 'private law' judge as opposed to a public law (including criminal law) judge. In the typical case, a civil law judge disposes of a dispute by issuing a ruling as to D's, the defendant's, liability—let us assume D is liable for committing a tort—and then issuing a further ruling in the form of an order against D to pay P, the plaintiff, damages. Now the judge has a further power, which is the civil law power analogous to the criminal judge's power to pass a sentence against a convicted criminal: if D fails to comply with the order to pay P damages, at the behest of P, the judge has the power to order execution against D, for example by empowering an official to seize sufficient of D's goods and sell them, giving the proceeds to P, or the power to fine or imprison D for contempt of court for failing to comply with the order. Again, to order execution against D or to fine or imprison D is like imposing a sentence upon a convicted criminal, in that it empowers officials to carry out certain actions against D. For the sake of brevity, I will call this set of powers, held by the civil law judge, the judge's 'power of execution'. For the purposes of the argument it is the civil law equivalent of the criminal law judge's power of sentencing.

Again, I begin with the IT analysis of the powers that precede the powers in question, ie, here, the powers of someone to create an office. Is it in the interests of the state to have a power to confer on an official, a judge, powers which must be exercised *only* in the interests of the state (in wishing to see justice done) or third parties, P and D (their interest in an authoritative resolution of their dispute), and *not* in the interests of the judge himself? An affirmative answer seems not only plausible but obvious. The rules of natural justice tell us that a judge is positively *disqualified* if any interest of his would be implicated by the exercise of any of his judicial powers in any given case. If a case comes before a judge whose resolution would implicate the judge's own interests, the judge would be required to recuse himself. The natural conclusion for anyone applying IT to this case would be that the judge has no personal interest in the exercise of these powers, thus no personal interest in having the powers themselves. Thus, the judge would not be considered as holding the powers of his office *as rights*. But Wenar and Kramer both think otherwise. We can begin with Wenar.

As we have seen,[46] Wenar thinks that properly describing a judge's relation to her powers as one of holding those powers as rights depends on framing the judge as fulfilling a role. One way of addressing this issue of 'role' would be to look at whether the creator of an office would wish to confer upon an office-holder an interest in fulfilling her role. In a sense, the obvious answer would be yes, but at first glance it is hard to distinguish this thought from the idea that the office-creator would wish the office-holder willingly, even enthusiastically, to comply with the duties of the office. Would the office-creator further wish that the office-holder viewed the fulfilment of the office as more deeply personally involving, in the sense of the role being in some way significantly constitutive or evocative of their personality or wellbeing? Perhaps I am a cynic but this strikes me as implausible.

In any case, both Kramer and Wenar make the judge's interest in fulfilling her role central to their disagreement. Though Wenar in his 2013 paper does not return to the specific case of the judge, he explains the rights role-holders have

[46] Text to n 16.

in terms of their role-based desires by way of two examples, from which we can extrapolate what he would say about the judge:

> One more set of examples illustrates a different type of case, in which one role-bearer imposes a duty on another. A meter attendant issues a parking ticket requiring the owner of a car to pay a fine. An army captain orders a corporal to peel potatoes. We are ordinarily inclined to say that a meter attendant does not have a right that the car owner pays his ticket, while the captain does have a right that the corporal do what she ordered. The formalization correctly sorts these structurally similar situations, where in one case we ascribe rights and in the other we do not.
>
> According to the formalization, the test for whether there is a right in such cases turns on whether we understand the role with the power to impose the duty as including a desire that the duty be performed. The job of the meter attendant is just to put tickets on cars illegally parked. Meter attendants as such do not care whether drivers pay their fines—as meter attendants, they are indifferent if someone they ticket dies the same day. However, army captains do care that their orders are carried out. The captain gives orders to get results, and she would have reason to care if the corporal had a seizure upon hearing her order. So the theory explains why captains have a right that the duties they impose are fulfilled, while meter attendants do not, by noticing what these role-bearers as such want.[47]

It is right to point out that central goal of Wenar's analysis of rights is to capture ordinary language,[48] ie, his theory should line up with what people ordinarily

[47] Wenar (2013: 213–14).

[48] This is particularly explicit in Wenar (2005: 249–51). Andrew Halpin has suggested to me a different basis, orthogonal to the WT/IT debate about holding powers as rights, for the idea that a judge or trustee has rights to their powers of office. Halpin argues that we can meaningfully speak of the rights of judges or trustees to their powers, or to the exercise of said powers in settings where the exercise is directly challenged (paradigmatically in court): where, for example, a litigant submits that a judge has no power to make a particular kind of order, or where a beneficiary argues that a trustee has no power to invest the trust property in a particular kind of way. In such cases, the focus is on what the power-holder 'had a *right* to do'. Judges and trustees as office-holders hold legal powers uncontroversially in this simple sense, with no further enquiry into the judge's interest or waiver or will regarding the power: to add an element of 'right' to that position, occurs when (and only when) the position of the power-holder is directly challenged, in confirming that the power-holder enjoys a right to exercise that power. But neither does this additional element of 'right' require further enquiry into the judge's interest or waiver or will regarding the power. This is an interesting thought, but in response I would say the following: it is true that when a judge rejects a litigant's submission that the judge has no power to make a particular order, it might be said that the judge asserts a right to the power. But that is not an end to the matter. The litigant can appeal to a higher court. The lower court judge does not make any claim to have the power in that latter proceeding. That to my mind shows that the individual judge's interests are not at stake. So Halpin's thought, interesting though it is, does not, as Halpin recognises, undermine the argument in the text about whether under IT the judge holds his powers as rights. Where, say, a beneficiary challenges a trustee's act on the basis that under the trust terms he exercised a power ultra vires or had no such power so to act in the first place, the trustee of course does appear in the suit and has representation. But on a conventional understanding of trust litigation, the trustee has to appear with representation to provide counter-arguments to those advanced by the complaining beneficiary, because he is required to do so to protect the interests of all the beneficiaries, including the complaining beneficiary under the trust, not his own interests. So again, whilst interesting as a different view of the meaningfulness of ascribing 'rights' to powers, this thought does not undermine the claim that the trustee does not hold his powers as rights under IT.

say, for example that people say that 'judges have rights to sentence', 'trustees have rights to invest trust property', and so on. On this point, I should only say that it is common to use the term 'right' to include powers, so such sentences can arguably just mean, returning to judges, 'judges have powers to sentence', and so on. It therefore does not seem to follow, to my mind, that people's use of 'right' in such circumstances bespeaks any commitment to the idea that judge's hold their powers as rights in the sense under discussion here. That is, on a natural reading these sentences simply state that, for example, the trustee or judge has the powers that each has, not that they hold these powers *as rights*. As regards the sentence: 'We are ordinarily inclined to say that a meter attendant does not have a right that the car owner pays his ticket, while the captain does have a right that the corporal do what she ordered', I think the same lesson applies. I disagree that these sayings properly reflect any intuition about whether or not the meter attendant or the captain hold their powers *as rights*. Let me explain.

As to the captain, the sentence merely affirms that the captain has the power to order the corporal to do things. It reveals no intuition that the army captain holds the power to do so as a right. The difference Wenar finds between the case of the army captain and the meter attendant seems in part to be that the recipient of the parking ticket is not answerable to the attendant if he fails to pay, but is answerable to the local authority (or whatever), whereas the corporal owes his duty to the captain in the sense that he is answerable to the captain if the potatoes remain unpeeled; but this difference does not reflect any difference in the way they hold their powers, or at least it is not clear how it does.

This thought can be bolstered by considering Wenar's notion of a role-based desire, and trying to figure out what he would say about a judge and others with a role to discharge. As far as I can tell, the judge would line up with the meter attendant, whilst a company manager would line up with the army captain, whereas a trustee would line up with both depending on which power of his was under consideration.

Like meter attendants, judges *as such* don't care whether litigants comply with their particular orders. They are 'indifferent if someone [against whom they make an order] dies the next day'. After they issue their rulings, they go home, have a drink and attend to the next case, just like the meter attendant. If P later seeks enforcement against D, she will not typically have to appear before the same judge. That is, on failing to comply with the judge's order, D is not typically answerable to that same judge; P can prove D's failure to pay before, and seek execution against D from any judge she can get in front of, according to openings in the court docket. So, contrary to Wenar's earlier view, judges *do not* on this new accounting hold their powers as rights.

However, like the army captain, a company manager, as agent of the company, normally exercises his powers *to get results*. So, the company manager does hold his powers as rights, despite the fact that he achieves those results for the benefit of the company, not himself. The case of the trustee is trickier. When he distributes the trust property, this is not 'getting a result'. Upon final distribution, the trust comes to an end and the trustee no longer has any concern with the beneficiaries. The distribution of the trust property is not a 'result' he gets; rather the distribution of the trust property is the discharge of his central trustee obligation(s), though he exercises the power to transfer title to the trust property in doing so. By contrast, when a trustee exercises his power of investment over the trust property, he certainly does mean to get results. He wants the value of the trust assets to rise, not fall, though his success, if he succeeds, and his failure, if he fails, will, like the company manager's, enure not to himself, but to the beneficiaries. So the trustee's power to invest would be one he held as a right, but not the power to distribute the trust assets to the beneficiaries.

With respect, none of this even begins to show whether these various characters hold their various powers as rights.

Kramer's argument for holding that a judge holds his power of sentencing as a right under Kramer's (capacious) version of IT is based on the idea that 'the possession of such a [power] is generally beneficial for someone who bears the legal responsibilities of a judicial office'.[49]

I must now quote from Kramer to set out Wenar's counter-argument, and Kramer's response to that:

> While continuing to focus on the examples of the judge and the policeman, Wenar contends that my 'line of reasoning [about the judge's power and the policeman's liberty] simultaneously relies upon and misunderstands the norms that are roles'. [Wenar] elaborates as follows:[50]
>
> > It is not as though there is a coherent role described as 'judge who has the responsibility to sentence but no power to sentence'—and then we make a separate determination that the life of someone filling that role would go better if they gained the power to sentence. The original description makes no sense: a role that assigns a responsibility to ϕ but with no normative ability to ϕ is not a role that fits into any recognizable human practice. Similarly with the patrolman. There is no intelligible job that is 'policeman who has the duty not to detain suspects whenever he has the duty to detain suspects'. Such a job could be imagined only at the edges of a fantasy, if there; speculation about the interests of such a job-holder is moot. In reality, offices such as 'judge' and 'policeman' always pair the responsibilities of office with the normative abilities appropriate for carrying out these responsibilities. 'Rights of office' are not optional add-ons that help a person do a job; rather, rights of office are an integral part of every job's description.
>
> Nothing in this passage has any bearing on the ways in which the capacious variant of my version of the Interest Theory applies to the examples of the judge and the policeman. Wenar's remarks would have such a bearing if the relevant *explananda* were the fact that the judge has legal powers of sentencing and the fact that the policeman has legal liberties to detain suspects. If I were trying to explain those facts, my explanations which advert

[49] Kramer (this volume: p 57).

[50] Quoting Wenar (2008: 260, fn omitted).

> to the interests of the office-holders would be ludicrous for the reasons indicated in this passage. However, once again, those facts are not the relevant *explananda*. Rather, the capacious variant of my version of the Interest Theory is aiming to explain why the legal powers of the judge are properly classifiable as legal rights and why the legal liberties of the policeman are properly classifiable as legal rights. I am addressing not a question concerning why the judge and the policeman hold certain entitlements, but instead a question concerning the status of those entitlements as rights. Wenar's observations do not bear on that latter question nor on my answer to it.[51]

It seems to me that Kramer has not appreciated the strength of Wenar's objection here, and that Wenar's thought can be built upon to show that Kramer's argument is misjudged.

Wenar's thought is essentially of this kind. Where a judge has a power, it is constitutive of his office. For Kramer's approach to the issue of whether a judge holds a power of his office as a right, we must look at the nearest possible world in which the person in question has the role but not the power, but where it would also be coherent for the person in the role to think that having the power (of which he has notionally been stripped) would be in his interest. Now Wenar's claim, as I understand it, is that this sort of thinking is muddled. A person's office is defined by whatever rights, duties, powers, liabilities and so on he actually has. It is essentially incoherent to ascribe to such an office-holder *qua* typical office-holder an interest in other rights, duties, powers and so on, for that would not be an interest he has as that office-holder, but is rather an interest *in holding a different office.*

Consider the following real-life example of the nearest possible world to being a judge, in which the person has all the powers of a judge save for the power of execution. Such a person is called an arbitrator.[52] Arbitrators can determine issues of liability between P and D but have no powers of execution. P needs to bring his arbitral award to a court of law in order to enforce it against D. Now we can ask, would it be in the interest of an arbitrator to have the power of execution? Put this way, it may seem at first glance that the answer is 'yes'. It would give the arbitrator

[51] Kramer (this volume: p 58).

[52] Like Wenar, by parity of reasoning I therefore agree that the criminal judge's powers of sentencing are conceptually constitutive of being a judge, or rather, of the office of a judge. Mark McBride questions this constitutive connection. At the margins of the concept of a criminal judge, McBride suggests that he can think of a judge without sentencing powers, and therefore that he is implicated in no conceptual error in so imagining. In reply I should say Wenar's position and mine is that offices are constituted by the rights, powers, etc that make them up, and that the burden of proof is on someone who wants to say that there is a concept of the role of an office-holder which goes beyond that so as to give him an 'office-holder' reason to acquire powers/lose powers, to better fulfil his role in that office. So, as to the example of the criminal law judge with no power to sentence, I can think of an official who had the right to determine guilt but not to sentence, in the same way that a conventional criminal law judge has the right to sentence, but no right to pardon, or no right to determine parole conditions. I can imagine arguments that an individual might have for separating or combining these powers in one office, but not a 'role-based' reason for doing so, a role which, remember, can only be elaborated in terms of the *actual* powers and so on which constitute the role.

more scope for resolving the dispute between P and D. But this superficially plausible view is misleading, because by wanting to have the power of execution, the arbitrator is really saying that he wished he were a judge, ie, wished he had that job rather than the job of an arbitrator.

Another way of putting this is that the arbitrator's interests are irrelevant. It is the people who enter into an arbitration clause in a contract whose interests are at stake, and if they choose arbitration (where the arbitrator has no power of enforcing the award) over litigation in court (where the judge has such a power) it would be positively against their interests, as they see them, for the arbitrator to have the power of enforcement he longs for. A further way of putting this would be that if the arbitrator got his wish it would do him no good, for he would lose all his business. No one would go to him to conduct arbitration, ie, go to him in his office *of an arbitrator*, because he would no longer be an arbitrator—he would be a judge.

Now consider another real-life example. At one time, the only way that a court of equity could enforce an order against D to transfer real property of his to P was by throwing D into gaol for contempt if he failed to do so. D would remain in gaol until he decided to comply. But that was the limit of what the court could do. Now, it might well have seemed to an equity judge that it would be a good idea if the court were to acquire a power to execute a transfer from D to P itself, and indeed, judges do now have that power by statute. Does this sort of case bolster Kramer's argument against Wenar?

Unfortunately, I don't think it does, or at least not following the explicit terms of Kramer's argument. As we have seen, Kramer says, 'the possession of such a [power] is generally beneficial for someone who bears the legal responsibilities of a judicial officer'. But if the judge has no power to execute a transfer from D to P, then ipso facto he can have no responsibility to do so. Of course, it is true that it might better serve the interests of justice and the normative relations between P and D if the judge were to have this power, but those are not the interests of any typical person because they happen to have the office of judge. A judge might be, and presumably is, in a very good position to see how such a power would advance the cause of justice and the right of the parties to an authoritative resolution of a dispute, but that doesn't begin to suggest that it would be in the personal interest of a typical judge to have such a power, *except and in so far as it would be in the personal interest of the judge to tweak his office so that he was now a judge'* (ie, is a judge-prime), a slightly different judicial office. But that would be an interest in there being a slightly different office, not an interest in the powers of that office.

What Kramer owes us then, to make his case for the capacious version of IT which maintains that a judge holds some of his powers of office as rights, is a notion of an office-holder as something which transcends, or can be understood apart from, the office as constituted by what we normally think constitutes it, ie, the rights, duties, powers and liabilities which make it the legal office that it is.

Three final technical points.

First, on Kramer's view it would seem plausible to hold that whether or not a judge held a power as a right would involve some discrimination across the range of his powers, such that he held some as rights, some not. For example, it seems very plausibly the case that, understood from a broader responsibility to do justice which was not constituted entirely by the norms (rights, duties, powers) that legally constituted his office, there might well be powers that are *not* in the interests of the typical judge to have. Take two examples. First, consider the power of a criminal judge to have a criminal defendant convicted of treason to be tortured to death by being hanged, drawn and quartered. Or, second, consider the power of a civil law judge to order imprisonment for debt, or to order trial by ordeal or by battle. We know historically that it was probably the case that typical judges held the view that these various powers were *not* powers which were (typically) good in the way of fulfilling their roles. We know this because of the way in which the exercise of such powers fell into desuetude, or were only very reluctantly exercised. They have all, of course, been abolished. If this is true, then Kramer's explication of the notion of an office-holder whose responsibilities transcend the actual legal incidents of his office will require more colour—distinguishing those powers he holds as rights from those which he does not.

The second point again involves thinking of the judge understood as a doer of justice apart from the incidents of his office. It might seem that a typical judge could have views about his interest in doing justice, not just in terms of his powers, but also in terms of his claim-rights, and more significantly still, in terms of his duties. Those duties, such as the duty to order disclosure against the parties, the having of which a judge would plausibly and typically regard as furthering his role in, say, presiding over the resolution of a dispute fairly between the parties, or a duty to provide reasons for judgment, he might say he held *as rights*. But it does seem to stretch the concept of a right-holding or holding 'as a right', to say that one can have a duty or hold a duty as a right, ie, that a judge has a right to the duties that properly, in justice, form part of the incidents of the office. Yet on a 'right-holding' version of IT,[53] which both Kramer and I endorse, there would seem to be no way to block the result that a person could hold a duty as a right, if Kramer's broader notion of the interests of a judge in the performance of his role were to prevail.

The third technical point was suggested to me by Leif Wenar. Wenar points out that judges and trustees can resign—meaning that they have the power to annul their powers of office. This, arguably, might be enough for WT to ascribe them a right. I disagree, though it of course depends on the contours of the particular WT. But compare—I can annul all my rights and powers simply by killing myself. As far as I know no Will theorist makes an argument of this kind to establish that all rights and powers are held as rights under WT. By parity of reasoning, when a judge or trustee resigns or retires this does not seem to count as the right kind of control to establish his holding of his powers as rights—what is required is some sort of control which he can exercise whilst still remaining a judge or trustee.

[53] See text to n 3.

VI. Conclusion

The main thrust of this essay is that the Kramer–Wenar debate over whether officials like judges hold their powers of office as rights has been misguided in several respects. The argumentative strategy, following the Razian version of IT I am endorsing, has been first to consider our moral powers, and then look at their customary legal equivalents. In doing so we first consider the interests of those power-holders themselves, before then considering the interests of those who acquire rights by the exercise of those powers. In the case of offices, the first question is whether it would be in the interests of the creators of those offices to be able to do so such that the holders of those offices do not hold the powers of their offices as rights, ie, not for the benefit of their own interests, and it was claimed that this is more or less obviously the case. It was then concluded that the introduction of 'role-based' interests or desires does not do the work advertised to overturn this intuitively sensible result.

References

Cruft, R (2004) 'Rights: Beyond Interest Theory and Will Theory?' 23 *Law and Philosophy* 347.

Hart, HLA (1982) 'Legal Rights' in HLA Hart, *Essays on Bentham: Jurisprudence and Political Theory* (Oxford: Oxford University Press).

Hegel, GWF (1942) (1821) *Hegel's Philosophy of Right* (trans Knox) (Oxford: Claredon Press).

Kramer, MH (1998) 'Rights Without Trimmings' in MH Kramer, NE Simmonds and H Steiner, *A Debate over Rights. Philosophical Enquiries* (Oxford: Oxford University Press).

—— (2010) 'Refining the Interest Theory of Rights' 55 *The American Journal of Jurisprudence* 31.

—— (2013) 'Some Doubts About Alternatives to the Interest Theory of Rights' 123 *Ethics* 245.

Kramer, MH and Steiner, H (2007) 'Theories of Rights: Is There a Third Way?' 27 *Oxford Journal of Legal Studies* 281.

MacCormick, DN (1977) 'Rights in Legislation' in PMS Hacker and J Raz (eds), *Law, Morality and Society: Essays in Honour of HLA Hart* (Oxford: Clarendon Press).

—— (1982) 'Children's Rights: A Test-Case for Theories of Right' in N MacCormick, *Legal Right and Social Democracy: Essays in Legal and Political Philosophy* (Oxford: Clarendon Press).

Penner, J (1996) 'Voluntary Obligations and the Scope of the Law of Contract' 2 *Legal Theory* 325.

—— (1997a) *The Idea of Property in Law* (Oxford: Clarendon Press).
—— (1997b) 'The Analysis of Rights' 10 *Ratio Juris* 300.
—— (2013) 'On the Very Idea of Transmissible Rights' in J Penner and HE Smith (eds), *Philosophical Foundations of Property Law* (Oxford: Oxford University Press).
Penner, J and Kwek, K (2016) 'The Law's Remedial Norms') 28 *Singapore Academy of Law Journal* 768.
Raz, J (1984a) 'On the Nature of Rights' 93 *Mind* 194.
—— (1984b) 'Legal Rights' 4 *Oxford Journal of Legal Studies* 1.
—— (1986) *The Morality of Freedom* (Oxford: Clarendon Press).
—— (1994) *Ethics in the Public Domain: Essays in the Morality of Law and Politics* (Oxford: Clarendon Press).
Shiffrin, S (2008) 'Promising, Intimate Relationships, and Conventionalism' 117 *Philosophical Review* 481.
Sreenivasan, G (2005) 'A Hybrid Theory of Claim-Rights' 25 *Oxford Journal of Legal Studies* 257.
Steiner, H (1998) 'Working Rights' in MH Kramer, NE Simmonds and H Steiner, *A Debate over Rights. Philosophical Enquiries* (Oxford: Oxford University Press).
Stevens, R (2009) 'Damages and the Right to Performance: A Golden Victory or Not?' in JW Neyers, R Bronaugh and SGA Pitel (eds), *Exploring Contract Law* (Oxford: Hart Publishing).
Wenar, L (2005) 'The Nature of Rights' 33 *Philosophy & Public Affairs* 223.
—— (2008) 'The Analysis of Rights' in MH Kramer et al (eds), *The Legacy of HLA Hart: Legal, Political, and Moral Philosophy* (Oxford: Oxford University Press).
—— (2013) 'The Nature of Claim-Rights' 123 *Ethics* 202.

6

Public Goods, Individual Rights and Third-Party Benefits

GOPAL SREENIVASAN

In this essay, I examine the question of whether individuals can hold a claim-right to any pure public good. Intuitively, it would seem that the answer is clearly 'no'. But, of course, people may differ in their intuitions and some people may not have any intuitions on this subject at all. More importantly, intuitions are not a decisive basis on which to settle philosophical questions in any case. I shall thus examine our question through the lens of various competing theories of rights. Two of the three 'major' theories of rights I shall canvass—namely, the Will theory and Raz's (1986; 1994) Interest theory—support the intuitive conclusion that no individual can hold a claim-right to a pure public good.[1] As we shall see, however, the rationales they respectively offer for their common verdict are very different.

By contrast to these three theories, Kramer's (1998; 2007) version of the Interest theory affirms without restriction the possibility of individuals holding claim-rights to pure public goods.[2] The fundamental reason for this difference is that pure public goods are, as we shall also see, third-party benefits par excellence. In affirming individual rights to them, the Interest theory therefore invites us to revisit the 'third-party beneficiary' objection (Hart 1955; 1982). Despite Kramer's (2007) valiant efforts, I shall conclude that this objection remains fatal to the Interest theory. So perhaps public goods represent an instance in which intuition was on to something after all.

To set the stage, I shall begin by describing an example from the health sector and reviewing the definition of 'pure public good' in terms of it. In section II, I shall explain why no individual can hold a Will theory claim-right to this (or any other) pure public good. In section III, I add a brief coda reframing this argument in terms of my Hybrid theory. Thereafter, I shall focus on the two main versions

[1] My own Hybrid theory also supports this verdict (Sreenivasan 2005). I shall review its argument for this conclusion briefly below. But, on this topic, it has much in common with the argument from the Will theory.

[2] Kramer's version does not differ from other versions of the ordinary Interest theory on this point. I focus on his version simply because it is the best version. For simplicity, and without intending any disrespect, I shall refer to the authors of Kramer and Steiner's (2007) paper as 'Kramer'.

of the Interest theory. In section IV, I shall examine Raz's version. As we shall see, Raz's position on our question is somewhat complicated to interpret. On his view, there are clearly many public goods—of which our health sector example is one—to which no individual can hold a claim-right. I shall suggest that, under the best interpretation of Raz's view, the same is true of all public goods. The remainder of my discussion is concerned with the ordinary Interest theory. In section V, I review Hart's (1955; 1982) well-known third-party beneficiary objection. In section VI, I shall examine and reject Kramer's (2007) most recent attempt to defend the Interest theory against Hart's objection. Section VII concludes that individuals cannot hold a claim-right to any pure public good.

I. Pure Public Goods, Defined and Illustrated

As my example of a pure public good, let me introduce *herd immunity* against contagious infectious disease.[3] Herd immunity is a form of health protection that is available to individuals in a population who lack personal immunity against particular contagious infectious diseases. Let me explain using measles to illustrate. Herd immunity against measles obtains when a sufficiently high proportion of individuals in a given population has personal immunity against measles. When this critical threshold is crossed in the 'herd', the immunised function as a protective barrier against the transmission of measles, reducing the likelihood that someone who lacks personal immunity against measles will come into contact with the disease—reducing it, that is, to a point at which her likelihood of contracting measles becomes negligible.

Personal immunity against measles is achieved by vaccinating the individual to be protected;[4] and it is a property of the protected individual herself. By contrast, herd immunity against measles is achieved by vaccinating individuals *other than* the individual(s) to be protected. Thus, with herd immunity the protection against measles enjoyed by someone who lacks personal immunity is conferred by a property of the population in which she resides, rather than by any property the protected individual has by herself. In this way, herd immunity is a third-party benefit. To achieve this property in a given community typically requires very high rates of vaccination. With measles, for example, it requires a vaccination rate greater than 92 per cent (Orenstein and Seib 2014). In practice, therefore, the achievement of herd immunity requires vaccination against a given disease to be *compulsory* (Malone and Hinman 2003).[5]

[3] This section excerpts from Sreenivasan (2012: section 5). Some infectious diseases are not contagious (eg, tetanus) and there can be no herd immunity against them.

[4] Personal immunity can also be achieved by previous exposure to measles. But, of course, that is not a public health intervention.

[5] In many jurisdictions, compulsory vaccination is clearly *legally* authorised, even in the United States (Malone and Hinman 2003). I shall assume that compulsory vaccination is also morally justified.

For individuals lacking personal immunity against various contagious diseases,[6] the existence in their community of herd immunity against those diseases represents a clear and important health benefit. Moreover, this health benefit is socially controllable, since herd immunity is produced by vaccination campaigns. Since the health benefit provided by herd immunity is also cost-effective, it is very plausible that the domestic state has a moral duty to provide herd immunity against measles (but against diphtheria and other contagious diseases, too).

Herd immunity counts as a pure public good because it exhibits all three features in terms of which pure public goods are commonly defined. The protection it confers against contracting a contagious disease is *non-rival*, meaning that its 'consumption' by one person lacking immunity does not diminish the protection available to other people lacking immunity. It is also *non-excludable*, meaning that if one person can consume this protection, then no one else in the herd can be excluded from consuming it (without excessive cost). Finally, the protection conferred by herd immunity is *indivisible*, meaning that each person who consumes it enjoys all the available protection.

For the purposes of this essay, then, I shall take it as a fixed point that domestic states have a moral duty to provide their citizens with certain pure public goods. While my example will be the state's duty to provide its citizens with herd immunity against measles, this focus is not meant to exclude other contagious diseases.[7] I should also emphasise that the intuitive dogma with which I opened the essay does not in the least deny this fixed point.[8] What it denies, rather, is something more precise, namely, that any individual citizen has a moral claim-*right that correlates* with her state's moral duty to provide herd immunity against measles. Let us now examine the extent to which this intuitive dogma can be vindicated by various theories of rights.

II. Why there are no Will Theory Rights to a Pure Public Good

Let us begin with the Will theory.[9] According to the Will theory, an individual citizen has a claim-right correlative to her state's duty to provide herd immunity

[6] Individuals may lack personal immunity against a given disease either because, for whatever reason, they have not themselves been vaccinated against it or because in their case the vaccine failed, as sometimes happens.

[7] Indeed, according to Anomaly (2011), the moral structure of the entire enterprise of public health is best defined by the production of pure public goods.

[8] The most controversial question in this neighbourhood is probably whether a state has a moral duty to provide its citizens with *every* socially controllable cause of health. But even a negative answer to this question (ie, the correct answer) is consistent with my fixed point because the provision of herd immunity against measles is very cost-effective, as I have said.

[9] This section excerpts from Sreenivasan (2016).

against measles just in case she has the moral power to *waive* her state's duty (to provide herd immunity against measles).[10] Assuming, however, that individuals have exactly the moral powers they are morally justified in having, it seems clear that no individual citizen has the moral power required under the Will theory. For the effect of a solitary individual's exercising that power would be to extinguish the state's moral duty to provide herd immunity against measles. Whatever her opinion in the matter, all her fellow citizens who lack personal immunity against measles still stand to gain a (cost-effective) health benefit from herd immunity; and the state still has a moral duty to protect *their* health. Hence, the original grounds for justifying the state's duty to provide the public good of herd immunity remain fully in force; and their remaining in force precludes an adequate justification for extinguishing that duty. No individual, then, is justified in having the moral power to waive this duty, since no individual would ever be justified in exercising it. It follows that no citizen has a Will theory claim-right to the existence of herd immunity against measles.

Some may be inclined to protest that I start this vindication off on the wrong foot, and thereby make things too easy for it. In particular, I assume that the duty an individual must be empowered to waive here (to qualify as a Will theory right-holder) is the state's *one and only duty* to provide herd immunity. Only on that assumption does a single individual's waiver have the crucial and indeed unjustified consequence that the state is left bereft of *any* duty to provide herd immunity. But why should this assumption be accepted? Would it not be equally reasonable, at least in some cases, to analyse the state's 'duty to φ' as a bundle of plural (perhaps, indefinitely many) *duties* to φ? In that case, the effect of a single individual's waiver would be limited to extinguishing one of these duties, leaving the state's other duties to φ in place; and that effect may well be perfectly justified, even when 'φ-ing' is 'providing herd immunity'.

Structurally, of course, the alternative analysis contemplated by this protest is perfectly coherent. It is also familiar from at least one everyday context, namely, promising.[11] There is nothing to stop me, for example, from promising the same thing to three different people, say that 'I will fast from sun up til sun down next Easter'. In that case, I will acquire three numerically distinct duties with exactly the same content. So even if one of the promisees 'waives my duty' (ie, releases me from my promise), I will remain duty-bound to fast at Easter. However, while this sort of example fully instantiates the contemplated alternative, it still fails to undermine the vindication I offered for the intuitive dogma.

The challenge is to secure the crucial feature of the plural coincident promises scenario—the existence of numerically distinct duties with identical content borne by the same agent—without recourse to the special machinery of promising. I do not need to claim that this is simply impossible. Perhaps there are cases, for

[10] I am simplifying the Will theory here. For the omitted details, see Sreenivasan (2005: section 2). Restoring these details would complicate the story without materially changing it.

[11] Compare my discussion of 'variant A' in Sreenivasan (2005: 269). I now think that I was insufficiently attentive there to the possibility that the relevant constellation of features is an artefact of the special machinery of promising.

example, in which the state is duty-bound to secure some good, and the good itself (a minimum income, say, or a fair trial) is also discretely individuable in some way, so that there is room to argue that the state's 'duty to provide [that good]' can be redescribed without loss as a bundle of indefinitely many duties to provide the relevant quantum of that good.

I can afford to leave the fate of any such argument up in the air. For however many goods are amenable to being treated along these lines, there is no possibility of pure public goods being among them. By definition, pure public goods are goods whose very existence is 'all or nothing' in various senses. What this means in the present context is precisely that a pure public good cannot be 'discretely individuated', and hence that there can be no plural quanta [of it] to which the plural duties in any redescribed bundle might refer. At least as far as pure public goods are concerned, then, the protester's alternative analysis is a non-starter. Promising aside, if the state is duty-bound to provide herd immunity against measles (or any other pure public good), there is no alternative to the assumption that the state has but one duty to provide it. From that point, the Will theory's vindication of the intuitive dogma can return to the races.

III. Coda on the Hybrid Theory

Elsewhere (2005) I have advanced my own theory of rights, which is a hybrid of the Will theory and the Interest theory. One feature that my Hybrid theory shares with the Will theory, and which also distinguishes it from either version of the Interest theory, is that its test for right-holding refers explicitly to the power to waive the correlative duty. In particular, the Hybrid theory makes it a necessary condition of an individual's holding a claim-right correlative to some duty that it be *justifiable* to empower her to waive that duty (here I extend the simplification of footnote 10 to the Hybrid theory). For present purposes, we do not require any deeper acquaintance with details of the Hybrid theory. That is because there is a very short route from this feature to a vindication of the intuitive dogma. As we saw in the previous section, no individual is justified in having the power to waive the state's duty to provide herd immunity against measles. It follows immediately that no individual holds a Hybrid theory claim-right to the existence of herd immunity against measles.

IV. Why there are no Razian Rights to a Pure Public Good

On Raz's version of the Interest theory, it is a more complicated question whether individual citizens have a claim-right correlative to their state's moral duty to provide herd immunity against measles. According to Raz's (1986) general definition of rights, an individual citizen has a claim-right correlative to her state's moral duty to provide herd immunity against measles just in case an aspect of her wellbeing is *sufficient*, other things being equal, to *justify* the state's duty. We might call this his 'general test' for rights. In the present case, 'sufficiency to justify the state's duty' requires the moral significance of a single individual's health to be capable of underwriting the whole burden of having to vaccinate close to the entire domestic population against measles. This burden includes not only the obvious material costs of a standing vaccination programme, but also the *moral* costs of compelling everyone else in society to submit to it.[12]

It is very doubtful that a single individual's health has the moral significance to underwrite either cost,[13] let alone both. Raz himself clearly concurs in the sum of these judgements. In relation to a different example of a public good (or, as he says, collective good), he declares that it is 'difficult to imagine a successful argument imposing a duty to provide a collective good on the ground that it will serve the interests of one individual' (1986: 203). A few pages later, Raz concludes even more explicitly that 'one may indeed doubt the possibility of a justification for a fundamental individual right to a collective good' (1986: 208).

At the very least, an imposing obstacle stands in the way of any individual's satisfying Raz's general test for holding a claim-right to a public good. On one natural understanding, this obstacle consists in a fundamental mismatch between the weight of a single individual's interest and the weight of the state's duty to provide (say) herd immunity against measles. For given that mismatch, the individual's interest cannot possibly be sufficient to justify the state's duty, as required by Raz's general test. The basic impossibility here is not conceptual, but rather turns, as Réaume (1988) observes, on a substantive moral judgement, albeit an extremely plausible one.[14]

Now complications arise in Raz's treatment of public goods because of an additional test he introduces in subsequent work (1994). In the first instance, this test—Raz's 'special test', as I shall call it—aims to augment the weight of certain

[12] While my assumption that compulsory vaccination is morally justified entails that *some* set of conditions is sufficient to justify these (moral) costs, the question in the text is whether a single individual's health constitutes such a set all by itself.

[13] This is consistent with my earlier claim that the provision of herd immunity is cost-effective because the accounting framework differs in the two cases. From the state's point of view, the denominator includes the entire population, which makes the relevant material cost a per capita cost. By contrast, from the individual's point of view, the denominator is one, so the entire material cost must be counted.

[14] For her part, Réaume (1988) proceeds to distinguish a subset of public goods, which she calls 'participatory goods,' in relation to which it is conceptually impossible for an individual to satisfy Raz's general test for holding a claim-right. Hence, her own denial that any individual holds a claim-right to a *participatory* public good does not depend on a substantive moral judgement. However, herd immunity against contagious disease is not a participatory good in Réaume's sense, so in this case there is no way to avoid a substantive moral judgement, one way or the other. Interestingly, Réaume herself (1988: 9) seems not to share the particular judgement that a single individual's interest in avoiding contagious disease is not sufficient to justify the state's duty to provide protection against it.

individual claim-rights consistently with his general test for rights. More specifically, it aims to augment their weight to a point where their weight (vastly) exceeds the weight of the individual right-holder's own underlying interest. According to Raz's special test, *third-party* interests can be counted alongside the individual's interest, for the purposes of satisfying his general test, as long as the third-party interests are served *precisely by serving* the individual's own interest (1994: 51–52). Thus, when they satisfy his special test, Raz is willing to count third-party interests as adding to the weight of an individual's interest, thereby enabling that individual's interest to justify imposing a much weightier duty (eg, on the state) than it would otherwise have been sufficient to justify.

Consider one of Raz's examples. The beauty of Oxford (the city) is a public good for its inhabitants. Among the factors contributing to the protection of this public good, we are asked to imagine, is the work of Juliet, an architect employed by the city council to devise and administer a preservation scheme for central Oxford. Like all employees, Juliet has a right not to be unjustly dismissed from her post (eg, as a result of scheming by property speculators). Given Juliet's position, the interest of every inhabitant of Oxford (in protecting the beauty of their city) is served precisely by serving Juliet's interest in not being unjustly dismissed. Hence, all of *their* interests in this public good weigh in her balance as well, and as a result Juliet's right (ie, the council's duty not to dismiss her unjustly) has a much greater weight than the weight of Juliet's own interest, though this apparent mismatch is explained away by the (hidden) contribution from the third-party interests that satisfy Raz's special test. More generally, Raz argues,

> in the case of the central civil and political rights of liberal societies, the main reason for the mismatch between the importance of the right and its contribution to the right-holder's well-being is the fact that part of the justifying reason for the right is its contribution to the common good (1994: 55).[15]

For our purposes, the most acute complication here is interpretative. As we shall see presently, not all public goods satisfy Raz's special test (nor does he claim otherwise). Nevertheless, some public goods do satisfy it. For those that do, a question arises concerning the significance of that very fact: does satisfying Raz's special test remove the imposing obstacle preventing individuals from satisfying his general test (for holding a claim-right to the public good in question), and thereby clear the way for individuals to hold Razian claim-rights to some public goods?

I shall canvass two different answers to this question. According to what I shall call the 'loose' interpretation, individuals *can* hold a Razian claim-right to a public good provided that the public good satisfies Raz's special test. After all, the reason an individual appeared to be disbarred from holding a Razian claim-right to any public good was that the weight of the candidate correlative duty (ie, the duty to provide some public good) was always much greater than any one individual's interest could plausibly be considered sufficient to justify. Yet when relevant

[15] For some discussion and criticism of this argument, see Sreenivasan (2005: section 4).

third-party interests satisfy Raz's special test, there will perforce be some interest belonging to the individual in question whose credited weight is now sufficient, thanks to Raz's special accounting, to justify the state's duty to provide the relevant public good.[16] The augmented weight credited to this individual's interest therefore enables her to pass Raz's general test for claim-right holding and, by extension, to qualify for a Razian claim-right.

Before we pass to the second answer, we should notice explicitly that even the loose interpretation does nothing to vindicate the proposition that individuals can hold claim-rights to public goods that do *not* satisfy Raz's special test. Moreover, our guiding example of a pure public good, herd immunity against measles, falls into this category. In this case, the individual's interest (in not contracting measles) and the third-party interests (everyone else's interest in not contracting measles) are each served by some common cause (herd immunity against measles), rather than the third-party interests being served *by* serving the individual's interest. For example, living in strict isolation would serve the individual's interest without thereby serving the third-party interests. However we interpret Raz, then, no individual citizen has a Razian claim-right to the existence of herd immunity against measles.

According to what I shall call the 'strict' interpretation, a public good's satisfying Raz's special test is *not* enough to qualify any individual for a Razian claim-right to that good. Let me elaborate this answer in relation to his example of Juliet the architect, taking as fixed points that the beauty of Oxford is a public good and that every inhabitant's interest in protecting it satisfies Raz's special test. For convenience and good measure, let us also stipulate that the weight of these third-party interests is sufficient to justify the state's duty to provide that public good.

Under these assumptions, the strict interpretation will accept the loose interpretation's claim that *some interest* of Juliet's will be credited, on Raz's accounting, with a weight sufficient to justify the state's duty to provide the public good of the beauty of Oxford. However, it does not follow that Juliet has a Razian claim-right *to that public good* (ie, a claim-right that correlates with *that* duty of the state's). Instead, more attention has to be paid to the content of the relevant interests.

Of course, like any of its inhabitants, Juliet herself also has an interest in the beauty of Oxford.[17] But that is not the interest of hers to which Raz applies his special test. It is not the interest of Juliet's, in other words, that the third-party

[16] More precisely, the augmented weight of the individual's interest will only be sufficient to justify the state's duty when the previous mismatch with the weight of that duty has been erased. While satisfying Raz's special test guarantees that the relevant third-party interests will *augment* the credited weight of the individual's interest, it does not itself guarantee that this will fully erase the mismatch. However, as long as the public good in question has a positive benefit–cost ratio (ie, it is 'worth' providing, narrowly speaking, in the first place), satisfying Raz's special test will fully erase the mismatch.

[17] This illustrates the second harmony in the 'dual harmony' that Raz claims often characterises the relation between a public good and individual interest (1994: 53). My statement of his special test only emphasised the first of these harmonies (third-party interests are served by serving the individual's interest), and to that extent may have simplified it.

interests in the beauty of Oxford are served by serving. Hence, according to the strict interpretation the satisfaction of Raz's special test here does nothing to augment the weight of Juliet's interest *in the beauty of Oxford*, which thus remains insufficient to justify the state's duty to provide that public good. Juliet therefore has no Razian claim-right to the beauty of Oxford, since her individual interest in that public good still fails Raz's general test.

On a plain reading, the interest of Juliet's that features in Raz's special test is rather her interest in not being unjustly dismissed.[18] The third-party interests in the beauty of Oxford are served by protecting Juliet's *job security* (and hence her preservation scheme, which is what secures the beauty of Oxford) from the scheming of property speculators. Since it is her interest in not being unjustly dismissed whose weight has thereby been augmented, the strict interpretation will accept both that Juliet has a Razian claim-right not to be unjustly dismissed *and* that this claim-right of hers (now) has a weight equivalent to the weight of the state's duty to provide the public good of the beauty of Oxford. Still, this equivalence in weight does not transform her claim-right against unjust dismissal into a claim-right to that public good. 'Sufficiency to justify' a specific duty—and thus, Raz's general test—requires that an individual's interest have both the right weight *and* the right content. Raz's special test clearly aims to change the (credited) weight of Juliet's interest in not being unjustly dismissed, but it wisely harbours no ambition to change the content of that interest.

More generally, the very structure of Raz's special test itself seems to require that the content of the third-party interests *differs* from the content of the individual's interest that they are 'served by serving'. All the examples Raz (1994) actually gives certainly fit that bill (and not merely the case of Juliet).[19] If that is right, then whenever third-party interests in a public good satisfy his special test, the individual interest whose weight gets augmented will never be an interest in that same public good. Consequently, a public good's satisfying Raz's special test never qualifies an individual for a Razian claim-right to that public good, whatever effect it may have on the weight of other claim-rights held by that individual.

On reflection, it seems to me that the strict interpretation is the better interpretation of Raz. To a considerable extent, the reasons for this are philosophical. The additional strictures observed by the strict interpretation, and on the basis of which it objects to the loose interpretation, seem to be drawn correctly. Beyond this, there are also purely interpretative reasons to favour the strict interpretation. To begin with, nowhere in the text does Raz (1994) himself conclude that (or even

[18] Or, as Raz also puts it, 'her interest in her contract of employment' (1994: 53).

[19] Further support for this interpretation comes precisely from Raz's celebration of *dual* harmonies (*cf* n 17 above). The second of these harmonies is a logically trivial reflection of the fact that, with any public good and given that she is also a member of the community, one of the individual's interests will always be identical to the third-party interests in question. But that also means that the individual's *other* interest (her contribution to the first harmony) must differ from the third-party interests; and that is the interest described in the text.

raise the question whether) individuals can have a claim-right to a public good. By contrast, as we have seen, Raz (1986) does explicitly conclude that individuals cannot have such claim-rights. Moreover, this contrast holds despite various other continuities between the two discussions, including some of the examples of public goods (such as the beauty of a city). Finally, Raz's later text also explicitly contains an alternative and perfectly adequate motivation for introducing the machinery of his special test (and for affirming the milder conclusions licensed by the strict interpretation). Namely, Raz wishes to demonstrate the fault in the widespread tendency of treating rights as inherently in conflict with the common good (and thereby, to reject that tendency): 'A major theme of this essay is that the image of right as a bulwark of the rightholder's interest against the claims of others distorts the nature of the concept and its role in our thought' (1994: 58).

Let us therefore accept the strict interpretation of Raz. In that case, no individual can hold a Razian claim-right to any public good and it makes no difference to this conclusion whether a public good satisfies Raz's special test or not.

V. The Third-Party Beneficiary Objection

As Raz recognises, it is in the nature of public goods to confer third-party benefits. However, Raz's general test for right-holding does not afford any role to third-party interests nor, under the strict interpretation, are third-party interests allowed to contribute to the satisfaction of his test. By contrast, the ordinary Interest theory does not distinguish third-party interests from other interests in the first place. All interests are on a par. As a result, this version of the Interest theory is infamously liberal in awarding claim-rights to third-party beneficiaries.

On the one hand, this means that, under the ordinary Interest theory, there is no particular impediment to an individual's holding a claim-right to a pure public good. On the other hand, as is well known, it also means that the ordinary Interest theory is vulnerable to a compelling objection, first raised by HLA Hart (1955). At first glance, then, it is not clear whether this entailment of the theory should be taken as a *modus ponens* or a *modus tollens*. To settle this question, let us begin by reviewing Hart's objection and the existing state of the debate about it.

In simple form, the third-party beneficiary problem runs as follows.[20] Suppose Xavier promises his brother to pay their sister £100. Ordinarily, we would say that Xavier's brother now has a claim-right against him or that Xavier now owes a duty to his brother to pay their sister £100. Hart questions whether the Interest theory yields this verdict. However that may be, the Interest theory certainly yields the verdict that Xavier's duty to pay his sister is (also) owed to his sister, and so that Xavier's sister (also) has a claim-right against him, since she benefits from

[20] The remainder of this section excerpts from Sreenivasan (2005: section 3).

the £100. Hart also maintains that this verdict is incorrect.[21] However that may be, it would certainly be the wrong verdict if Xavier's duty to pay his sister were also owed *to his sister's child*, on whom—let us say—she will spend the £100, so that Xavier's niece had a claim-right against him. But the Interest theory clearly appears to yield that verdict as well.

More generally, the objection is that, intuitively, there is a limit to the number of claim-rights that arise under a third-party promise or contract. It is therefore a condition of adequacy on the Interest theory that it suitably limits the number of people it classifies as correlative claim-holders (*cf* Kramer 1998: 80–81). For the most part, this condition of adequacy has not been met. However, Kramer's (1998) defence of the Interest theory is worth examining in detail in this connection, since it has a promising claim to be an exception to this indictment.

Kramer (1998) offers somewhat different sufficient conditions for holding a claim-right from other versions of the ordinary Interest theory. His preferred sufficient conditions are adapted from Bentham's test for the assignment of rights under a law, as glossed by Hart (1982: 177–79). According to Hart, Bentham's test identifies holders of a claim-right correlative to a given duty by asking what findings are *necessary* to establish a breach of that duty by the duty-bearer. In particular, it asks whether detriment to the candidate right-holder is necessary to establish a breach. Kramer adapts the test by substituting 'sufficient' for 'necessary' (1998: 81–82).

Thus, on Kramer's test if detriment to A is *sufficient* to establish a breach by the duty-bearer, then A holds a correlative claim-right and otherwise not (1998: 81). In terms of our example, we are to ask what findings are sufficient to establish that Xavier has breached his duty to pay his sister £100. Since proof that his sister suffered the detriment of 'not having been paid £100 by Xavier' suffices to establish that he breached this duty, it follows on Kramer's test that she holds a claim-right correlative to Xavier's duty. By contrast, proof that her child suffered the detriment of 'not having been given a £100 present' does not suffice to establish a breach of Xavier's duty, since Xavier may have paid his sister £100, only for her to have changed her mind about spending it on her child. Hence, the child does *not* hold a correlative claim-right. So Kramer's test certainly rules some beneficiaries out as claim-right holders; and may even seem to draw the line in the right place.

Appearances, however, can be deceiving. To begin with, we should ask how, on Kramer's test, Xavier's brother (the promisee) qualifies as a claim-right holder. Presumably, it is because of his interest in having his wishes fulfilled (*cf* Kramer 1998: 79–80). The idea is that proof of the detriment to Xavier's brother of not having their sister get her £100 will suffice to establish a breach of Xavier's duty. But it is not clear that this will do the trick. Imagine that Xavier's grandmother has an interest in having her grandchildren behave themselves, receive benefits, and so

[21] Kramer (1998: 66–68) protests that it begs the question for a Will theorist to deny that Xavier's sister has a claim-right against him (on the ground that she lacks a power to waive his duty).

on. Will proof of the detriment to her—of not having her granddaughter get her £100—suffice to establish a breach of Xavier's duty? If so, his grandmother will also hold a correlative claim-right.

An adequate test of claim-right holding should draw the line between Xavier's grandmother and his brother. Yet it is not clear how Kramer's test can exclude the former without also excluding the latter. I can make out three options, none of them satisfactory. First, Xavier's grandmother may be excluded because she is not a party to the promise. But this fails to distinguish her from Xavier's sister, who is said to hold a correlative claim-right. Second, his grandmother may be excluded because her interest is parasitic—it smuggles in reference to Xavier's sister's detriment. But this fails to distinguish Xavier's grandmother from his brother, who would otherwise fail to hold a correlative claim-right.[22] Third, his grandmother may be excluded because her interest is not important enough. But the one clear way of interpreting this option is not available to Kramer. One might require the detriment to be so important that proof of it is necessary to establish a breach of the relevant duty. However, this would be to adopt precisely the structure of Hart's gloss on Bentham's test, which Kramer explicitly rejects.

Furthermore, if we examine the notion of what 'suffices to establish' a breach a little more closely, a different sort of trouble soon emerges. Consider the special case where Xavier's brother waives Xavier's duty to pay their sister. In this case, their sister's detriment is not 'sufficient to establish' a breach of Xavier's duty. Having once seen this, we should then recognise that her detriment does not *suffice* even when Xavier's brother does not waive Xavier's duty, since he might have done. In fact, even Xavier's brother's parasitic detriment does not really suffice to establish Xavier's breach, since detriment on the brother's part does not, strictly speaking, entail that he did not waive Xavier's duty. Kramer's test therefore fails to vest the one uncontroversial claim-right holder—the promisee—with a claim-right against Xavier.[23]

VI. Difficulties with Kramer's Revised Defence of the Ordinary Interest Theory

Kramer (2007) generously credits my previous discussion of his 1998 solution to the third-party beneficiary objection with having revealed a need to clarify the terms of that solution. In response to each of my two criticisms, Kramer introduces some

[22] Changes in the description of Xavier's brother's interest can be mirrored by changes in their grandmother's interest. In principle, the description of his interest should not explicitly refer to the breach or fulfilment of Xavier's promise, since this would make Kramer's test vacuous (see n 23 below). For that matter, however, Xavier's grandmother may also have an interest in promises to her grandchildren being kept.

[23] Kramer (1998) does sometimes slip in the qualification 'unexcused detriment' (eg, at 82–83), which might be exploited to cover cases where the duty is waived. But this makes his test vacuous. Compare the equivalent notion of a 'detriment in breach,' which explicitly drains the test of content.

refinements to his theory. He then contends that, so refined, his Interest theory is proof against the challenge raised by Hart's objection. Although I certainly appreciate his candour, and also find it very refreshing, I am afraid that I do not agree in either case. To see why not, let us consider each of Kramer's replies separately.

The principal issue raised by my first criticism of his 1998 solution is how to qualify the promisee (Xavier's brother) as a claim-right holder without also qualifying some intuitively irrelevant party (for concreteness, Xavier's grandmother). Or, moving the shoe to the front foot, the issue is how to *disqualify* his grandmother without also disqualifying his brother, who is the one clearly uncontroversial claim-right holder in the entire affair. As my discussion in section V tried to make clear, replies to this challenge are subject to certain constraints. For present purposes, two specific constraints are salient.[24] On the one hand, the grandmother's disqualification cannot rest on the fact that her interest in the matter is *parasitic* (ie, it refers to Xavier's sister's detriment, where his sister is the direct beneficiary of the promise). On the other hand, neither can the grandmother's disqualification rest on the fact that she is not a party to the promise. We can review the rationales for these constraints in the course of evaluating Kramer's refinements. For as we shall see, it would appear that, in the process of trying to steer between them, Kramer's 2007 defence of his Interest theory actually runs afoul of both constraints.

As Kramer brings out, my 2005 description of the candidates for the relevant interests here (the brother's and grandmother's, respectively) presented some unnecessary obstacles to understanding.[25] However, my main point remains perfectly valid: in principle, the grandmother's situation parallels the brother's, so that the distinction between them cannot lie in the detailed contents of their interests. Whatever detail may seem to do the trick for the brother can always be credited to the grandmother as well, whereupon the apparent distinction would disappear (again). What makes their situations parallel is the fact that, for these purposes, the glaringly obvious difference between them—the brother is the promisee, whereas the grandmother is not—is 'out of bounds'. Given that Kramer wants to credit Xavier's sister (the eponymous third party in Hart's original scenario) with a claim-right correlative to Xavier's duty, he cannot make 'being party to the promise' a necessary condition of holding a claim-right correlative to the promissory obligation, since Xavier's sister is not a party to the promise (either).[26]

We can illustrate these strictures in relation to Kramer's refined suggestion for how to understand the brother's relevant interest. He writes:

> Greater precision is needed. The interest of the brother is in the preservation of the dignity of his status as a moral agent. Given that a promise has been made to him, the

[24] We can leave aside a third constraint that Xavier's grandmother's disqualification cannot appeal to the inadequate significance of her interest.

[25] In reprising this material in section V, I profited from the opportunity to correct these mistakes.

[26] I shall consider below the possibility that being party to the promise may function instead as part of a sufficient condition for holding such a claim-right.

> realization of that interest will be advanced through the fulfilment of the promise (except in special circumstances that are not relevant here). Conversely, that interest will have been set back if the promise is not kept (2007: 302).

By contrast, Kramer maintains, the grandmother's 'standing as a moral agent, unlike the brother's standing as a moral agent, is not at stake in X[avier]'s keeping or breaking of the promise' (2007: 302). Accordingly, this represents an attempt, anyhow, to do what I just said cannot be done, namely, to distinguish the brother from the grandmother by reference to the content of their interests. Of course, it is intuitively very plausible that the grandmother's 'standing as a moral agent' is not at stake in Xavier's keeping or breaking of the promise. But why is that? Alternatively, why *is* the brother's parallel standing at stake, if it is (as is, at least, more plausible)? All that Kramer says to distinguish the cases is 'Given that a promise has been made *to him*' (2007: 302; my italics). Yet, as I have already said, this cannot be taken to make being a party to the promise a necessary condition of holding a correlative claim-right.

But perhaps being the promisee can belong to a sufficient condition for right-holding, so that it can serve to explain the brother's claim-right without implying anything about his grandmother (or his sister)? For the moment, the important point to note is that something else still needs to be added to yield a legitimate sufficient condition. On the intuitive way of understanding it, the brother's 'standing as a moral agent' is at stake here because promisees are right-holders. However, Kramer is obviously not entitled to that assumption. Nor, of course, can the circumstances that either advance the brother's relevant interest or set that interest back, as the case may be, be legitimately described as circumstances in which *X's promise has been* 'fulfilled' or 'not been kept'.[27] Thus, it remains an open question why exactly Xavier's brother qualifies as a claim-right holder correlative to Xavier's duty.

The second, perhaps more substantive refinement Kramer introduces (in response to this first criticism) is to affirm explicitly that, in order to be eligible to bear on the question of whether somebody holds a claim-right, the person's interest 'cannot be wholly vicarious'. In other words, Kramer excludes interests that 'reside wholly in the furtherance of somebody else's interest' from the scope of his test for right-holding (2007: 303). Later he wonders rhetorically whether I might find this exclusion arbitrary (only to reject the suggestion). On the contrary, my concern is rather that his new stipulation is too similar to my constraint that Xavier's grandmother cannot be disqualified on the ground that her interest is 'parasitic'. Too similar, that is, to serve Kramer's purpose of fending off my objection. Or so it can at first appear.

To begin with, it is not clear to me how Kramer's new stipulation avoids the (unintended) effect of disqualifying Xavier's brother. That was my rationale

[27] Evidently, circumstances that 'entail' that Xavier's promise has not been kept will also 'suffice to establish' that Xavier has breached his promissory obligation. But that is only because they *say* that Xavier has breached it. Compare nn 22 and 23 above.

for imposing the constraint in the first place (that this effect must be avoided). Kramer does not consider the application of his stipulation to the brother's case because (I presume) he thinks the brother's status is already in the clear, thanks to the refined description he has provided. As we have seen, however, Kramer's refined description of the brother's interest is at best incomplete. What brings my concern that excluding parasitic interests will disqualify Xavier's brother into play is the likelihood that completing the description of the brother's interest will require the operative description of the circumstances affecting that interest either to include or entail the fact that Xavier's sister has not been paid £100, ie, the fact of *her* detriment.

Still, in relation to Kramer's second refinement, a different problem is perhaps more pressing. For it is not clear that his refinement even succeeds in disqualifying Xavier's grandmother. A lot depends on precisely how we understand which interests count as 'wholly vicarious'. Summarising his discussion of this point, Kramer writes as follows: 'An interest that underlies R's status as a right-holder—which might be an altruistically oriented interest, of course—has to be R's own interest rather than someone else's interest' (2007: 304). On a natural interpretation of this formulation of the underlying idea, Kramer's stipulation fails to exclude Xavier's grandmother as a claim-right holder because the grandmother's interest in Xavier's sister's welfare (ie, her granddaughter's welfare) counts as the grandmother's *own interest*. As I am imagining things, this grandmother has 'taken an interest' in her granddaughter's welfare,[28] which not all grandmothers need have done. Since the grandmother's interest refers to someone else's welfare, it counts as an altruistic interest. But, as Kramer is very reasonably at pains to emphasise, 'an altruistic stake in the matter is a personal stake of the sort required' (2007: 303). That is to say, the grandmother's altruistic interest remains *her own* interest (who else's interest could it be?) Hence, it is not a 'wholly vicarious' interest after all and Kramer's stipulation does not actually help his cause.

Against this natural interpretation, there is a curious wrinkle in the passage in which Kramer first clarifies that his exclusion of 'wholly vicarious' interests does not have the (undesirable) effect of requiring eligible interests to be 'selfish in any way' (2007: 303). Kramer's clarification emerges in the specific context of a modified scenario in which Xavier has made *two* promises to his brother. Xavier's second promise is 'to inform their grandmother that the payment has been made' (2007: 303). It therefore *names* their grandmother in the way that Xavier's first promise names their sister. Moreover, Kramer's acceptance that the grandmother's altruistic interest gives her the required 'personal stake' (to qualify as a claim-right holder), which I quoted previously with approval, is restricted to the duty in which

[28] In a complete account, something would have to be said about what exactly counts as 'taking an interest' in someone else's welfare. Not just anything goes. But whatever the correct account, there will be a version of the grandmother's story according to which she satisfies it. So, while Kramer may be right that the bare relation of 'grandmother' is not adequate to the task, this need not trouble the objection.

she is named.[29] He explicitly denies, that is, that the grandmother's (altruistic) interest in relation to Xavier's *original* duty (to pay his sister £100) gives the grandmother the same personal stake: 'she does not have any non-vicarious interest in the fulfilment of [Xavier's original duty]' (2007: 303).

On a competing interpretation, then, some qualifying condition is attached to altruistic interests; and altruistic interests that fail it are still classified as 'wholly vicarious'. Thus, if the grandmother's altruistic interest in her granddaughter's receiving £100 fails that qualifying condition in relation to Xavier's original duty, Kramer's second refinement really does exclude the grandmother from holding a claim-right correlative to that duty. Unfortunately, however, this competing interpretation introduces three new difficulties.

The first difficulty is simply to say what the qualifying condition is. While I hesitate to conjecture how it should be formulated, one candidate on the surface of Kramer's text is 'being named in the duty'. (An alternative, related to our previous discussion, is the disjoined condition 'being a party to the promise or named in it'.) The second difficulty is to establish the *relevance* of the favoured qualifying condition, whatever it is, to the consequent partition of altruistic interests into those that are and those that are not the person in question's '*own* interests'. Being named in the duty, for example, is clearly irrelevant to this partition, which presents an impediment to any fully satisfactory interpretation of Kramer's passage as it stands. Similarly, the relevance of being the promisee remains obscure, given that we cannot appeal to the explanandum that promisees are right-holders. Without an adequate answer to this difficulty, the partition of altruistic interests (which is now doing the heavy lifting in excluding the grandmother) really will wind up as an arbitrary stipulation.

Finally, the third difficulty is to show that the favoured qualifying condition is also consistent with the Interest theory—in particular, with Kramer's test for the assignment of claim-rights. On the face of it, for example, the operation of any such qualifying condition prevents detriment to an (eligible) altruistic interest from being 'sufficient to establish' a breach of any duty. I shall simply leave these difficulties as open questions about Kramer's refinements.

So far we have been discussing the refinements Kramer introduces in response to my first criticism of his 1998 solution. My second criticism concerns the significance of the possibility that promissory obligations may be waived by the promisee. Although this possibility plainly has some significance—to begin with, it exists—it is not clear, as a general matter, that the ordinary Interest theory can accommodate its significance. More recently, for example, Kramer (2013: 264) has explicitly built into the formulation of his Interest theory the denial that having the power to waive a specified duty is either necessary or sufficient for holding the correlative claim-right. But the question of whether Interest theorists wish to accord the power to waive a duty any official role in their theory is actually

[29] Why should interests be individuated in relation to duties?

separate, at least in the first instance, from the question of whether the fact that a promissory obligation can be waived is consistent with Kramer's 1998 test for right-holding—consistent with his test, that is, under the assumption that the promisee holds a correlative claim-right. My second criticism was only concerned with the latter question.

To recapitulate briefly, my second criticism was that, however we describe the promisee's interest, the detriment to it implied by the promisor's non-performance is *not* 'sufficient to establish' that the promisor has breached her duty. It is not sufficient because it must also be true that the promisee did *not waive* the promisor's duty; and this is a separate fact, not entailed by the detriment to the promisee's interest. Hence, Kramer's test fails to identify the promisee as a claim-right holder.

In response to this criticism, Kramer introduces two further refinements to his theory. His first refinement is to distinguish two classes of duty, according to whether there is a meaningful distinction between the time at which the duty is ascribed and the time at which the duty is to be fulfilled (or breached). An example of the first class of duties is the duty not to assault anyone and an example of the second class of duties is a duty (eg, a contractual duty) to deliver a load of widgets on a specified date. Unlike the second duty, the time to perform the first duty is 'always'.

Kramer's final refinement is rather complicated, involving time indices in the (re-) formulation of his test for right-holding and commitments on the truth conditions of future contingents. Fortunately, however, we do not have to investigate its details. For Kramer only invokes them to deal with the special features of the *second* class of duties, where the times for ascription and performance can be distinguished. He restricts the scope of his final refinement to this case because, so he claims, the problem raised by my second criticism only arises there: 'Sreenivasan's complaint applies solely to duties of this latter type, and we shall therefore train our scrutiny here only on such duties' (2007: 306). As we shall now see, though, Kramer is mistaken about that: the problem applies equally to the first class of duties.[30]

The nub of the problem arises because 'non-performance' of some duty to φ should, strictly speaking, be distinguished from 'breach' of the same duty, but the notion of 'detriment' to someone who is potentially a beneficiary from performance of that duty (ie, from φ-ing) is not sensitive to this distinction. A fortiori, Kramer's test for right-holding is not sensitive to it either. Relatedly, there are (at least) two rather different ways in which a duty to φ can go out of existence: it can be waived or it can expire.[31] These points are related because an agent who was duty-bound to φ, and yet omits to φ, does *not count* as having 'breached' her duty

[30] It is possible that Kramer believes that the problem is confined to his second class of duties because he also believes that the fact that the duty under discussion has not been waived can be treated as a presupposition of his test for right-holding. We shall discuss this second belief further below, where we shall see that it is also mistaken (and for more or less the same reason).

[31] If duties are partly individuated by their bearers, a third way in which a particular duty to φ can go out of existence, I suppose, is that its bearer (ie, the agent) can herself go out of existence.

to φ if the duty either expired or was waived prior to her omission. By contrast, if such an agent omits to φ, she can still be described as having 'not performed' it,[32] even if her duty to φ had gone out of existence by then. By itself, then, 'non-performance of [a duty to] φ' never entails 'breach of a duty to φ'. At the same time, 'non-performance of [a duty to] φ' always entails *detriment* to anyone who will benefit from φ-ing by the agent in question. Whence my question about how that notion of detriment can ever 'suffice to establish' breach of a duty, as Kramer's test requires.

Kramer's final refinement inserts a clause into his test that excludes 'the' scenario in which the duty has already *gone out of existence*. Naturally, if we hold fixed the truth that the agent 'remains duty-bound to φ', then her non-performance of φ will indeed entail a breach of her duty to φ. However, the Interest theory is not entitled to hold that truth fixed. Kramer motivates his new clause by reference to the need to control for the possibility that the duty in question may have *expired*. Yet, so far as mere expiry is concerned, it is overkill to exclude the scenario in which this duty has 'gone out of existence', since this excludes both expiry and waiver. Kramer's refinement therefore has the convenient additional side effect of controlling for the possibility that the duty in question has been *waived*, but without having to declare as much.[33] If I am right about all of this, we should be able to flush the troublesome possibility out into the open, shorn of the cover provided by Kramer's refinement, simply by turning our attention to the class of duties that never expire.

Consider a man, Muhammad, who has a duty not to assault a colleague, Joe.[34] Since this duty belongs to Kramer's first class of duties, his refined test for right-holding does not apply here. Rather, his 1998 test applies. Officially, there is no need to control for a scenario in which Muhammad's duty has gone out of existence, since the time for his performance is 'always', meaning that Muhammad's duty never *expires*. Kramer's position, then, is that Joe qualifies as a correlative right holder because the detriment to Joe of 'having been punched by Muhammad' suffices to establish that Muhammad has breached his duty (not to assault Joe). I shall take it that this is the correct (indeed, a mandatory) result, since Joe very plausibly has a claim-right against Muhammad not to be assaulted.

Of course, Joe also has the power to waive Muhammad's duty not to assault him. We do not have to understand this as a power to make Muhammad's duty 'expire' (ie, cease to exist forever more). It can instead be understood as the power to *suspend* Muhammad's duty for a time (ie, to make it go out of existence

[32] One might fuss here about whether 'did not perform her *duty* to φ' implies that the non-performer *had* a duty to φ at the time. But this is actually immaterial, since the person can clearly be described as having 'not *φ-ed*,' where her not φ-ing still causes the relevant *detriment* to the potential beneficiary in question. As we shall see, that is enough to generate my problem.

[33] I am not suggesting that any intentional sleight of hand was afoot.

[34] When I composed this section, and even later during the conference in Singapore, Ali was still alive. Singapore is the closest I have been to Manila. All hail to the bee.

temporarily, for some prescribed interval).[35] Accordingly, suppose that Joe waives Muhammad's duty not to assault him during a specified interval of time—'the round', as we might call it. Let the round be inaugurated by a clapping of hands and terminated by the ringing of a bell. So now if Muhammad punches Joe—pummels him, even—*during* the round, Muhammad will not have breached his duty. However, if he punches Joe after the bell, Muhammad will have breached his duty.

If Muhammad punches Joe, Joe will suffer some specific detriment; that is, some interest of Joe's will be set back (it does not matter which one). Let us call his detriment, 'being stung'. Crucially, the timing of Muhammad's punch makes *no* difference to Joe's interest. Whether Muhammad punches Joe during the round or after the bell, the detriment Joe will suffer is exactly the same. In that case, my original criticism of Kramer's Interest theory remains in full force.[36] Joe's having been stung cannot itself 'suffice to establish' that Muhammad breached his duty, even if it occurs after the bell, since if it had occurred during the round there would have been no such breach to establish. Properly to establish a breach of Muhammad's duty, one has explicitly to include the fact that Joe was stung *after the bell* (or before the clapping of hands). Alternatively, if Joe was stung after the bell, and the fact that he was stung *is* taken, without reference to its timing, as sufficient to establish a breach of Muhammad's duty, then the fact that Joe was stung during the round must similarly be taken as sufficient to establish a breach of Muhammad's duty. But this, of course, would be the wrong result. Hence, Kramer's 1998 test fails to qualify Joe as a correlative right-holder and his 2007 refinements do nothing to rectify this error.

The fundamental problem is that the truth-conditions for the attribution of claim-rights are undeniably sensitive, as the example of Muhammad and Joe illustrates, to the exercise of powers of waiver over certain duties. At a minimum, then, a theory of claim-rights has to be able to accommodate this fact. As a technical matter, one could always achieve this accommodation by inserting a further clause into Kramer's test, explicitly excluding the possibility that someone has *waived* the duty in question (for the interval in question). But this would only force the question of whether such a clause is consistent with the Interest theory (and how). I presume that it is not, though advocates of the Interest theory are free to show us that this is a mistake. Without some such clause, however, Kramer's test gives the wrong results. For example, it fails to qualify Joe as holding a claim-right correlative to Muhammad's duty not to assault anyone. I therefore reaffirm my original conclusion that Hart's third-party beneficiary objection is fatal to the ordinary Interest theory.

[35] Nor do we have to assume that Joe's having this power is tied to his holding the correlative claim-right. We merely need to suppose that he (justifiably) *has* the power described in the text. We can then focus, in the first instance, on whether Kramer's 1998 test for right-holding is consistent with this part of the ordinary facts on the ground.

[36] I continue to assume, very plausibly, that Joe has a claim-right not to be assaulted by Muhammad (outside the round, in any case).

With these pieces in place, we can now return to the question of whether the fact that Joe (say) has *not* waived Muhammad's duty not to assault him could legitimately be treated as a presupposition of Kramer's test, as Kramer is perhaps tempted to treat it (2007: 305). The idea, I take it, is that if Joe has waived Muhammad's duty (for the round, anyhow), there is no risk of discovering that Kramer's test gives the wrong significance to Joe's detriment (of having been stung during the round), since the test has a presupposition that is not satisfied and hence simply does not apply to Joe's detriment.

This suggestion raises two further questions that I cannot fully settle here. On the one hand, there is a question about whether these two different means of accommodating the significance of waivers within the ordinary Interest theory are actually equivalent. That is to ask, is an unarticulated presuppositional structure equivalent to an explicit reference to the consequences (under Kramer's test) of the exercise of powers of waiver over the duty in question? Insofar as they are not equivalent, the presuppositional interpretation leaves Kramer's test vulnerable to counter-examples in the mould of Muhammad and Joe. So let us assume they are equivalent.

On the other hand, there is also the very basic question of whether the presuppositional interpretation of Kramer's test is legitimate as a defence of the Interest theory. This reprises the question I already asked about explicit references to waivers. Since we are assuming they are equivalent in effect, it would seem that the presuppositional interpretation is legitimate if and only if explicit reference to waivers is legitimate. Here it may help to spell out that my concern is about whether incorporating references to waivers over duties into Kramer's test (either explicitly or implicitly) turns his Interest theory into a version of the Hybrid theory (not my version, but some version). It is clearly a significant step in the direction of a Hybrid theory. But a lot depends on how the line between Interest theories and Hybrid theories should be drawn. I shall leave that as a question for defenders of the Interest theory.[37]

VII. Conclusion

We began with the question of whether individuals can hold a claim-right to any pure public good. In this context, the ordinary Interest theory has a special place among theories of rights, since it is the only major theory that returns an unqualified affirmative answer. As we have seen, though, it is precisely the feature of that

[37] However, with respect to our specific organising interest in individual claim-rights to pure public goods, it should be noted that taking even this first step towards a Hybrid theory already imperils the conclusion that the resultant theory—even if it remains an 'Interest' theory—clearly awards individuals with claim-rights to public goods.

theory that licenses its affirmative answer—namely, its liberal assignment of claim-rights to third-party beneficiaries—that also turns out to be its Achilles heel. Following Hart, we should thus reject the ordinary Interest theory of rights. The remaining major theories of rights *all deny* that an individual can hold a claim-right to a pure public good. In particular, to reprise our central illustration, they all deny that an individual can hold a claim-right correlative to her state's duty to provide herd immunity against measles (or any other contagious disease). Let me end by suggesting that we accept their common negative verdict, and thereby take the intuitive dogma on this question to have been vindicated.[38]

References

Anomaly, J (2011) 'Public Health and Public Goods' 4 *Public Health Ethics* 251.

Hart, HLA (1955) 'Are There Any Natural Rights?' 64 *Philosophical Review* 175.

—— (1982) 'Legal Rights' in HLA Hart, *Essays on Bentham: Jurisprudence and Political Theory* (Oxford: Oxford University Press).

Kramer, MH (1998) 'Rights Without Trimmings' in MH Kramer, NE Simmonds and H Steiner, *A Debate Over Rights: Philosophical Enquiries* (Oxford: Clarendon Press).

—— (2013) 'Some Doubts About Alternatives to the Interest Theory of Rights' 123 *Ethics* 245.

Kramer, MH and Steiner, H (2007) 'Theories of Rights: Is There a Third Way?' 27 *Oxford Journal of Legal Studies* 281.

Malone, K and Hinman, A (2003) 'Vaccination Mandates: The Public Health Imperative and Individual Rights' in R Goodman et al (eds), *Law in Public Health Practice* (New York: Oxford University Press).

Orenstein, W and Seib, K (2014) 'Mounting a Good Offense Against Measles' 371 *New England Journal of Medicine* 1661.

Raz, J (1986) *The Morality of Freedom* (Oxford: Clarendon Press).

—— (1994) 'Rights and Individual Well-Being' in J Raz, *Ethics in the Public Domain: Essays in the Morality of Law and Politics* (Oxford: Clarendon Press).

Réaume, D (1988) 'Individuals, Groups, and Rights to Public Goods' 38 *University of Toronto Law Journal* 1.

[38] This essay was presented at a conference on Contemporary Debates Over Legal Rights at the National University of Singapore's Faculty of Law. As will be evident, it draws on various bits of discussion in previous papers of mine. I am very grateful to Mark McBride for his invitation to present at the conference and for the consequent opportunity to pull these disparate pieces together into a more comprehensive treatment. I also thank the other participants in the conference for a very helpful discussion. I am especially grateful to Matthew Kramer and Mark McBride for their comments.

Sreenivasan, G (2005) 'A Hybrid Theory of Claim-Rights' 25 *Oxford Journal of Legal Studies* 257.
—— (2012) 'A Human Right to Health? Some Inconclusive Scepticism' 86 *Proceedings of the Aristotelian Society, Supplementary Volume* 239.
—— (2016) 'Health Care and Human Rights: Against the Split Duty Gambit' 37 *Theoretical Medicine and Bioethics* 343.

7

The Tracking Theory of Rights

MARK McBRIDE

I. Introduction

A. Overview

In debates over the correct theory of rights, two theories—viz the Interest Theory (IT) and Will Theory (WT)—have dominated.[1] Until recently, that is. Recently, several sophisticated attempts have been made to transcend the stark dichotomy between IT and WT by offering alternatives thereto. Most prominently, perhaps, Gopal Sreenivasan (2005; 2007; 2010), and Leif Wenar (2005; 2008; 2013), have offered fascinating theories of rights purporting to be viable alternatives to both IT and WT. Unsurprisingly, theorists of rights invested in defending IT against WT (Kramer (and Steiner) 2007; Kramer 2013; and in this volume), and WT against IT ((Kramer and) Steiner 2007), have reacted by, either denying that the new theories are genuine alternatives to IT/WT, or by, accepting that the new theories are genuine alternatives, and attempting to cast doubt on their attractiveness. My focus in this essay is on a latter such case (with reaction to Wenar's theory being a former such case). In response to Sreenivasan's Hybrid Theory (HT) of rights, Matthew Kramer (an IT) (2007; 2013) and Hillel Steiner (a WT) (2007) have accepted that Sreenivasan's HT of rights offers a genuine alternative to both IT and WT, but gone on, by means of a putative (generalisable) counterexample, to deny HT's attractiveness as a theory of rights. My claim will be that the counterexample in question—the leading counterexample to HT thus far—is of the wrong shape. I'll show this by bringing to the fore a feature of Sreenivasan's HT which Sreenivasan himself has, thus far, not fully developed.

[1] In what follows, I use 'IT' and 'WT' to refer, at different junctures, to both the theories, and the theorists espousing the theories. The context makes clear which is germane.

The conclusion will be that Sreenivasan's HT is undented by the counterexample in question, and thus—albeit, in modified form (more on which, presently)—remains standing as a promising new alternative (to both IT and WT) theory of rights.

This result is particularly important, given the independent merits of Sreenivasan's HT. Space prevents detailed exposition of HT. But, its treatment of criminal law, for example, is particularly nuanced—more so than either IT or WT (Sreenivasan 2005: 268–69; 2010: 487–88). In effect, supposing powers to demand/waive criminal law duties are held, not by citizens, but rather by the public prosecution service, it allows whether such citizens have corresponding rights or not to depend on the *justificatory reasons* for giving such citizens no measure of control over such duties, and vesting such control, instead, in the public prosecution service. In a nutshell, if the operative reasons are trained on the interests of the citizen, that citizen will have a right; if not, that citizen will not have a right. Hence the nuance: by contrast, IT will categorically ascribe a right to this citizen (on account of the duty's protection of the citizen's interests); and WT will categorically deny a right to this citizen (on account of the citizen's lack of control over the duty). And we'll return, presently, to HT's—on my understanding thereof—distinctive way of cashing out the notion of *justification* operative therein.

B. Genealogy

This last sentence is particularly important, and warrants a brief digression on the genealogy of this essay. It began as an effort to defend *Sreenivasan's* HT—indeed, its original title was 'The Hybrid Theory [ie, Sreenivasan's HT] of Rights is an Efficient Alternative'. During communication with Sreenivasan—before, during and after the conference in Singapore from which this volume has emerged—it has become clear to me that my precise means of responding to the counterexample to HT, but also, and much more importantly, the positive theory which emerges from my grappling with the counterexample, are not Sreenivasan's. And the key to discerning this is the different means by which Sreenivasan and I attempt to accommodate and explain the *justificatory status* of being a right-holder. In sum, and contrary to my initial intentions, I have constructed a new theory of rights—a new alternative to IT/WT. The new theory did not arise, one might say, by design. The theory in question is palpably a hybrid theory, and evidently owes much to Sreenivasan's HT; but it is *my* HT. For reasons to become clear shortly it is the *Tracking Theory* of rights. Nonetheless, in what follows I shall preserve my initial aim of responding to the counterexample on behalf of Sreenivasan's HT, and note divergences between it and the Tracking Theory (TT) as they emerge.

II. Sreenivasan's HT, and Why it is a Genuine Alternative to Both IT and WT

A. Formulation of HT

Here is Sreenivasan's (2005: 271; 2010: 488) last-pass formulation of his HT, called the *Complex Hybrid*:

> (CH) Suppose X is duty-bound to ϕ. Y has a claim-right against X that X ϕ just in case: Y's measure (and, if Y has a surrogate Z, Z's measure) of control over a duty of X's to ϕ matches (by design) the measure of control that advances Y's interests on balance.

Now we can best bring out the nature of this proposal, and its difference from IT and WT, by briefly considering some cases, and how the results it delivers differ from both IT and WT.[2]

B. HT's Extension vis-à-vis WT

Essentially, HT is *more* inclusive than WT in the following way. As is well known, WT, in its most general formulation, makes the holding of a power to demand/waive enforcement of the duty in question necessary and sufficient for the holding of a right.[3] As is equally well known, such a thesis (on account of its necessity precept) precludes WT from ascribing rights in the case of duties which are unwaivable, and also in the case of incompetent adults and children. In the foregoing cases, such powers are not in play, thus WT, counterintuitively, cannot ascribe rights. By contrast, HT can ascribe rights in such cases: in the case of unwaivable duties, a right is in play provided the candidate right-holder's lack of a power of waiver matches (by design)[4] his interests on balance. And, plausibly, in many such cases—for example, unwaivable duties not to torture or enslave another—this is the case. For HT, then, I (and you) have a right not to be tortured or enslaved: my interests are, arguably, advanced on balance by lacking a power

[2] There are previous disjunctive formulations Sreenivasan offers of his HT (2005: 267–70), which bring out even more clearly HT's difference from IT and WT; however as those formulations are not extensionally equivalent to CH, and as CH is Sreenivasan's last-pass formulation of HT, best to focus on CH.

[3] Sreenivasan talks of 'claim-right', on the supposition that, for WT, the holding of a claim-right stands and falls with the holding of such a power. I will simply talk of a 'right', as this, more ecumenically, doesn't require making the foregoing assumption. Indeed, there is a general point here (from which I prescind): Sreenivasan elaborates his theory in terms of 'claim-rights' specifically, and not 'rights' more generally.

[4] Complexities involving the 'matching' and, particularly, 'design' conditions will be introduced later. For now, I leave these notions intuitive.

(having a disability) to waive such duties. Likewise, *mutatis mutandis*, in the case of incompetent adults and children.[5]

C. HT's Extension vis-à-vis IT

By contrast, HT is *less* inclusive than IT—on which, as is well known, at a very general level, necessary for the holding of a right is that it furthers the right-holder's interests—in the following way. As is again well known, IT has been argued to face the so-called 'third-party beneficiary' objection (Sreenivasan 2010: 485–86; and in this volume). This objection is a pressing instance of a more general challenge for IT—the challenge of principledly delimiting the set of interest-holders who get to become right-holders. We'll return to this more general 'delimitation challenge' presently, but now let's focus on this specific instance of the challenge. We're asked to assume that 'B promises A to do something which explicitly favours C and implicitly favours D (whom C will favour, as it happens, if B performs)' (Sreenivasan 2005: 268). And we assume, as is ordinarily the case, that only A has a power to demand/waive enforcement of the promise. In brief, the most developed version of IT *explicitly* 'answering' this objection (Kramer 2010), involves asking 'what facts [concerning a person's detriment] are minimally sufficient to constitute a breach of the contract or norm'.[6] By the lights of this test, according to IT, A and C, but not D, are ascribed rights under this contract or norm. By contrast, HT assigns a right only to A under this contract or norm. A's (assumed) power to demand/waive enforcement of the terms of the promise, matches (by design) his interest in seeing a promise made to him fulfilled. By contrast, C's and D's (assumed) lack of such a power does not match (by design) their interests on balance. On the contrary, each of C and D has a strong interest in seeing the promise in question being fulfilled. Thus, their measure of control—viz none—does not match (by design) their interests on balance. Now Sreenivasan (2005: 262–64; and in this volume) offers arguments designed to show that (Kramer's) IT cannot restrict the candidate right-holders under this contract or norm to just

[5] In such cases, issues involving *surrogacy* may well arise. Surrogacy issues are not relevant in what follows. Finally, see Steiner (2013) for a fascinating argument that (absolutely and unconditionally) *inalienable* rights are not possible.

[6] I don't develop this (arguably necessary and sufficient) test for right-holding ('Bentham's test'), and leave the contained notion of minimal sufficiency intuitive; I simply put the test, and the notion, into operation. For more on the foregoing, though, see Kramer (2010). Interestingly, Sreenivasan thinks (2005: 265; 2010: 486, fn 56) Raz's (1986) IT answers this objection with the same result as (or at least similarly to) HT. Thus, HT isn't *clearly* less inclusive than Raz's IT. Sreenivasan (2005: 265–67), however, thinks Raz's IT suffers from the independent defect of *instrumentalising* rights (a defect from which HT doesn't, for Sreenivasan, suffer). Finally, see May (2012), whose focus is on the moral realm, for an interesting argument that both Raz's IT *and HT* suffer from the foregoing defect; and, moreover, that *each* theory can be reformulated to *avoid* this defect. May thus concludes that the instrumentalisation objection cannot separate the two theories.

A and C. We don't need to adjudicate on those arguments here. Nor, indeed, do we need to adjudicate on whether denying C a right (as HT does, in this case) is more or less intuitive than conferring on C a right (as IT does, in this case). All we need to establish for now is that HT is less inclusive than (Kramer's) IT in the foregoing respect.

D. Closing Notes

As a closing note, even if, contrary to fact, HT proved to be *extensionally* equivalent to either IT or WT, HT *could* still be an alternative thereto, provided—as is the case—its *justificatory basis* for ascribing/withholding rights differed; provided, that is, it is *intensionally* inequivalent. Nonetheless, establishing HT's extensional inequivalence from IT and WT seems important, both motivationally for Sreenivasan, and in confirming HT's distinctiveness.

Finally, note that my foregoing remarks on HT's degrees of inclusiveness are *not* to say either that WT is a (proper) subset of HT, or that HT is a (proper) subset of IT. In fact, neither of these set-theoretic relations would appear to hold. As for whether WT is a (proper) subset of IT, much will depend on how we fill in the details of each of these two theories.

III. Kramer's and Steiner's Counterexample to HT, and Why it Doesn't Work

A. The Counterexample

Here, then, is the counterexample (Kramer 2013: 15)[7]—call it *K&S*:

> Suppose that Mark is legally obligated to pay Paul $20,000. A third-party, Liam, does not have any legal power to waive Mark's duty. His not having any power of that sort is very much in his interests, since Paul (who is far stronger) would be violently furious if Liam were ever to exercise such a power. Objectively, the furtherance of Liam's interests in that fashion is a sufficient justification for his not being vested with the power to waive

[7] A counterexample not materially different from this one first appeared in Kramer and Steiner (2007). As such, I am able to: (1) classify the (2013) counterexample as Kramer's *and Steiner's* (given Steiner has not withdrawn support from the (2007) counterexample); and (2) reproduce (with name switches) Sreenivasan's (2010) reply to the (2007) counterexample as a reply to the (2013) counterexample. As a final note, Kramer (and Steiner) draws a distinction between 'objective' and 'subjective' justification, but sets up the counterexample as a case in which, putatively, these two forms of justification are aligned. Given this, and given Sreenivasan (2010: 490, fn 66) 'do[es] not have anything particular to say about the special case(s) when objective and subjective justifications come apart', I omit this complication from the counterexample (but *cf* n 18 below).

> Mark's obligation. Now suppose that the judge or other legal official whose directive has placed Mark under a duty to pay Paul was focused on Liam's interests when determining whether Mark's duty should be waivable by Liam ...[8] Accordingly, Liam's wholesale lack of any control over Mark's duty is justified ... by reference to Liam's own interests. His measure of control—no control at all—is precisely the measure that advances his interests on balance.

Kramer and Steiner contend that HT leads to the conclusion that Mark's duty is owed, not only to Paul, *but also to Liam*. (And the case is generalisable.) They contend, that is, that Liam's lack of a power of waiver matches (by design) his interests on balance. And they conclude (2013: 16) that this (and other like) counterintuitive conclusion(s) fells HT:

> In a situation where Liam is not involved in any way in Mark's bearing of a duty or performance of a duty to pay $20,000 to Paul—and where Liam has deliberately been kept uninvolved by the judge who imposed the duty—no tenable theory of rights will generate the verdict that Liam has a right to Paul's being paid $20,000 by Mark. Since Sreenivasan's theory does generate that verdict, his theory is unsustainable.

B. Sreenivasan's Reply: Tersely

Sreenivasan (2010: fn 68) replies (somewhat tersely) as follows:

> [W]hile [Liam] therefore satisfies the matching condition by coincidence, he fails the design condition. Hence, on (CH) [ie HT], [Mark] does not owe his duty to [Liam]. [Liam] fails the design condition because the assignment of control over [Mark]'s duty does not track the assignment that advances [Liam]'s interests on balance. Indeed, as Kramer and Steiner tell the story, it seems there is no one whose interests on balance are tracked by that assignment.

A chief purpose of mine in the remainder of this essay is to flesh out this rather condensed reply of Sreenivasan's, and to show how Kramer's and Steiner's counterexample doesn't dent HT. In essence, the point will be that Kramer's and Steiner's case lacks the requisite *counterfactual dimension*.[9]

C. Sreenivasan's Reply: Less Tersely

In *K&S*, in the *actual case* Liam has no power of waiver, and it serves his interests on balance to have no power of waiver: the 'matching condition' is met. I take it

[8] My note: I've here omitted a lengthy passage articulating the judge's reasoning. I refer to this reasoning later.

[9] Sreenivasan's *direct* reply to K&S is indeed, as noted, somewhat brief. However, that reply should be read in conjunction with the surrounding main text (489–91), which gives more information on how to understand the 'design condition'. In particular, Sreenivasan provides suggestive remarks on the aforementioned counterfactual dimension of HT: 'the design condition requires that the matching condition remain satisfied over a range of relevant counterfactual scenarios' (490).

what Sreenivasan is asking, by way of the 'design condition', is for consideration of the possible world(s) closest to the actual in which it *does* serve Liam's interest to have a power of waiver, and for Kramer and Steiner to show that, plausibly, in that possible world Liam *is* vested with a power of waiver.[10] (The assignment of control must 'track' the interest; not vice versa.)[11] Sreenivasan says Liam fails the 'design condition' because the required 'tracking' does not obtain (and thus, for Sreenivasan, Liam doesn't have a right). There are clear echoes here, in a way to be pursued in greater detail shortly, of Robert Nozick's (1981: ch 3) 'tracking' account of knowledge.

D. Tracking

Here is my best shot at figuring out what Sreenivasan is getting at, which involves—but is not limited to[12]—asking the following counterfactual 'tracking' question:

> (T) In the closest possible world in which it is in Liam's interests on balance to have a power of waiver, is he granted a power of waiver?[13]

(It's not: in the closest possible world in which Liam is granted a power of waiver, is it in his interests on balance to have such a power?)[14] If the answer to T is 'yes' (*modulo* our assumption in footnote 12), tracking obtains (and thus, for Sreenivasan, Liam has a right); if the answer to T is 'no' (all assumptions aside), tracking doesn't obtain (and thus, for Sreenivasan, Liam doesn't have a right). In essence, Sreenivasan's HT—here, by means of T—as (on one view) with tracking accounts of (conditions on) knowledge, is a (putative) way of *extracting* justification from counterfactuals or modal relations.

[10] Invocation of possible worlds does not commit us to any overly abundant ontology (*cf* Lewis 1986): it is simply a revealing way of cashing out the notion of intuitive relevance. We can assume *pro tem*, as here, an intuitive (standard, 'Lewis–Stalnaker') approach to evaluating (context-dependent and/or vague) counterfactuals. (For complications on this, see the Appendix.) Moreover, see Lewis (1979: 472) for a proposed 'system of weights or priorities' when establishing a 'similarity relation' between possible worlds.

[11] Regarding the former, apposite 'tracking' question, it is an interesting exercise to attempt to generalise and formalise it (and, indeed, the 'matching' condition). I make a first-pass at this in the Appendix. And regarding the latter, alternative 'tracking' question, it would nonetheless be interesting to ask it, and to consider what import our answer to this question might have.

[12] I simplify somewhat here, leaving complications to the Appendix (*cf* n 11 above). In brief, 'tracking' requires more than matching in two cases. More specifically, a 'yes' answer to (the coming) T is *not* sufficient, though it *is* necessary, for tracking. As noted, I deal with what else must be present for tracking to obtain in the Appendix. I focus for now on T as it is the most urgent tracking question; and if the answer thereto is 'yes' we can safely assume, pro tem, the other requirements for tracking are met.

[13] T could be reformulated thus (*cf* n 10 above): If it were in Liam's interests on balance to have a power of waiver, would he be granted a power of waiver? (*Mutatis mutandis* for the immediately subsequent question in the main text.) To note a point of departure between Sreenivasan and me in this context: Sreenivasan nowhere invokes the apparatus of possible worlds, and has communicated to me his unease with doing so here.

[14] *cf* n 11 above.

Before evaluating T, this last sentence marks an important point of departure between Sreenivasan's HT and my HT—the Tracking Theory. In ways to become clear shortly, we each want to put a slightly different gloss—put different weight—on the way in which the justificatory status of right-holding can be *extracted* from the holding of the relevant counterfactuals. As has become clear in communication with Sreenivasan, while he does take *some* justification to be extracted from counterfactual tests being satisfied, it's not the case for him that *all* the justificatory status of right-holding is to be explained thereby. Put differently, for Sreenivasan, the obtaining of said counterfactual relations between control, and interest in having control, is *part*, but not *all*, of the justificatory picture of right-holding. This is all to say that, for Sreenivasan, some extra *justification-generating* machinery/tests are at work in his HT, beyond the bare satisfaction of counterfactual tests. I leave it to Sreenivasan to make fully explicit what this extra machinery is, what these extra tests are, for him (*cf* Sreenivasan (2005: section 6), and section V.E below).

But—the divergence—note this: for *my* HT, the Tracking Theory, *no* such extra *justification-generating* machinery/tests are invoked. This is to say, for the Tracking Theory, in a way to be explained shortly, *all* the justificatory status of right-holding is to be explained by—extracted from—the obtaining of certain counterfactuals or modal relations between control, and interest in having control. Whether this can be pulled off remains to be seen. But, if it can, and insofar as (as is the case for many participants in these debates) it is a desideratum on a theory of rights to abstain as far as possible from evaluative (pre)commitments, this would be a strong point in favour of my theory (and against Sreenivasan's HT). Indeed, a more general claim can be ventured: the Tracking Theory of rights clearly seems *the most evaluatively austere* theory of rights going.

And a concluding parallel with Nozick's 'tracking' account of knowledge can profitably be noted here. Nozick—though his focus was on knowledge—could be taken to be trying to extract epistemic justification *wholly* from the obtaining of certain counterfactuals or modal relations between a subject's beliefs, and the facts. One might, somewhat vernacularly, gloss Nozick's ambitions here as attempting to abstain from operating with an *oomphy* notion of epistemic justification, in favour of a focus on bare modal relations between a subject's beliefs, and the facts, shorn of any evaluative (pre)commitments. As with my theory, whether Nozick pulled this off is a moot point.

E. Evaluating T

Let's, then, return to *K&S*, and evaluate T. So, let's first make the antecedent of the conditional *enshrined* in T true, viz: if it were in Liam's interests on balance to have a power of waiver, then he would be granted a power of waiver (*cf* footnote 13). Plausibly, in this possible world (or set of worlds), the risk of injury to Liam is defeated by the benefits to Liam of holding a power of waiver. The next question arises as to what these benefits to Liam could be. Two options present themselves.

Possibility 1 would be Liam's benefit in (seeing) justice being done; here, specifically, by ensuring Mark doesn't become destitute (call this the 'moral benefit'). (Liam is, Kramer and Steiner (2007: 309; Kramer 2013: 259) posit, 'a humane person'.) If this possibility were allowed, given the moral sensitivity displayed in the judge's reasoning in the actual case, it's plausible Liam *would* be granted a power of waiver, and, arguably counterintuitively for Sreenivasan, tracking obtains, and thus Liam has a right. (Effectively, Kramer and Steiner (2007: 309; Kramer 2013: 259) posit, the judge is sensitive, in his decision not to allocate a power of waiver to Liam in the actual case, not only to Liam's interests in not being pummelled, but also to Mark's interests in not becoming destitute (*cf* footnote 8).)[15] However, Kramer (and Steiner) would be precluded from making this reply, as Liam's interest here seems, in his sense, 'wholly vicarious', and thus not 'an interest of the requisite sort' which could form 'the bases for attributions of rights' (2007: 303). And this is all just to say that possibility 1 is *not*, for Kramer (and Steiner), a case in which the antecedent of T is true (in the technical sense of 'interests' adopted by Kramer (and Steiner)).

For Kramer (and Steiner), a wholly vicarious interest is an interest 'resid[ing] wholly in the furtherance of somebody else's interests' (2007: 303). I recognise that Kramer (and Steiner) makes clear here that an interest can be benevolently other-directed and nonetheless not wholly vicarious. But, if Kramer (and Steiner) is to argue that Liam's interest in being assigned the power to waive Mark's legal duty (here, for the sake of justice) is *not* wholly vicarious, we need to hear more as to why this is so (*cf* Sreenivasan 2005: 263–64; and in this volume). This will involve saying more about the vicarious/non-vicarious distinction. And, in turn, this will involve a further encroachment on Kramer's claim (1998) that his theory only requires a 'thin evaluative stance'. (Steiner is, of course, not an IT; hence the parentheses around 'Steiner' are particularly important at this juncture.)

In sum, the Kramer (and Steiner) approach with respect to possibility 1 can be broken down into two discrete stages. At stage 1, Kramer (and Steiner) must acknowledge his commitment to the aforementioned vicarious/non-vicarious distinction, with wholly vicarious interests not counting in the determination of whether someone is a right-holder. Then, at stage 2, Kramer (and Steiner) must argue that Liam's interest in possibility 1 of *K&S* is not wholly vicarious. We'll have cause to invoke these two distinct stages presently (see footnote 16).

F. *Ad Hominem*?

Have I, then, merely established the *ad hominem* conclusion that *Kramer (and Steiner)* is precluded from making this reply; compatibly with which *any other*

[15] In these foregoing respects, there is *an implicit* counterfactual dimension to *K&S*, but it is not the *requisite* counterfactual dimension which engages Sreenivasan's HT—viz a dimension asking question T.

philosopher could? No. Let's begin by noting that *K&S* can be wielded only by a philosopher (like Sreenivasan) committed to the notion (*arguendo*, in Steiner's case) that interests *can* form (part of) the bases for attributions of rights. Any such philosopher will consequently face the aforementioned third-party beneficiary objection—and, more generally, the challenge of principledly delimiting the set of interest-holders who get to become right-holders. Kramer (and Steiner) introduced the vicarious/non-vicarious distinction to deal with a challenge from Sreenivasan (2005: 263–64; and in this volume) to distinguish, in our contract or norm from section II.C above, A (an IT right-holder) from A-and-C's-grandmother (intuitively a non-right-holder).[16] (In Sreenivasan's example, A, C *and B* are *all* siblings.) According to Kramer (and Steiner), A has a non-vicarious, whereas A-and-C's-grandmother has a wholly vicarious, interest in the contract or norm being performed. In effect, my (and Sreenivasan's) challenge to Kramer (and Steiner) is to explain why Liam's interest in being assigned a power of waiver is *not* wholly vicarious while A-and-C's grandmother's interest in the contract or norm being performed *is*.

Of course, the former's interest relates to *holding* a power of waiver, while the latter's relates to the performance of a contract or norm *by another party*. But why should this be determinative of the matter? And recall, in a strict sense Liam's interest is the interest in being *assigned* a power of waiver, rather than the interest in its *exercise*. To be sure, the former interest might derive (in part) from the latter interest—specifically, its exercise *should propitious circumstances arise*; however the two interests are clearly distinct. Thus, any response by Kramer (and Steiner) to my challenge would be ill-advised to put weight on any *active agency* being *essentially* involved in the relevant interest of Liam's. At all events, the key point here is that *any philosopher* wielding *K&S* must address this thorny delimitation issue.

[16] Sreenivasan, in constructing this challenge (2005: 264), in fact himself introduces a distinction seemingly equivalent to the vicarious/non-vicarious distinction, viz the parasitic/non-parasitic distinction. Moreover, he can be read as endorsing the position that wholly parasitic/vicarious interests should not count in the determination of whether someone is a right-holder. If all this is so, Sreenivasan would be in the same boat as Kramer (and Steiner) with respect to possibility 1, stage 1. Where Sreenivasan and Kramer (and Steiner) plausibly differ, given Sreenivasan does not regard *K&S* as a genuine counterexample to HT, is at stage 2. That is, it's plausible that Sreenivasan holds that Liam's interest in *K&S is* wholly parasitic/vicarious. Finally, (drawing on conversations with Sreenivasan), given all the foregoing, does (or should) HT definitionally rule out wholly parasitic/vicarious interests from counting in the determination of whether someone is a right-holder? If it does, we could short-circuit the whole *ad hominem* worry at source: as a *definitional* matter, *anyone* would be prevented from inputting wholly parasitic/vicarious interests into the right-hand-side of CH (Sreenivasan's last-pass formulation of HT). Several quick points are relevant here. First, until Sreenivasan explicitly incorporates this restriction on the types of interests which can be inputted into the right-hand-side of CH, we cannot conclude, by definition, that the *ad hominem* worry has been deflected. Second, it seems to me to be inadvisable for Sreenivasan to restrict CH in this way: it's not clear *every* philosopher faced with the foregoing 'delimitation' challenge will respond to it by invocation of the foregoing typing of interests (*cf*, eg, Raz). Third, even if Sreenivasan *does* come to explicitly incorporate the foregoing restriction into the right-hand-side of CH, it is still, of course, open to Kramer (and Steiner)—and, indeed any wielder of *K&S*—to respond by (at stage 2) denying that Liam's interest in *K&S is* wholly parasitic/vicarious.

The 'elephant in the room' here is Raz. We've already seen that Sreenivasan thinks Raz's IT, while never explicitly addressing the third-party beneficiary objection, has the resources to provide a satisfactory answer thereto (*cf* footnote 6). Extrapolating from this, it might be thought that Raz's IT has the resources to answer the more general 'delimitation' challenge for IT, here exemplified by the cases of Sreenivasan's 'granny' and *K&S*'s Liam. Two (hardly conclusive) observations are in order. First, Raz certainly is not committed to Kramer's 'thin evaluative stance': on the contrary, in order to determine which interests are 'sufficient reason for holding some other person(s) to be under a duty', we are directed to consult (what we might term) Raz's 'thickly evaluative' theory of well-being (1986). Second, and relatedly, however, it is (in part) this 'thickly evaluative stance' itself which renders doubtful the extent to which Raz's IT can perform the subtle aforementioned distinguishing work required to tackle the 'delimitation' challenge. Indeed, I've elsewhere argued (MS) that the 'other things being equal clause', contained in Raz's definition of a right, also threatens to drain the definition of its ability to determinately generate results as to right-holders (and duty-bearers). Though I recognise (see footnote 17) that we should not expect an analysis of rights to generate wholly determinate answers in (certain) *hard cases*, the concern here is that the indeterminacy infecting Raz's IT is more thoroughgoing.

Thus, in conclusion, though I continue, for ease of prose, to train my focus on Kramer (and Steiner)—my chief interlocutors—any whiff of the *ad hominem* has been dispelled, and I've shown that there are problems in the offing—albeit, potentially subtly different problems—for Kramer (and Steiner) *and any other wielder of K&S*.

G. Evaluating T Continued

So, pursuing possibility 2—regarding the question as to what the benefits to Liam could be in being granted a power of waiver—in this world Liam would have some personal, likely pecuniary, interest in being able to waive the duty in question (maybe he is likely to get the money himself in that case; call this the 'prudential benefit'). However, the judge's reasoning in the actual case (his morally sensitive outlook, outlined in the previous paragraph) *doesn't* suggest that Liam would be granted a power of waiver in this world. Far from it. One can, though, stipulate this to be the case.[17] But now, while we have Liam's having (or

[17] The ordering of possible worlds is centred on *K&S*. It's in the nature of thought-experiments that they're underdescribed. Thus, by 'stipulation' here, I simply mean building more, or different, detail into the thought-experiment, with such (extra) detail *filling in* the world on which we're centred, and resultantly determining a different closeness ordering. Such orderings are not always going to be uncontentious (*cf* n 10 above); but, this is no more a reason to ditch a theory of rights relying on counterfactuals than it is to ditch a theory of knowledge reliant thereon. Indeed, contentiousness in

not) a power of waiver tracking his interests, we've effectively stipulated a case of a contract (or norm) 'designed' (in part), if you like, to *prudentially benefit* Liam.[18] Now we have a case which, given the counterfactual posit, is exceedingly bizarre[19] and, moreover (and relatedly), it's no longer so bizarre to suggest Liam has a right.[20] Indeed, even on possibility 1, were Kramer (and Steiner) not precluded from taking this option, we'd be stipulating a contract (or norm) 'designed' (in part) to *morally benefit* Liam. And the 'bizarreness' issue appears to rear its head again.

IV. (Interim) Conclusion

A. HT Undented

In sum, these possibilities seem to exhaust the alternatives. (This is to simplify things somewhat. What we might call 'mixed' cases, involving both moral *and* prudential benefits, are of course possible. But they can be of no assistance to Kramer and Steiner: they will inherit the deficiencies of each of the 'unmixed' cases.) Possibility 1 (the moral benefit case) is ruled out for Kramer (and Steiner) (and, in any event, appears to face my 'bizarreness' objection). On possibility 2 (the prudential benefit case), my hybrid theorist is, I take it, saying that in the closest possible world in which the antecedent of T is met, its consequent isn't (on account of the ordering of worlds generated by the way the judge reasons in the actual case).

hard cases may be what we should expect a theory to deliver. (Wenar agrees (2013: 222): '[T]racking uncertainty is not a failure in a conceptual analysis so much as an advertisement for it ... This tracking of uncertainty is even more acute in ... analysis [of human rights].') Which, for example, of possibility 1 or 2 is closer to the actual world as described in *K&S*? I don't commit on this.

[18] Here is a way (suggested to me by Sreenivasan) to short-circuit the possibility 2 approach to wielding *K&S* at source. *K&S* is set up such that objective and subjective justification are aligned (*cf* n 7 above); more concretely, the judge is (subjectively) focused on (objectively) correct moral matters when deciding over allocating a power of waiver to Liam. By contrast, possibility 2 seemingly countenances the judge (subjectively) focused on (objectively) incorrect prudential matters when so deciding. In other words, in possibility 2, we no longer have convergence between objective and subjective justification—and such convergence was part of the set-up of *K&S*. But this is all just evidence that pursuing possibility 2—as recognised in the main text—involves 'tweaking' *K&S*. To think that the possibility 2 approach to *K&S* is ruled out a priori involves a substantive claim that objective and subjective justification *must* be aligned. And that's a substantive claim I'm unwilling to make. In particular, divergence between the two forms of justification (in cases like that envisaged in possibility 2) would appear to be required to leave room, on HT, for 'legal-but-not-moral' rights. And it's not only legal positivists who would want to leave room for such rights.

[19] *K&S even without* the counterfactual posit is already *pretty* bizarre; its bizarreness is magnified with that posit's insertion.

[20] This is an instance of a more general accusation levelled against philosophers relying upon intuitions in bizarre cases—particularly in ethics: essentially (in its mildest form), the more bizarre the case, the less stable/reliable/probative will be the intuition.

Thus, tracking doesn't obtain; and thus Liam doesn't have a right. If Kramer and Steiner then stipulate things as I mention at the end of the previous paragraph, they encounter my 'bizarreness' objection.

Thus, either way, Sreenivasan's Hybrid Theory of rights (the last pass of which is the Complex Hybrid Theory) is both a genuine and, so far, attractive theory of rights.[21]

V. A Set of Pro Tem Counterexamples to Sreenivasan's Hybrid Theory, Prompting a Modification Thereto

A. Counterexamples' Shape

K&S tries to get traction from the clear fact that HT *can* grant a right notwithstanding the right-holder has *no* degree of control at all over the relevant duty in the actual case, provided that matches the right-holder's interests. Now Sreenivasan takes this to be an advantage of HT, in that, as we saw above (section II.B), it allows HT—unlike WT—to ascribe rights to, for example, categories of people, such as incompetent adults and children, provided certain conditions are met. And *K&S*, we've seen, tries to turn what Sreenivasan takes to be an advantage of HT into a disadvantage: it's a case contending that this feature of HT leads an *explosion* of right-holders. My two ensuing pro tem counterexamples—pro tem, in the sense that I want to immediately suggest a modification to HT to handle them—get a foothold from the same feature of HT as *K&S* does. (These are counterexamples numbers *II* and *III*, with *K&S* serving as number *I*.) They begin, that is, with an actual case in which the putative right-holder has no degree of control at all over the relevant duty (and that matches the right-holder's interests). And this is no surprise: this feature of HT is a natural focus, or locus, for counterexamples. The reason I belabour all this is that it is not clear to me that a solid, like counterexample can be offered in the *other* set of cases in which we can have a right-holder, viz where the right-holder *has* some degree of control over the relevant duty in the actual case (and that matches the right-holder's interests). This is an interesting phenomenon, and I want to return to it—and its upshots—shortly.

[21] In establishing this—established by my essay *in conjunction with Sreenivasan's papers* (*cf* section I.A above)—we've also established something else: what (rough) shape *genuine* counterexamples to HT must take, if they are to exist. I don't presently have a *knockdown* counterexample to hand (*cf* section V below); though this is not to say that one cannot be provided.

B. Nozick's *Granny*

Before getting to my first counterexample—which, for reasons to be made clear shortly, I will call *Happenstance-Basis*—we need to make another quick detour to Nozick. We've already mentioned, *en passant*, parallels between Nozick's 'tracking' account of knowledge and Sreenivasan's HT. To understand the origins of this counterexample, we need to spend some time making a brief detour to a case produced by Nozick, and which prompted a modification to Nozick's account as he was developing it—the case of Nozick's *Granny*:

> A grandmother sees her grandson is well when he comes to visit; but if he were sick or dead, others would tell her he was well to spare her upset. Yet this does not mean she doesn't know he is well (or at least ambulatory) when she comes to see him (1981: 179).

In brief, there is a strong intuition in *Granny*, that the grandmother has knowledge, via visual perception. Yet 'tracking' (in particular, the *sensitivity* condition) fails for the grandmother in the counterfactual world in which the grandson is sick or dead: in that world, she believes *falsely* he is well, via *testimony*. To avoid this result, Nozick amends his 'tracking' account to require *fixed methods* of belief formation across possible worlds: in a nutshell, if visual perception is the method used in the actual world (as in *Granny*), we hold that method fixed across counterfactual worlds (as is not the case in *Granny*).[22]

C. Carry-Over to HT

Now this Nozickean modification has received much scrutiny and criticism. Is it ad hoc? Even if not ad hoc, is it confronted by insurmountable difficulties concerning the individuation of methods? The success or otherwise of these objections is a moot point. What is clear, however, is that Nozick's 'tracking' account *needs* to be modified in this way for it to be viable. What I want to suggest is that the same goes for HT.

What follows is my *Granny*-inspired counterexample. The keen reader will notice that, though it is inspired by Nozick's *Granny*, it is not the exact structural analogue thereof. Nozick's *Granny* was a clear case of knowledge, but which failed Nozick's bare conditions on knowledge (in particular, sensitivity). My counterexample here, meanwhile, is a clear case of the non-existence of a right, but which meets Sreenivasan's bare conditions on a right (matching by design). And I think this is no accident. I think one will struggle to generate exact structural analogues of Nozick's *Granny*: clear cases of a right, but which fail to meet Sreenivasan's bare

[22] Both in my elucidation of the epistemological puzzle, and in my transposition to rights, I hope to sidestep *overdetermination* issues regarding methods (*cf* Nozick (1981: 180–84)).

conditions on a right. Exploring why this might be so would be an interesting task; but one for another day.

D. *Happenstance-Basis*

Here is the counterexample:

> *II. Happenstance-Basis*: Suppose it is in John's interest that he does not have the power of waiver over Jill's contract with Jack, and the law does not give him a waiver. John is a pure bystander. And, as such, the law—unreflectively[23]—does not give him (or any indefinite number of other bystanders) a power of waiver. The law 'does' (refrains from) this on what we can call the 'happenstance' basis. But suppose, plausibly, the closest world in which it is in John's (and any indefinite number of other bystanders) interest to have such a power of waiver, is a world in which John acquires a joint interest with Jill, becomes her trustee, etc. And suppose, again plausibly, that in such a world the law does give John (and any indefinite number of other bystanders) a power of waiver on the basis of the joint interest, becoming her trustee etc.

Intuitively, John does *not* have a right. This seems undeniable. A way to vindicate this intuition, however, would be to point out that if John were to have a right, so too would an indefinite number of bystanders whose situation parallels John's. Explosion of rights. Yet, HT's conditions *are* met. The 'matching' condition is met: in the actual world, John's measure of control (none) matches his interest in having a measure of control (none). And the 'design' condition is met: in the relevant closest possible world, John's measure of control (power of waiver) matches his interest in having a measure of control (on the basis of the joint interest, becoming her trustee etc). Problem for HT.

E. *Bystander-Basis*

Now before considering how HT might—must—be modified in light of this case, it's worth considering a possible rejoinder from Sreenivasan. Sreenivasan has recently said:

> [T]he design condition *requires* that the matching condition remain satisfied over a range of relevant counterfactual scenarios (my emphasis) (2010: 490).

Now this leaves open that the counterfactual dimension of the 'design' condition is necessary, but not sufficient, for that condition to be met. On such an interpretation, presumably the required 'extra ingredient' would be some kind of *advertence*

[23] One can—I presently shall—tell a similar story on which the law does this reflectively (one can call this the 'bystander' basis), but, especially insofar as we want our counterexample to be generalisable, the story does *risk* losing its plausibility.

constraint in the actual world—a constraint not met in *Happenstance-Basis* due to the law's *unreflective* nature in that case. As it happens, I would caution Sreenivasan against going this route: part of the (potential) beauty of a tracking account such as HT (and the point generalises), is that they offer a (putative) way of *extracting* justification from counterfactuals or modal relations (section III.D above). There is something alchemical in play: moving from the latter base metals to the gold of justification. And the more one enriches one's base metals with *advertence constraints*, the less alchemical one's result becomes.[24] Insofar, then, as Sreenivasan adopts this rejoinder, it marks another departure between him and me.

Let me, though, explain further, and address, any such advertence constraint on HT, by way of a second counterexample:

> *III. Bystander-Basis*: As *Happenstance-Basis*, except here the law *reflectively* does not give him[25] (or any indefinite number of other bystanders) a power of waiver. The law does this on what we can call the 'bystander' basis.

Now, switching from *Happenstance-Basis* to *Bystander-Basis*, should there be any advertence constraint on the 'design' condition, we have a case satisfying it. So, 'matching' and 'design' conditions met; yet still, intuitively, no right. Again: problem for HT.

F. The Tracking Theory

In sum, we have strong grounds now for thinking that a modification forced on Nozick is also forced on any hybrid theorist. That modification, for my Tracking Theory, involves stipulating that the *basis* on which the match occurs is held fixed across the counterfactuals (and I make this explicit in the coming Appendix). With such a restriction, the foregoing counterexamples do not get off the ground: Sreenivasan's matching by design conditions—which I formalise and incorporate into my Tracking Theory—are no longer met. And this point is generalisable to counterexamples of a like shape.

Now any such modification to the hybrid theory will need to confront all the concerns which we've noted were expressed with respect to Nozick's modification (see section V.C above). And that is, again, a challenge for another day (though we can note that this modification to the hybrid theory will not unsettle its verdicts either in core cases we've considered, or in *K&S*). But just as Nozick's account of knowledge *needs* to be modified in this way for it to be viable, so too, I want to

[24] *cf* Nozick (1981: 183), who *doesn't* require knowledge or awareness of the method one uses to form a belief.

[25] To generalise the counterexample (and generate the explosion of rights problem), one would need here to appeal to the ensuing: '(or any indefinite number of other bystanders)'. How plausible this story is here, I leave to the reader.

suggest, does Sreenivasan's HT. And this modification, woven into my formalisation of Sreenivasan's 'matching by design' conditions, constitutes—just is—my Tracking Theory of rights. The Tracking Theory—as we shall presently see—simply comprises bare (or pure) counterfactuals; that is, counterfactuals that operate without any *prior* substantive assumptions about justification in the background (with the aspiration being that justification *emerges* therefrom). For the foregoing reasons, while the theory is heavily indebted to Sreenivasan's HT, it constitutes a new hybrid theory of rights. And I take it to inherit all the attractions of Sreenivasan's sophisticated HT, while avoiding several of its defects.

Appendix: The Tracking Theory Formalised

First-pass at generalising and formalising the Tracking Theory and its 'matching' and 'design' conditions: Let 'I' = it is in Y's interests on balance to have control over X's duty to ϕ; 'C' = Y has control over X's duty to ϕ; '$\wedge$' = conjunction; '$\sim$' = negation; 'N$\rightarrow$' = 'Nozick-subjunctively implies';[26] and '$\rightarrow$' = subjunctively implies.

For three reasons what follows can only be a first-pass. (1) The coming question marks by (4) and (4*) indicate that I'm not *absolutely committed* on whether these conjuncts are necessary ('tracking' must stop somewhere); though my present position is that they indeed *are* necessary. Indeed, more generally, it might ultimately be (and Sreenivasan has hinted to me that this is his current position) that counterfactuals just aren't the right tool for the job for framing, or modelling, a hybrid theory. I still think making a first-pass at formalisation, though,

[26] Recall, from n 10, we assumed, pro tem, a Lewis–Stalnaker account of the semantics of subjunctive conditionals. And we also noted, in n 12, that 'tracking' requires more than matching in two cases. In order, in my first-pass at formalisation, to demonstrate what more is required, the best approach is to introduce a modal relation I call Nozick-subjunctively implies—a modal relation which doesn't render 'true–true' subjunctive conditionals trivially true (Nozick 1981: 680–81, fn 8). (An alternative approach to this 'true–true' problem would be to reject Lewis's (strong) centring constraint—a constraint which makes 'true–true' subjunctive conditionals trivially true. But, this form of cherry-picking with the Lewis–Stalnaker account would not deliver the modal relation we need for formalising the Tracking Theory.) Crudely speaking, this modal relation, in evaluating [A N$\rightarrow$ C], invites us to check whether the closest *band* of A-worlds are *all* C-worlds. Conditions (2) and (2*) force us to introduce this modal relation: if we simply operated with the Lewis–Stalnaker account of subjunctive conditionals, if (1) and (1*) are met, (2) and (2*) would be trivially met. But (2) and (2*) are substantive conditions. Therefore (by *modus tollens*), we must move beyond the Lewis–Stalnaker modal relation. And we can introduce this new modal relation consistently with assuming, pro tem, the correctness of the Lewis–Stalnaker approach for the semantics of (natural language) subjunctive conditionals. Finally, note that this modal relation, as it features in (2) and (2*) is analogous to Nozick's (1981: ch 3) 'adherence' condition (a component of his 'tracking' account of knowledge). (To develop this analogy in more detail: a proposition is to a subject's belief in that proposition, as a subject's interests in having control over a duty are to that subject's control over that duty.) To complete the analogy, (3) and (3*) (and, if included in the formalisation, (4) and (4*)) are analogous to Nozick's 'sensitivity' condition on knowledge.

is a useful task for any hybrid theorist to undertake. Moreover, it is an essential task for anyone espousing the Tracking Theory. (2) A more complete pass would not leave 'control' a simple binary predicate: recall, Sreenivasan's formulation of (CH) (ie, HT) speaks of Y's 'measure' of control. And (3) A more complete pass would provide a semantics for the subjunctive implication relation (but *cf* footnote 10 for my working assumption). Operating as I currently do, with a blend of Nozick-subjunctively implies relations and (standard) subjunctively implies relations gives me more flexibility (see reason (1))—which is a boon, given we're merely at the first-pass stage.

The Tracking Theory (TT)

Abbreviated

'Matching by design'—which is, for the Tracking Theory, necessary and sufficient for the holding of a right[27]—as a disjunction of two conjunctions:

Either (A): (1) [I ∧ C] ('matching condition') ∧ (2) [I N→ C] ∧ (3) [~I → ~C] ∧ (4?) [~I N→ ~C] ((2), (3) (and (4?)) 'design condition(s)'). **Where the *basis* on which the match occurs is held fixed across the counterfactuals.**[28]

Or (B): (1*) [~I ∧ ~C] ('matching condition') ∧ (2*) [~I N→ ~C] ∧ (3*) [I → C] ∧ (4*?) [I N→ C] ((2*), (3*) (and (4*?)) 'design condition(s)'). **Where the *basis* on which the match occurs is held fixed across the counterfactuals.**

[27] It is also necessary and sufficient for Sreenivasan's HT. On my interpretation, though, Sreenivasan cashes out the 'design' condition differently—in particular, as we've seen in the essay, it cannot, for him, be reducible to the bare obtaining of a set of modal relations.

[28] Recall: counterexamples which prompted this modification were (necessarily?) focused on the ensuing second disjunct. But, despite the failure to provide a like counterexample focused on the first disjunct, reasons of consistency militate in favour of including this modification here also.

Unabbreviated

Y has a right against X that X ϕ if and only if:

(A)

(1) It is in Y's interests on balance to have control over X's duty to ϕ & Y has control over X's duty to ϕ. ('matching condition'; remainder 'design')

&

(2) If it were in Y's interests on balance to have control over X's duty to ϕ, then Y would have control over X's duty to ϕ (this read as a Nozickian subjunctive conditional).

&

(3) If it were not in Y's interests on balance to have control over X's duty to ϕ, then Y would not have control over X's duty to ϕ (this read as a non-Nozickian subjunctive conditional).

&

(4?) If it were not in Y's interests on balance to have control over X's duty to ϕ, then Y would not have control over X's duty to ϕ (this read as a Nozickian subjunctive conditional).

Or:

(B)

(1*) It is not in Y's interests on balance to have control over X's duty to ϕ & Y has no control over X's duty to ϕ, ('matching condition'; remainder 'design'.)

&

(2*) If it were not in Y's interests on balance to have control over X's duty to ϕ, then Y would not have control over X's duty to ϕ (this read as a Nozickian subjunctive conditional).

&

(3*) If it were in Y's interests on balance to have control over X's duty to ϕ, then Y would have control over X's duty to ϕ (this read as a non-Nozickian subjunctive conditional).

&

(4*?) If it were in Y's interests on balance to have control over X's duty to ϕ, then Y would have control over X's duty to ϕ (this read as a Nozickian subjunctive conditional).

Where, throughout, the *basis* on which the match occurs is held fixed across the counterfactuals.

The Tracking Theory's reply to *K&S* amounts, on this first-pass, on which only the second disjunct (viz (B)) is relevant, to saying that conjunct (1*)—itself a conjunction—but not all of conjuncts (2*) and (3*) (and (4*?)—subjunctive conditionals—is met therein. And conjunct (3*) *corresponds* to question T (from section III.D above).

Also, note that conditions (2) and (4*), and (2*) and (4), are ostensibly the same. However, this is merely ostensible identity, as the different disjuncts will determine different worlds on which we are centred. Finally, note that (Nozick-)subjunctive conditionals don't (on the standard view) contrapose. Thus, for example, [~I → ~C] is not equivalent to [C → I], and [I → C] is not equivalent to [~C → ~I] (*cf* footnotes 10 and 12).[29]

References

Kramer, MH (1998) 'Rights Without Trimmings' in MH Kramer, NE Simmonds and H Steiner, *A Debate over Rights: Philosophical Enquiries* (Oxford: Oxford University Press).
—— (2010) 'Refining the Interest Theory of Rights' 55 *The American Journal of Jurisprudence* 31.
—— (2013) 'Some Doubts About Alternatives to the Interest Theory of Rights' 123 *Ethics* 245.
Kramer, MH and Steiner, H (2007) 'Theories of Rights: Is There a Third Way?' 27 *Oxford Journal of Legal Studies* 281.
Lewis, D (1979) 'Counterfactual Dependence and Time's Arrow' 13 *Nous* 455.
—— (1986) *On the Plurality of Worlds* (Oxford: Blackwell Publishers).
McBride, M (MS) 'Raz's Definition of a Right'.
May, S (2012) 'Moral Status and the Direction of Duties' 123 *Ethics* 113.
Nozick, R (1981) *Philosophical Explanations* (Harvard, MA: Belknap Press).
Raz, J (1986) *The Morality of Freedom* (Oxford: Clarendon Press).
Sreenivasan, G (2005) 'A Hybrid Theory of Claim-Rights' 25 *Oxford Journal of Legal Studies* 257.
—— (2007) 'In Defense of the Hybrid Theory' in E Villanueva (ed), *Law: Metaphysics, Meaning, and Objectivity* (Amsterdam: Rodopi).
—— (2010) 'Duties and Their Direction' 120 *Ethics* 465.
Steiner, H (2013) 'Directed Duties and Inalienable Rights' 123 *Ethics* 230.
Wenar, L (2005) 'The Nature of Rights' 33 *Philosophy & Public Affairs* 223.
—— (2008) 'The Analysis of Rights' in M Kramer et al (eds), *The Legacy of HLA Hart* (Oxford: Oxford University Press).
—— (2013) 'The Nature of Claim-Rights' 123 *Ethics* 202.

[29] Thanks to Andrew Halpin, Matt Kramer, Gopal Sreenivasan and John Williams for detailed written comments. Thanks also to participants at the conference itself for helpful discussion.

8

The Circularity of the Interest and Will Theories of Rights

ROWAN CRUFT

Theories of the nature of rights—which for present purposes I shall take to be the same as theories of what it is for a duty to be owed to someone, and of what it is for violation of that duty to wrong someone[1]—standardly bifurcate into (1) a 'will' theory, which claims that a given duty is owed to whoever has some control over this duty as a matter of their will,[2] and (2) an 'interest' theory, which claims that a given duty is owed to whoever's interests bear an appropriate relation to it.[3] In this essay, I argue that versions of both theories can be developed which are extensionally accurate, but that the theories in these forms cannot avoid circularity.[4] My conclusion will be that if we want a broadly reductive account of the nature of rights and directed duties, we need to look beyond both interest and will theory. To put it roughly, the best versions of these theories cannot avoid saying (in will theory mode) that to be owed a duty is to have the kind of control over it (including control on one's behalf by another) that comes with being owed it, or (in interest theory mode) that to be owed a duty is for it to serve one's interests in the way that a duty owed to one does.

I. Will Theory's Circularity

The will theory famously struggles to explain how duties could be owed to beings who lack the type of will that could give them control over duties. The standard version of the will theory contends that to be owed a duty is to have the power to

[1] For more on this way of taking the theories, see Cruft (2013a).

[2] The type of control differs for different theories; I explore some options in section I below. For classic statements of the will theory, see Hart (1955; 1973); Simmonds (1998); Steiner (1994; 1998).

[3] The conception of the 'appropriate relation' between interests and a duty's direction varies across different interest theories. For discussion, see sections II and III below. For classic statements of different forms of the theory, see MacCormick (1982); Raz (1986); Kramer (1998; 2010).

[4] For anticipation of this point, see Thompson (2004: 349–51).

waive it; but young babies and non-human animals such as rabbits do not have the kind of will that could exercise a power to waive.[5] In response, a defender of the will theory might argue that duties are owed either to those who have the power to waive them, or to those who—because they are incapable of holding this power—have others hold this power on their behalf. But it is not clear that the will theory has the resources to explain what it is about an incapable being that makes a duty owed to her while someone else holds the power of waiver on her behalf. And it is also unclear that the will theory can explain what it is about the surrogate or trustee (who holds this power of waiver on behalf of the person to whom the duty is owed) that makes it the case that the duty is not owed to them, as power holder.[6]

Before developing this point in a new direction, I should also note the second famous problem for the will theory: it struggles to explain unwaivable rights, even including such rights when borne by fully capable adult humans. If the duty not to enslave me is one that I cannot waive (for moral or legal reasons), then the will theory seems to force us to conclude that this duty is, despite appearances, not really owed to me.[7]

In response to the latter point, defenders of the will theory might relax their focus on waiver, and think more broadly about the kinds of ways in which a person can actively exercise her will in relation to a given duty. In particular, I would suggest that even in relation to unwaivable rights like my right not to be enslaved, I hold the powers to demand and protest, if not waive.[8] That is, a revised will theory could say that the reason your duty not to enslave me is owed to me, correlating with a right of mine, is because I hold special powers to demand and protest against being enslaved, even if I lack the power to waive your duty.[9]

But in either its waiver or its demand version, the will theory suffers a problem of circularity that has not been fully developed so far in the literature. Criticism in the literature focuses on the way in which the will theory fails to give a necessary condition for a duty's being owed to someone—by focusing on those to whom the duty seems to be owed but who lack any control (to waive or demand) over this duty. Yet the will theory also fails to give a sufficient condition for duties being owed to someone. For, as the surrogate or trustee idea mentioned earlier shows, having power over a duty or having it under control of one's will does not guarantee that the duty is owed to one. When two companies enter into a contract to merge, the Competition and Markets Authority in the UK has the Hohfeldian power to cancel this contract if it would damage the state of the market. Is this power a 'waiver' power of the type that would make the duties owed to the Authority as well as to the contractors? I do not see how a will theorist can avoid saying it is, without

[5] MacCormick (1982); Kramer (1998: 69–70); see also Hart (1955: section I(C)).

[6] These concerns are implicit in, eg, Sreenivasan's 2005 discussion of the will theory.

[7] MacCormick (1977); Kramer (1998: 72–73).

[8] Unlike the power to waive a duty, powers of demand and protest are not obviously *Hohfeldian* powers. I set this point aside for now.

[9] These ideas are present in Feinberg (1970), and are also associated with Skorupski's Millian enforceability conception (Skorupski 2010: 307–13).

circularly appealing to our prior intuition that the Authority is not owed these duties. Similarly, if a passing bystander has the (non-Hohfeldian) power to demand that a farmer stop mistreating her cows, how can we avoid seeing the farmer's duty (not to mistreat the cows) as owed to the bystander as much as to the cows? We would, I claim, want to say in these cases, that the Authority and the bystander are exercising powers but are not themselves right-holders—and further we would want to say that in the bystander case the power is exercised *on behalf of* separate right-holders (the cows). But the will theory lacks the resources to explain these points without circularity.[10]

In my view the best version of the will theory is circular: it says that a duty is owed to any person P who can either (i) waive or demand its fulfilment *on her own behalf* or (ii) have some other(s) waive or demand its fulfilment *on behalf of P*—where the notion of 'on behalf of' here has to mean (in both (i) and (ii)) on behalf of *the being to whom the duty is owed*. Such a circular conception of waiving or demanding on behalf of P is required to distinguish such waivers or demands from other notions of 'on behalf' that would deliver the wrong conclusion. For example, will theorists must rule out the idea that whenever someone demands fulfilment of a duty *while thinking of P*, then that duty is demanded on behalf of P or that whenever someone demands fulfilment of a duty *on their own without prompting*, then that duty is demanded on the demander's own behalf—or indeed that when waiving or demanding a duty *in one's role as regulator or bystander*, the duty is waived or demanded on behalf of the regulator or bystander. These notions of acting 'on behalf of' oneself or another would deliver incorrect directions for the duty.[11] The will theorist needs and cannot avoid the circular notion of waiving or demanding as or on behalf of *the person to whom the duty is owed*.

II. Interest Theory's Circularity 1: Raz and Sreenivasan

Raz's interest theory tells us that a duty is owed to whoever's interest is sufficiently important to ground it.[12] ('Interest' here means 'aspect of wellbeing'. It need not be something one is interested in.)[13] A familiar problem with this theory is that there seem to be duties owed to people whose interests play no major part, or in some cases no part at all, in the duty's grounding. Raz's own examples include the right, within the British welfare system, to child benefit payments: the duty to

[10] For a similar thought, see Raz (1984: 5).

[11] A will theorist might try to cash out 'on behalf of P' by appeal to P's *interests*—but then their theory turns into the rival interest theory.

[12] Raz (1986: 166). How exactly to interpret 'sufficiently important' is difficult. For discussion and implications of different views, see Cruft (2013b: 204–06).

[13] Raz (1986: 166).

make such payments is owed to *parents* even though *children's* interests are what ground it.[14] In my view, most property rights are a further, and perhaps less esoteric, example: your duty not to run off with my shirt is, in my view, not grounded primarily by my own interest in that shirt (I am wealthy enough that if I lose this one, I can buy another); rather, your duty not to run off with my shirt is grounded in how the property system as a whole serves the common good. But according to Raz's account, it then looks doubtful that your duty really is owed to me because my interests are not what ground it.

Raz thinks he can accommodate this type of case by making the right-holder's interest gain duty-grounding importance from how serving this interest serves the further interests of others. Thus, he suggests that a journalist's right to withhold the names of her sources is grounded by the journalist's interests—but he adds that the journalist's interests ground the relevant duties precisely because serving these interests serves the common good; the journalist's interests have no independent duty-grounding importance.[15] Similarly, in discussing the rights of officials and corporations, Raz writes: 'rights protect the interests of right holders. But these interests need not be intrinsically valuable. The reason for protecting them may be that by doing so one does protect the interests of others'.[16]

This move is unsustainable for it would absurdly multiply right-holders. For any given duty, there are often a great many interests that are served by it. Raz's move seems to allow us to interpret any one of these interests as of duty-grounding importance, because any one of these interests is such that serving this interest by respecting the duty in question is a way of serving the further interests which really ground the duty. For example, my duty not to assault you—grounded, I suggest, ultimately on your interest in not being assaulted—serves your family, the wider community (who, due to my respect for the duty, do not have to bear the medical cost they would have to bear if I assaulted you), your pets, and your local shopkeepers (who benefit from custom they would lose if I assaulted you). Serving any one of these interests by not assaulting you is a way of serving all the others. Any one of these interests can thereby, according to Raz's strategy, inherit the importance generated by what I see as the genuine ground of the duty, namely, your interest in not being assaulted. Does it follow that your family, your community, your pets and your local shopkeepers are all owed my duty not to assault you? Surely not—or at least, if we do want to say that some of these people are owed the duty, Raz's approach delivers this conclusion much too easily.[17]

[14] Raz (1994: 50). Raz also mentions journalists' rights grounded in how they serve the common good (1986: 179) and pregnant women's rights not to be executed grounded in the interests of the unborn child (1994: 50).

[15] Raz (1986: 179).

[16] Raz (1984: 20).

[17] For different but cognate points, see Kamm (2002: 485) (arguing that if it needs the support of others' interests in order to ground a duty, then a journalist's interest cannot be *sufficient* to ground that duty) and Sreenivasan (2005: section 5) (arguing that the *instrumental* importance of one's interest is inappropriate as the ground for one's right). Mark McBride has pointed out to me that we can distinguish those interests which are served *necessarily* by a duty's fulfilment from those which are served

Sreenivasan's ingenious hybrid theory suffers from the same problem. For Sreenivasan, a duty is owed to whoever has a level of control over it which is grounded in her interests. This level of control might be zero, but so long as this zero control is grounded in her interests—as it might be if she is a child who is unable to exercise control—then the duty in question is owed to her.[18] As with Raz, Sreenivasan suffers from the fact that some duties, and in particular our level of control over them, are grounded by factors independent of the interests of those to whom they are owed. Again, property is a good example: my control over your duties to refrain from using or taking my yacht is justified, I think, not by my own interests but by how the common good is served by a system which gives me this control. Sreenivasan's theory seems compelled to conclude that your duty not to take my yacht is therefore not owed to me.[19]

Both theories can be rescued, as Thompson points out in relation to Raz, by a more circular interpretation.[20] Such an interpretation is, I think, already implicit in Raz's account of the journalist's right, the right to child benefit payments or officials' and corporations' rights as outlined earlier. By saying that the journalist's or the parents' interests ground the duty in question via how they serve others' interests, Raz makes clear he does not mean that the former interests are the real source of the duty. But I suggested two paragraphs ago that he also should not mean to imply that a duty is grounded in the relevant sense by just *any old* interest which is served by how the duty serves those interests which are really its source. Instead, implicit circular reasoning is going on: a claim that a duty is 'grounded' by an interest, for Raz, makes most sense simply as a claim that the duty in question is already *owed to* the being whose interests are in question. 'Ground' here really means nothing on this account; what we have is circularity.[21]

However, it is worth noting that unlike the will theory, and unlike the versions of the interest theory to be discussed next, Raz's theory when interpreted

contingently, and that a restriction to those served *necessarily* would avoid many of my problem cases. My view is that Raz cannot make this move without excluding too many duties as not owed to people (eg, I think property rights often only contingently serve appropriate interests of owners). If Raz modified the position to accommodate these sorts of cases by claiming that while rights must *necessarily* serve their holders, they need only do so in ways that are *typically* beneficial, then Raz's theory will have turned into Kramer's; I explore this approach in section III below.

[18] Sreenivasan (2005; 2010).

[19] This example suggests that Sreenivasan's account fails as a *necessary* condition for right-holding. For the case against Sreenivasan's account as a *sufficient* condition, see Kramer and Steiner (2007: 308–10); and May (2012: 123). Mark McBride noted that my case against Sreenivasan's account as a necessary condition depends on reading what Sreenivasan calls the 'design' condition as a justificatory or grounding one; I think this reading is supported by, eg, Sreenivasan (2010: 25–27). But I think property works as a counterexample even for a weaker 'counterfactual match' condition: the yacht is mine, along with the powers of waiver over the trespassory duties that make it mine, so long as I gain the yacht in accordance with the rules of the property system, independently of how these powers reflect or serve my interests.

[20] Thompson (2004: 349–50).

[21] Of course, I am not saying that Sreenivasan or Raz would endorse this reading of their theories; they have their own responses (eg, Raz (1994); Sreenivasan (2010)).

non-circularly does deliver a *sufficient*, though not a necessary, condition for right-holding. That is, if a duty is grounded solely or overwhelmingly by a given animal's or human's interest, then the duty must be owed to that animal or human. I do not have the space to argue for this here, but I defend it elsewhere: if an animal's or human's interests manage to work as the principal source of some duty, then that duty is owed to them.[22] The trouble for Raz is simply that some duties are also owed to animals and humans whose interests do not ground them.

III. Interest Theory's Circularity 2: Kramer and Wenar

By identifying to whom a duty is owed with the person whose interests ground it, Raz's theory offers one solution to what had become known as the 'third-party beneficiary' problem for interest theories of rights: the problem of explaining why not *every* beneficiary of a duty holds a right correlative to it. (Hart's classic example involves one person promising to perform some task for another person's parent; even though the parent benefits from this duty, the promisee is the right-holder, not the parent.)[23] But I have shown that Raz's overly expansive view that an interest can 'ground' a duty via what it does for other interests reopens this problem.

Kramer develops a different and attractive solution to this problem, identifying the person to whom a duty is owed as any person for whom fulfilment of the duty is *necessarily*—as opposed to *contingently*—beneficial. To accommodate those cases (problematic for Raz too) in which a right does nothing whatsoever for its holder—such as property rights I inherit from an unknown relative over ugly, worthless garden gnomes[24]—Kramer specifies that a given duty to *phi* is owed to any human, animal or group who is necessarily placed, by the duty-bearer's *phi*-ing, in a state or situation that it is *typically* beneficial for a human, animal or group to be in.[25] Note that unlike Raz, Kramer does not make the right-holder's interests the *ground* or *justification* of their right.

[22] See Cruft (forthcoming).

[23] Hart (1955: section I(C)).

[24] See Cruft (2004: 372–73).

[25] I here follow Kramer's 2010 exposition (at 32). In Kramer (1998), the idea that rights must *necessarily* serve their holders is outlined via 'Bentham's test' (where Kramer puts it as the thesis that when detriment to someone is sufficient to establish a duty's breach then the duty is owed to them; see 81–83); the explication of 'serving' and 'detriment' in terms of what is *typically* beneficial comes at 93–97. I discuss the indexing to humans, animals and groups in the main text shortly; obviously this should be read as saying that for a duty to be owed to a given *human*, its fulfilment necessarily has to place that human in a state or situation that would be typically beneficial for a *human*; for it to be owed to a given *animal*, we should read it indexed to 'animal' and so on. Note also that Kramer's thesis refers to the benefits of the full action enjoined by the duty. Even if part of an action (or an action under a partial description) would necessarily be beneficial for the typical human, a duty enjoining this action will not be owed to the person it affects unless the full action (under the description used in specifying

Wenar offers an original and insightful new theory that, with its language of roles, kinds and desires, seems distinct from the interest theory. But on close inspection I see it as akin to Kramer's theory. For Wenar, a duty to *phi* is owed to any person who (1) is someone to whom the *phi*-ing is done and (2) has a role- or kind-based desire that this *phi*-ing be done.[26] The first clause is interesting and I explore it elsewhere;[27] here my focus is on the second clause, because it is here that Wenar comes close to Kramer and the interest theory. In focusing on role- or kind-based desires, Wenar explicitly follows Raz's suggestion that

> rights are vested in right-holders because they possess certain general characteristics: they are the beneficiaries of promises, nationals of a certain state, etc. Their rights serve their interests as persons with these characteristics, but they may be against their interests overall.[28]

Whereas Kramer takes this idea as linking rights to what is *typically* in the interests of a human, animal or group, Wenar links them to the desires one holds *given one's kind or role*. What makes Wenar's approach distinctive is that one's desires *as bearer of a particular kind or role* can be distinct both from one's particular interests or desires as a specific embodied person, and from the interests or desires statistically typical to persons in general or to the type of person one is. Wenar makes clear how free-floating his notion of role- and kind-based desires is:

> When travelling through King's Cross station in London you may hear a recorded announcement saying that members of the station's staff will be happy to help passengers. Even if every individual who works at King's Cross is entirely misanthropic, we still say that all staff members, qua staff members, are happy to help passengers.[29]

The trouble for Wenar's presentation of his theory as distinct from the interest theory is that once we enter the realm of roles and kinds, it seems very unclear that there is any distinction between a role- or kind-based *desire* and a role- or kind-based *interest*. Considered independently of the idea of roles and kinds, there might indeed be a distinction between interests and wants: one's wants might mean psychological items in one's head, while one's interests will be aspects of one's wellbeing which might diverge from what one wants. For example, I might

the duty) places the person in a position that would be beneficial for the typical human. Thus, Kramer avoids Wenar's ingenious concern that a duty to waterboard a prisoner of war might be owed to that prisoner because it is beneficial for the typical human to lie down sometimes (Wenar 2013: 205, fn 9). Finally, Kramer's own exposition gives necessary but insufficient conditions for a duty's direction because he states his theory in a way that does not assume that any duty exists (2010: 32). It is, I contend, fair to read his account as giving a sufficient condition of the type outlined: a condition whose fulfilment is sufficient to establish a duty's direction. See n 49 below.

[26] Wenar (2013: 218–19). I here ignore Wenar's third, enforceability clause, because Wenar sees his first two clauses as sufficient for determining a duty's direction; the third clause simply distinguishes those directed duties which we can call 'rights' (ibid 214, fn 24)—and my focus in this essay is on duties' direction (see above, first sentence of this essay).

[27] Cruft (forthcoming).

[28] Raz (1986: 180), referenced by Wenar (2013: 205–06).

[29] Wenar (2013: 215).

want great wealth even though it will not in any respect enhance my wellbeing. But to accommodate cases like the gnomes, Wenar needs a conception of role- or kind-based wants which are, I suggest, indistinguishable from role- or kind-based interests. They are role- or kind-based entities which are distinct from any psychological items in one's head, and distinct also from what will independently make one flourish. On this basis, I see Wenar's theory as continuous with Kramer's: both offer rival versions of the thesis that a duty is owed to whoever it necessarily places in a position that is beneficial; to get Kramer's theory, we add '*typically*' before 'beneficial'; to get Wenar's, we add '*as a matter of one's role or kind*'.[30]

In my view, both Kramer's and Wenar's theories are very attractive. Wenar has suggested that Kramer's theory cannot account for many legal rights, including morally unjustified rights (eg, he mentions the legal right to arrange one's child's marriage) and morally justified rights of office (eg, the right of a judge to sentence prisoners). Wenar's thought is that fulfilling the relevant duties here—allowing parents to arrange the marriage, or allowing and respecting the sentencing judgment[31]—will not necessarily serve the interests of the people to whom they are intuitively owed; such duty-fulfilling actions do not even place those they affect in a situation that would *typically* be beneficial for a human.[32] Similarly, Wenar suggests that even if a particular kind of Marxist was correct to argue that owners have no genuine interest served by their property rights, nonetheless these would still qualify as rights.[33] Against this, Kramer has retorted that there are plausibly interests at stake in the right way for his theory in each of these situations, for example, allowing a judge to exercise her power to sentence does something for the judge which would typically be beneficial for any human: it allows her to do her job.[34]

It is extremely hard to think of counterexamples to either Kramer's or Wenar's theory, but I think this is because it is natural to take both theories, implicitly, in a circular way: to ascribe typical or role/kind-interests whenever, and only whenever, one already thinks a duty is owed to someone. We can begin to see this, I suggest, by investigating the plausibility of Kramer's response about the judge

[30] Let me make clear that I am *not* claiming that the two theories are ultimately the same. The focus on roles and kinds in Wenar, and on what is typically beneficial in a broadly 'objective' sense in Kramer, make for different though related theories.

[31] Note that because our target is theories of what it is for a duty to be owed to someone (ie, theories of the Hohfeldian *claim*-right), the two examples must be taken as focused not on the Hohfeldian *powers* they involve (eg, the parents' legal powers to place their children under duties to marry so-and-so; the judge's powers to impose new duties on the convict and criminal justice officials by sentencing) but rather on the associated Hohfeldian *duties* that are plausibly owed to the power-holders in protection of their roles (namely, the legal duties not to impede the parents or the judge in exercising their powers etc). On how Hohfeldian positions can aggregate in a single right, see Halpin's contribution to this volume.

[32] For the arranged marriage case, see Wenar (2013: 205); for the judge (focused primarily on the Hohfeldian power rather than—as in my text—on the claim), see Wenar (2008: 258–60).

[33] Wenar (2013: 205, fn 9).

[34] See Kramer's contribution to this volume, especially at sections V.A–V.C.

above. Does *being unimpeded in executing one's power to sentence* really necessarily place a judge in a situation that would typically be beneficial for a human being? This seems typically beneficial only for a human being who is a judge—rather than for a human being in general. Kramer makes this move, allowing us to ask not whether a duty-bearer's *phi*-ing would typically benefit a human, but rather whether it would typically benefit a human *in context*—for example, in the context in which one is a judge.[35] In making this move, Kramer brings his theory closer to Wenar's: the idea of what would typically benefit a 'human who is an X' is clearly close to the idea of what would serve someone's desires-as-an-X. With this move, Kramer's theory says that a duty to *phi* is owed to someone if *phi*-ing necessarily places that person in a situation which, in their context, would typically be beneficial to a person in such a context.[36]

My worry is that even with this adjustment, it is not clear that Kramer's theory accommodates cases like the judge. Is it *really* beneficial for a judge to be unimpeded in their power to sentence? Kramer notes that this lets the judge do her job, but is *this* really beneficial? Perhaps being singled out as the one judge who lacked any claim to be unimpeded in sentencing would place one in a position that was indubitably bad for one. But I am simply unclear on whether being enabled smoothly to do one's job as a 'normal' modern judge is something that is, typically, good for a human being who is a judge. This is partly because I am unclear whether the modern role is a good one or not.[37] And whether the duty to enable me to perform that role is owed to me or not should, I suggest, be independent of these issues which link it to beneficialness.

So why do I nonetheless find myself assenting readily to Kramer's contention that allowing a judge to exercise her power to sentence is beneficial for the typical judge by allowing her to do her job? I suggest that my readiness here is due to my prior commitment to the thesis that the judge has a *right* to do her job, and that my duties are *owed to* her. My perception of the relevant human interest is determined by my perception of the rights, rather than vice versa.

The same point can be made in relation to Wenar. We readily ascribe to judges the relevant kind of role-based desire or role-based interest in being unimpeded in sentencing; but I suggest that this is because of a prior commitment to the view that the duty not to impede sentencing is *owed to* judges. To make this point clearer, it is helpful to consider a case in which *duties* rather than *powers* take centre stage. Consider the conventional duty borne by private soldiers to salute sergeants.[38] It seems to me that this duty to salute sergeants could, in principle, be owed to sergeants (as it is in the modern British army), or it could be owed to

[35] ibid.

[36] Recall that we must consider the full *phi*-ing in context, not just some aspect of it—see n 25 above.

[37] See, eg, debates about penal abolitionism: Christie (1981).

[38] See my earlier discussion in Cruft (2013b: 210–12); there I failed to see how problematic the circularity is.

the monarch, or it could be undirected and owed to nobody.[39] Note that the latter two possibilities still concern the duty to *salute sergeants*: the thought is simply that in these two cases, this duty to salute when sergeants are present will be owed either to the monarch or to nobody; sergeants themselves will not be wronged if a private soldier fails to salute them—but the monarch will be wronged if a private soldier fails to salute the sergeants, or in the final case 'a wrong' will occur when this happens even though nobody will be wronged by this wrong. Now, it seems to me that we most naturally ascribe to sergeants a role-based desire to be saluted by private soldiers because we make the prior assumption that the duty to salute is owed to sergeants. It is not clear that we would ascribe such a role-based desire to sergeants in the possible scenarios in which the duty was owed to the monarch or was undirected. Without the duty being owed *to the sergeants*, it is unclear why sergeants need come to see this duty to salute them as good for them or something they want. If they think the duty is owed to the monarch, then they will see the saluting as good for the monarch, as what monarchs want *qua* monarchs. But if this is correct, then we are circularly ascribing a role-based desire or interest because of our commitment to the existence of a right, rather than vice versa.[40]

IV. Interests Created by Rights

We naturally fall into these circular interpretations of Kramer's and Wenar's theories, I suggest, because there are two ways in which someone's interest can be conjured into being by their holding a right. First, all morally justified rights necessarily generate a distinctively status-based interest, on the part of the right-holder, in their own fulfilment. Consider the full range of morally justified duties owed to a person, including morally justified but legally or conventionally created duties owed to that person, such as my duty to do what the person says because she is my manager, or my duty to hand my work in to her on time because she is also my tutor. These duties—including both the conventional directed duties just mentioned and what we might see as the natural or basic directed duties correlating with natural basic rights (eg, my duty not to assault her)—delineate the sphere of moral respect for the person in question. If I assault them, or indeed if I simply fail to do what they requested as my manager, or fail to hand my essay in on time to them, I show disrespect to them. These morally justified directed duties constitute ways of wronging someone which mark what it is to show disrespect to them. Further, it is natural to think that everyone has an interest in being

[39] It could, of course, be owed to both sergeants and the monarch at the same time; Kramer will question the claim that it could be owed to nobody, for he sees all duties as directed (1998).

[40] For the same argument applied also to Wenar's handling of property rights, see Cruft (2013b: 211): we only see Sarah as having a role-based desire that Jo keep off Greenacre if we make the prior assumption that Jo's duty to keep off Greenacre is *owed to Sarah*. See also discussion below.

respected and being shown respect; that is, each person's wellbeing is necessarily diminished in a certain way if they are not respected. The interest here can plausibly be described as a status interest.[41] These facts about respect and status mean that any morally justified right is one whose fulfilment necessarily serves the right-holder's interests in a certain way: namely, in this status way. But this interest is parasitic on, rather than determinative of, a duty's direction.[42]

Is there a parallel status interest in the fulfilment of morally unjustified rights? It is tempting to think this, for example, to ascribe to the organised crime boss a status interest in the 'respect' shown by those who pay her protection money. But—for reasons I cannot defend fully here—I would favour a more moralised conception of respect, and hence of the attendant status interest. In my view, the crime boss's wellbeing is not really enhanced by the 'respect' shown in such payments, and this is because they do not show true respect. (I would even deny that the payments themselves enhance her wellbeing, though that requires a much stronger moralised conception of wellbeing.)

There is a second way in which many rights—morally justified and unjustified—contingently create further interests in their own fulfilment. Such interests are *not* a necessary feature of certain rights, in the way that the status interest *is* necessary to morally justified rights. The second way in which rights create interests is, rather, contingent on particular circumstances, and involves rights, and respect for them, *causing* the development of interests in their own fulfilment. Examples of what I have in mind include the way that once a legal right becomes the social norm, people develop expectations based on 'their rights' that generate genuine interests. We should be careful in identifying the circular interests here. An undirected duty to *phi* might, contingently and over time by causal mechanisms, create interests which are served necessarily by *phi*-ing—but such interests are created by an *undirected duty* rather than by a *right*. The interest theory might have to say that in such a situation what was previously an undirected duty has now, by creating interests in its own fulfilment, become a right.[43] But this is not circularity for the interest theory. The circular case involves those interests of mine which are created, again contingently and over time via causal mechanisms, by the existence of a *duty owed to me* (or a *right of mine*). For example, it is quite plausible to say that because I am a property owner, I might contingently come to gain interests generated specifically by the fact that duties not to use particular items *are owed to me*. Perhaps I come, through various psychological mechanisms, to gain great pleasure (and hence develop an interest) in people's thinking of me as 'propertied',

[41] For theorists who stress this status interest, but look in my view primarily at the status constituted by *natural* rather than *legally created* duties owed to the person, see Kamm (1996) and Nagel (2002). See also Cruft (2013b).

[42] Ripstein makes a somewhat similar point in referring to the 'rights theory of interests' (2013: 180). Note that I do not suggest that *all* interests are conjured into existence by being owed a duty; only this special status interest is.

[43] By denying that any duties are undirected, Kramer would deny this possibility (1998).

and this requires that my property rights be respected.[44] Referring to this *rights-created* interest in order to explain why the duty not to use certain property is owed to me would be circular.

V. Avoiding Circularity for Kramer and Wenar

Non-circular versions of Kramer's or Wenar's theory must exclude both rights-created *status* interests and rights-created *contingent* interests from those 'typical' (Kramer) or 'role/kind-based' (Wenar) interests which purportedly identify the people to whom a duty is owed.[45] But once these circular interests are excluded, Kramer's and Wenar's theories fail to give adequate necessary and sufficient conditions for a duty's being owed to someone.

I have to confess that I cannot make up my mind whether Kramer's theory fails as a *necessary* condition on a duty's being owed to someone. The vast majority of rights enjoin actions which are typically beneficial, in the relevant non-circular sense, for the right-holder. On the basis of my controversial moralised conception of interests, I would argue that fulfilment of *morally unjustified* conventional or legal rights—such as the crime boss's right to her protection money—do not typically serve the right-holder's interests, yet they are still genuine rights. But I recognise that this is too controversial a conception of interests on which to rest my argument without further defence.[46] My real concern is with morally justified duties owed to people to allow them to perform morally justified roles. Such is our friend, the judge's right to be unimpeded in sentencing. To determine whether fulfilling a duty to *phi* is owed to the role-bearer, Kramer's theory tells us to ask whether the duty-bearer's *phi*-ing necessarily places the relevant person in a situation that would typically be in the interests of a human in context.[47] To avoid circularity, we must overlook both the status interest created by the right and any interests typically causally created by (and hence 'downstream' of) the right. But what interests, in being unimpeded in sentencing, borne by humans who are judges, does this latter requirement exclude? If the relevant role-creating duties were undirected or were owed to someone else (so judges were not wronged by being impeded, even though such impeding would be wrong), would they still have interests in sentencing unimpeded? Or are these interests causally downstream of

[44] Note that this is distinct from the status interest my property rights create, for this status interest is served by respect for my right independently of whether I take pleasure in such respect.

[45] To put this in terms of Kramer's 'Bentham's Test' (*cf* Kramer 1998: 80–83; 2010), detriments which consist solely of either *rights-created status detriments* or *detrimental impacts on interests contingently created downstream from rights* must be excluded from the range of detriments which, through their sufficiency for a breach, identify those to whom a duty is owed.

[46] Kramer has shown himself willing to adopt a more subjective conception of interests which would ascribe interests to the crime boss (see Kramer 2001: 84–85); I reject this conception but cannot defend my rejection here.

[47] I here set aside the animal and group case.

the duty's being directed at judges? Kramer would robustly claim that the relevant interests are straightforwardly unproblematic and non-circular here: interests in, among other things, doing one's socially defined duty. But I do not think there is such a general interest: it all depends what one's socially defined duty is. If, as in the case of the modern judge, we should feel at least some moral uncertainty about the value of this socially defined duty, then this I think generates a matching uncertainty about one's interest in being able to perform this duty. *Perhaps* we should be penal abolitionists in which case being impeded in sentencing would help the judge avoid unjustifiably harming the convict. If penal abolitionism were correct, then I am not sure that fulfilling the duty to let the judge sentence unimpeded would typically serve judges—not even merely *pro tanto* serve them; yet surely this would not stop judges having the legal right to sentence without impediment. So, if penal abolitionism were correct, we might have a counterexample in which judges have a right but fail to satisfy Kramer's theory.

Yet on balance I am unpersuaded by penal abolitionism, even though I retain nagging concerns about the role of judge. And while this saves Kramer's theory as a necessary condition, it should I think leave us with doubts about whether the condition he identifies is really what determines to whom a duty is owed. Surely if the legal system is set up in the way that it is actually set up, then judges have the right in question independently of the merits of their role—and hence, it turns out, independently of some of the central interests of judges.[48]

This concern manifests itself in the fact that Kramer's theory is less successful as a *sufficient* condition for right-holding.[49] One way to put this concern is to say that by allowing interests generated contingently downstream from the existence of a (initially undirected) *duty* to qualify as interests to which we can refer in working out whether fulfilling the duty would necessarily be typically beneficial for a human, we risk overgenerating rights. Consider again the conventional duty borne by private soldiers to salute in the presence of sergeants. It is possible, I have suggested, for an army to take such a duty to be owed only to the monarch and not to sergeants. This is possible whether or not the typical sergeant has an interest in being so saluted, given contemporary mores. Of course, it is very likely—given how the structure within which saluting occurs helps sergeants get on with their work—that sergeants will have an interest in private soldiers fulfilling their duty to salute, whether or not this duty is conceived as owed to sergeants. But even if sergeants do have this interest, which being saluted serves necessarily, we should be willing to see the duty as owed not to them but rather the monarch if, for example,

[48] I would make similar points, *mutatis mutandis*, about parents' rights to punish their children (see Kramer's essay in this volume, sections V.E–V.G); I am simply unsure how far parents have an interest in punishing their children that is independent of the interests created by their role-constituting *rights* to punish them.

[49] Note that Kramer himself eschews giving sufficient conditions for right-holding (see, eg, 2010: 32). But Bentham's test in Kramer (1998) and as refined in Kramer (2010) is clearly best interpreted as giving a condition sufficient for identifying to whom a given duty is owed (ie, who holds a right correlative to a given duty).

the military code makes this explicit ('private soldiers owe it to the monarch (and not to anyone else) to salute in the presence of sergeants'). Such a conception of the duty seems possible no matter the interests of sergeants. Similarly, being a *named beneficiary* to a contract or promise means that fulfilment of the relevant contractual or promissory duty necessarily benefits one; but again I think it should be an open question whether the duty in such a case is owed to one.[50]

Wenar's theory, if taken non-circularly, also comes close to extensional accuracy but faces counterexamples. Exceptions to it as a necessary condition include property rights. Suppose that everyone except Sarah, the owner of Greenacre, has a duty to keep off Greenacre. *Qua owner of Greenacre,* Sarah will necessarily desire that, or have an interest that, others fulfil this duty. But, as Wenar notes, the role 'owner of Greenacre' circularly presupposes that the role-bearer holds the rights correlating with duties to keep off Greenacre.[51] To avoid this circularity, Wenar needs to claim that *as the person associated with Greenacre on certain legal deeds, or associated with Greenacre via a certain process specified non-circularly (gift, inheritance),* Sarah in this non-circular role necessarily desires or has an interest in others keeping off Greenacre. And it is just not clear that this is true. *Must* Sarah, as the person associated with the deeds for Greenacre held at the Land Registry, necessarily want others' duties to keep off Greenacre to be fulfilled? Without already ascribing to Sarah a status-based interest in Greenacre *as right-holder* (eg, without assuming that being named at the Land Registry makes her a right-holder), we cannot find a role for Sarah that guarantees her a role-based interest or desire of the type we need. Yet she is owner of Greenacre nonetheless, and is owed others' duties to keep off it.

May's essay in this volume gives exceptions to Wenar's theory as a sufficient condition for a duty's being owed to someone.[52] He considers the duty, under the laws of cricket, borne by a bowler to inform the umpire if he wishes to change his mode of delivery. As May puts it,

> the umpire has a duty-derived [and hence role-based] desire to conduct the match in accordance with the laws of the game, and accordingly desires that the players cooperate with her in this regard. ... She therefore wants the bowler to inform her if he intends to start bowling around the wicket.[53]

But, May suggests plausibly, the bowler's duty to inform the umpire is not owed to her: 'It is the batsman on strike, not the umpire, who would most plausibly be wronged if the bowler tried to take him by surprise unfairly'.[54] May gives several further, more morally significant examples.

[50] See Kramer's essay in this volume, section X.A, and also Sreenivasan's essay in this volume, section V, for a full exposition of how Kramer's account struggles with third-party beneficiaries to contracts.

[51] Wenar (2013: 212, fn 21).

[52] May, this volume.

[53] ibid 94.

[54] ibid. (Note that in this paragraph I follow May's use of male and female pronouns.) Against May's contention, one might claim that the umpire also has a right correlative to the bowler's duty. I must

The key point—recognised by May's careful distinction between different sorts of role-based desires including role-based desires about one's *own* actions and role-based desires about the cooperative actions of *others*[55]—is that some role- and kind-based desires and interests are generated by the fact that the relevant role or kind involves holding *rights*, while other role- and kind-based desires and interests are generated by separate, rights-independent aspects of the role or kind. At one point, Wenar focuses attention on roles defined centrally by duties, and the role-based desires these create: desires to be able to do one's duty, such as parents' desire to be able to fulfil their duty to look after their children.[56] But it is doubtful, I think, that the presence of a *duty-derived* role-based desire *must necessarily* make any additional supportive duties borne by others to help the duty-bearer fulfil her own duties into supportive duties *owed to that duty-bearer*. Wenar assumes this, however, in arguing that because parents have a duty-derived role-based desire to look after their children, other people's or institutions' duties to help parents (including the state's duty to pay child benefits) will be *owed to* parents.[57]

I do not think that the presence of a *duty-derived* role-based desire should compel us to conclude this: while the British child benefit system takes the duty to make child benefit payments to be owed to parents, alternative systems could plausibly take such duties (to make certain payments to parents in order to help them fulfil their role) to be owed to *children* or to something else (perhaps *the community at large*). I think the polity can decide how it wants to conceive of such duties—without being bound to take them as owed to parents, despite the fact that parents have a role-based desire to care for their children. Wenar's theory denies this.[58] My own view, instead, is that some role- or kind-based desires or interests are *duty-derived*, some are *kind or role norms*,[59] but others are *rights-derived*. It is only the presence of the latter that compels us to see duties whose fulfilment satisfies these desires or interests as *owed to* the bearer of the role- or kind-based desire or interest. This, of course, is because rights-derived desires or interests circularly owe their existence to the prior existence of a directed duty (right), a directed duty partly constitutive of the relevant role.

confess that I do not see it, and I certainly would not want to be compelled—as Wenar's theory compels us—to see this. Thanks to Mark McBride for pressing this point. One might also question whether the umpire *qua* umpire really wants the bowler to inform her of the change, or simply wants to umpire the match in accordance with the rules by imposing appropriate penalties etc. Again, I do not see this: to my mind, the role of umpire comes with a role-based desire that each player abide by the rules. Thanks to Leif Wenar for pressing this.

[55] ibid 95.

[56] Wenar (2013: 215–16).

[57] ibid.

[58] Note that Wenar's theory does not deny that the relevant duties could be owed to children or the community at large (for these bodies might have the relevant kind-based desires); what it denies is that they could be *unowed* to parents, given the kind-based desires parents bear for their children's wellbeing. I think a polity could decide that the duties are not owed to parents; Wenar rules this out.

[59] Wenar discusses both of these at ibid and again (2013: 221–23).

VI. The Way Forward

Because any morally justified rights generate a status interest (on the right-holder's part) in the right's being fulfilled, and many rights—justified and unjustified—also contingently create further 'downstream' interests in their own fulfilment, our assessment of interest theories of rights can easily be led into circular reasoning, locating purportedly rights-marking interests on the basis of our prior convictions that rights are present. This, I suggest, is one reason why it is hard to find counterexamples to either Kramer's or Wenar's theory.[60] Purged of the circular interests, the theories struggle. While I do not think the considerations in the previous section are unassailable, to my mind they suggest that we should look elsewhere for a theory of rights.

But they also suggest that whatever we find in other places should do justice to the truth in the interest (and indeed the will) theory: that *almost all* morally justified rights enjoin actions that necessarily are typically beneficial to the right-holder in context; that these actions will necessarily serve some *right-derived* role- or kind-based interest of the right-holder; and that these actions will be demandable on the right-holder's behalf.[61] Another point that any theory should accommodate is that Raz's account is correct as a sufficient but not necessary condition of right-holding: *if* a human's or animal's interest generates a duty, then the duty is owed to that human or animal. It is just that many duties are owed to right-holders but grounded on factors other than the right-holder's interests (even though in the vast majority of cases fulfilling such rights serves the right-holder's interests). A further point to accommodate is that morally justified rights mark the sphere of respect for the right-holder, and hence generate the status interest outlined in section IV. A good theory should accommodate all this. Nonetheless, we have not (yet) arrived at a theory that delivers non-circular conditions both necessary and sufficient for right-holding. What makes it the case that a duty is owed to someone, and hence is a right, will, I think, be something beyond either interest or will theory—something which explains the truths we have gleaned from the two theories.[62]

[60] By making rights *grounded* in interests, Raz guards against this circularity: looking for a ground diverts attention away from interests created by the rights. (Something similar is true of Sreenivasan's approach.) But see section II above for the suggestion that such circularity enters into Raz's own interpretation of his theory.

[61] The last point is what I see as the truth gleaned in section I above from discussion of the will theory.

[62] For my own alternative theory—that rights are '*addressive*' duties, duties whose form makes apt (in appropriate circumstances) the same sort of first-personal apprehension by right-holders that all duties make apt for duty-bearers; see Cruft (forthcoming). Many thanks to Mark McBride, Leif Wenar and all the participants at a workshop at the National University of Singapore for assistance.

References

Christie, N (1981) *Limits to Pain: The Role of Punishment in Penal Policy* (London: Martin Robertson).

Cruft, R (2004) 'Rights: Beyond Interest Theory and Will Theory?' 23 *Law and Philosophy* 347.

—— (2013a) 'Introduction' (Symposium on Rights and the Direction of Duties) 123 *Ethics* 195.

—— (2013b) 'Why is it Disrespectful to Violate Rights?' 113 *Proceedings of the Aristotelian Society* 201.

—— (forthcoming) *Human Rights, Ownership, and the Individual* (Oxford: Oxford University Press).

Feinberg, J (1970) 'The Nature and Value of Rights' 4 *Journal of Value Inquiry* 243.

Hart, HLA (1955) 'Are There Any Natural Rights?' 64 *Philosophical Review* 175.

—— (1973) 'Bentham on Legal Rights' in AWB Simpson (ed), *Oxford Essays in Jurisprudence: Second Series* (Oxford: Oxford University Press).

Kamm, FM (1996) *Morality, Mortality, Vol II: Rights, Duties, and Status* (New York: Oxford University Press).

—— (2002) 'Rights' in J Coleman and S Shapiro (eds), *The Oxford Handbook of Jurisprudence and Philosophy of Law* (Oxford: Oxford University Press).

Kramer, MH (1998) 'Rights Without Trimmings' in MH Kramer, NE Simmonds and H Steiner, *A Debate Over Rights. Philosophical Enquiries* (Oxford: Clarendon Press).

—— (2001) 'Getting Rights Right' in MH Kramer (ed), *Rights, Wrongs and Responsibilities* (Basingstoke: Palgrave Macmillan).

—— (2010) 'Refining the Interest Theory of Rights' 55 *The American Journal of Jurisprudence* 31.

Kramer, MH and Steiner, H (2007) 'Theories of Rights: Is There a Third Way?' 27 *Oxford Journal of Legal Studies* 281.

MacCormick, DN (1977) 'Rights in Legislation' in PMS Hacker and J Raz (eds), *Law, Morality and Society: Essays in Honour of HLA Hart* (Oxford: Clarendon Press).

—— (1982) 'Children's Rights: A Test-Case for Theories of Right' in N MacCormick, *Legal Right and Social Democracy: Essays in Legal and Political Philosophy* (Oxford: Clarendon Press).

May, S (2012) 'Moral Status and the Direction of Duties' 123 *Ethics* 113.

Nagel, T (2002) 'Personal Rights and Public Space' in T Nagel, *Concealment and Exposure & Other Essays* (New York: Oxford University Press).

Raz, J (1984) 'Legal Rights' 4 *Oxford Journal of Legal Studies* 1.

—— (1986) *The Morality of Freedom* (Oxford: Clarendon Press).

—— (1994) 'Rights and Individual Well-Being' in J Raz, *Ethics in the Public Domain: Essays in the Morality of Law and Politics* (Oxford: Clarendon Press).

Ripstein, A (2013) 'Possession and Use' in in J Penner and HE Smith (eds), *Philosophical Foundations of Property Law* (Oxford: Oxford University Press).
Simmonds, NE (1998) 'Rights at the Cutting Edge' in MH Kramer, NE Simmonds and H Steiner (eds), *A Debate Over Rights: Philosophical Enquiries* (Oxford: Clarendon Press).
Skorupski, J (2010) *The Domain of Reasons* (Oxford: Oxford University Press).
Sreenivasan, G (2005) 'A Hybrid Theory of Claim-Rights' 25 *Oxford Journal of Legal Studies* 257.
—— (2010) 'Duties and Their Direction' 120 *Ethics* 465.
Steiner, H (1994) *An Essay on Rights* (Oxford: Blackwell).
—— (1998) 'Working Rights' in MH Kramer, NE Simmonds and H Steiner (eds), *A Debate Over Rights. Philosophical Enquiries* (Oxford: Clarendon Press).
Thompson, M (2004) 'What is it to Wrong Someone? A Puzzle about Justice' in RJ Wallace, P Pettit, S Scheffler and M Smith (eds), *Reason and Value: Themes from the Moral Philosophy of Joseph Raz* (Oxford: Oxford University Press).
Wenar, L (2008) 'The Analysis of Rights' in MH Kramer et al (eds), *The Legacy of HLA Hart: Legal, Political, and Moral Philosophy* (Oxford: Oxford University Press).
—— (2013) 'The Nature of Claim-Rights' 123 *Ethics* 202.

9

Adequacy Constraints for a Theory of Rights

SIEGFRIED VAN DUFFEL

The twentieth century saw a long debate over the nature of rights. Recently the dynamics of that debate have somewhat shifted. For decades, it had been dominated by two sharply opposed accounts. Proponents of the 'Will Theory' of rights have regarded individual freedom, autonomy, control or sovereignty as fundamental to the concept of a right, while proponents of the 'Interest Theory' have argued that rights protect people's interests or (aspects of) their wellbeing—and those interests could be other than our interest in freedom or control. In recent years, however, the dispute between Interest Theory and Will Theory is increasingly perceived as having reached a stalemate. Despite the fact that arguments have been going back and forth for several decades and that defences of both theories have become more sophisticated, it is clear that proponents on both sides have not been able to respond adequately to the best objections raised against their preferred analyses. Hence, more and more philosophers are becoming convinced that the truth about rights may well lie elsewhere than in an improved version of either Will Theory or Interest Theory.

Questions regarding the nature of rights can be pitched at different levels. First, one type of enquiry is to ask which normative incidents are commonly or properly regarded as rights. At the beginning of the twentieth century, Hohfeld distinguished four different *fundamental conceptions* which he thought lawyers have in mind when they use the word 'right'. Since then philosophers have debated whether all of these are genuine rights. Virtually no one has doubted that claim-rights are rights, but the status of liberties, for example, has been much more controversial. Some have argued that all rights are clusters of these fundamental conceptions. The aim of such enquiries is to reveal the (proper) reference of the word 'right'.

Second, when we have determined the reference of the word, another question we may ask is why these, and only these, normative incidents are commonly identified as rights. Or, to put this question slightly differently, what guides our identification of certain normative incidents as rights? One possible answer to this question is to identify what rights do for right-holders. Leif Wenar (2005), for example, has argued that any right has one of six different functions.

Third, even when we are convinced that rights do indeed have these different functions, we may still ask (as indeed Wenar does) why 'these particular six functions [are] associated with our concept of a right?' (2005: 251). Is there nothing more than mere linguistic coincidence to the fact that rights should be characterised by one of these functions? Is there something that rights have in common? The only difference with the second level, then, is that at the third level we will want a unified explanation of what makes some normative incident into a right. I shall suggest that a new analysis of rights which attempts to answer this last question should satisfy some adequacy constraints. Some of the constraints, however, are to do with issues at the two other levels.

Different authors have approached this question with divergent interests and assumptions, so it will help to clarify mine. First, my aim is to elucidate the nature of rights in general, not specifically that of legal rights. Differences between moral and legal rights will for the most part be set aside. Second, my purpose is to clarify the ordinary understanding of rights. It is often assumed that this ordinary understanding may in important respects be different from that of scholars. I do not want to deny this. Nevertheless, in their debates over the concept of rights scholars often rely on intuitions that they expect their audience to share. Here I will assume that the aim is to provide a conception of rights that accommodates these commonly held intuitions. Third, it is sometimes suggested that the ordinary understanding of rights may be too vague, or perhaps even inconsistent, to be of any use for philosophical reflection. Consequently, philosophers often see it as their task to carve out a coherent subset of these intuitions so as to provide scholars with an adequate tool for scholarly research. Wenar (2008: 265) has remarked that it has not been established that our ordinary understanding of rights is frequently vague and contradictory. In his contribution to this volume, Kramer takes issue with this. He points to Hohfeld as someone who has painstakingly pointed out many instances of confusion and mistaken inferences by lawyers and judges alike and to his own discussion of examples involving legal philosophers. Hohfeld uses his examples to show that the failure of jurists to distinguish claim-rights from liberties or powers or immunities sometimes led them to make invalid inferences. In other words, his concern is with the first level that we identified above, and he suggested that judicial reasoning could be improved by clearly distinguishing between the different concepts that underlie the indiscriminate use of the word 'right'. There is no point in denying that jurists and philosophers alike can profit from such disentanglements and clarifications of ordinary rights. However, if Kramer wants to insist that a coherent account of rights cannot be accomplished without stipulating away some of our strongly held intuitions about the topic, then he will have to do more than simply detail confusions in ordinary uses, or—for that matter—confused statements of legal philosophers. Frankly, I do not know what could be said to establish such a claim. On the other hand, it seems clear that the only way to disprove it would be to provide an account of rights that captures our stable intuitions on the topic. In my 2012 article I have thrown doubt on the idea that the classical statements of both Will Theory (eg, Hart 1982: 162) and Interest Theory (eg, Raz 1986: 165) are best construed as attempts to capture 'all and only rights-assertions that make sense to competent users of the language' (Wenar 2013: 203). I do not assume, however, that there is a need to stipulatively discard commonly held assumptions about rights in order to arrive at a coherent conception of rights.

Any new theory or conceptual analysis should do better than the alternatives it seeks to replace. For an analysis of rights, 'better' means that it should more adequately capture our common understanding of which rights there are, how they function in moral and legal thought, and what these rights do for their possessors. In view of the current state of the debate, any new analysis of rights should aspire to combine the best features of (respective versions of) Will Theory and Interest Theory, while avoiding the defects of each. I will identify four adequacy constraints on a new conceptual analysis. The first three can be broadly construed as part of extensional adequacy, whereas the fourth falls squarely under the heading of intensional adequacy.

I. Extensional Adequacy

By 'extensional adequacy', I shall mean the idea that the overall adequacy, success, or acceptability of an analysis of rights is augmented to the extent that it identifies as 'rights' those normative incidents that we commonly regard as rights and does not classify as rights any normative incidents that are not commonly recognized as rights. Extensional adequacy of existing accounts has been fiercely debated in the recent literature. Will Theorists have, for example, blamed Interest Theory for identifying the wrong person as the right-holder in cases involving third-party beneficiaries. Interest Theorists on their part have chastised Will Theory for failing to accommodate rights of children and the mentally disabled, or for denying that criminal law generates legal rights for citizens. Since many will agree that Interest Theory more adequately covers the incidents we normally regard as rights, my discussion of extensional adequacy will mainly focus on the shortcomings of Interest Theory. It will be a major advantage for a new analysis of rights if it can improve on (the best version of) Interest Theory and even better if it can also accommodate the incidents that are more adequately captured by versions of Will Theory. To see how it might do so, I shall start by identifying Interest Theory's three main weaknesses in terms of extensional adequacy.

A. Identification of Possible Right-Holders

The first weakness has to do with the identification of possible right-holders (*Rechtssubjekte* in German). The duties of parents to protect the wellbeing of their children are routinely construed as correlative to rights held by those children.

But Will Theory seems committed to denying that children can have rights.[1] Since most of us think there is something awkward about not ascribing rights to children, this counts against Will Theory as an adequate analysis of our concept of rights. Will Theory, it seems, excessively restricts the class of possible right-holders. Interest Theory, however, faces the challenge of cutting off an implausible proliferation of possible right-holders. When parents have duties not to mistreat their children, we are inclined to think that these children have rights correlative to their parents' duties. Duties of people not to walk on lawns also protect the wellbeing of the grass, but we don't think of the blades of grass as having correlative rights. The best explanation of the difference, it seems, is that children *can have rights*, whereas plants cannot. That is, we do not think of blades of grass as possible right-holders. If that is the case, then a conceptual analysis would need an account of the distinction between beings that can, and beings that cannot, have rights.

Not everyone believes this to be an issue that can, or should, be resolved at the level of conceptual analysis. Matthew Kramer tells us that it is 'necessary but insufficient for the actual holding of a right by a person X ... that the right, when actual, preserves one or more of X's interests' (1998: 62). In a follow-up article, he clarifies that Interest Theory's 'focus on the preservation of well-being rather than on the exercise of choices enables it to leave open the possibility of ascribing legal rights to animals and dead people and mentally incapacitated people' (2001: 30). Interest Theory 'enables' such ascription, but does not require it. The same holds for other organisms and things: Interest Theory does not, according to Kramer, proscribe ascriptions of legal rights to lawns (when the law forbids us to walk on the grass) or even buildings, but such ascriptions are not entailed by the theory either. Since Interest Theory enables, but does not require, recognition of children or animals as right-holders, the analysis must be supplemented with moral argumentation before we can decide whether or not to ascribe rights to children or animals (Kramer 2001: 32ff, 37).

The question whether or not a conceptual analysis of rights *should* aim to provide a criterion for deciding whether or not to ascribe rights to children or animals raises complicated issues, though, in the end, I don't believe it can be answered *in abstracto*. Why should anyone think that conceptual analysis can't, or shouldn't, answer this question? Consider, as an example, the suggestion that the change in our willingness to regard animals as possible right-holders is itself the result of moral argument. The influence of utilitarianism could be seen as paving the way for a more expansive conception of possible right-holders. If a utilitarian has convinced us that suffering matters morally, and that the ability to suffer is a basis for having rights, then the realisation that animals may suffer would be a reason to think of them as having rights. And if one grants that this development did not

[1] A Will Theorist may, of course, insist that children can have rights but are unable, until maturity, to exercise them. Still, this move seems motivated primarily by the desire to avoid a counterintuitive conclusion.

involve a change in the concept of rights, then one is committed to the independence of the concept from the identification of possible right-holders. And if the concept of rights is independent of how we identify possible right-holders, then an analysis of the concept of rights will have nothing to say about who may hold rights. The problem with this suggestion is that, even if we grant that people's stance towards possible right-holders may change, it is difficult to see how any amount of moral argument might lead us to conceive of lawns or solar systems as having rights. And if we were to encounter someone who did think of lawns as having rights, it would seem appropriate to think of her as having a different concept of rights. Again, this is not an issue that can be settled *in abstracto*, but my suggestion is that we should not in advance rule out the possibility that a conceptual analysis might explain the relevant facts. And if we find that it can, a conceptual analysis that can explain why we do not see lawns as possible right-holders would seem decidedly preferable.

Joseph Raz does include a criterion for a possible right-holder in his Interest Theory. He suggests two criteria for 'having a right', namely (1) that one *can have* rights, and (2) that an aspect of one's wellbeing (one's interest) is a sufficient reason for holding some other person(s) to be under a duty. An individual is capable of having rights, according to Raz, 'if and only if either his well-being is of ultimate value or he is an "artificial person" (eg, a corporation)' (1986: 166). Raz also thinks that those 'who regard the existence and well-being of (some) dogs as merely derivatively valuable … are committed to the view that dogs can have no rights' (1986: 178). Personally, I find it hard to assess whether I, or anyone else, judges the *wellbeing* of human beings to be of ultimate value, simply because I find the notion of 'ultimate value' rather obscure. Similarly, I wonder whether those who see no conceptual awkwardness in saying that animals have rights are committed to judging *their existence and wellbeing* to be of ultimate value. If we do grant this, however, Raz's proposal seems to be on the right track.

The chief drawback of Raz's proposal is that it achieves extensional adequacy of possible right-holders at the cost of two oddities. First, it is at least peculiar that we should be committed to regarding the wellbeing (and existence) of animals to be of ultimate value before we can regard them as right-holders, while we have no problem acknowledging that corporations—whose value we certainly do not regard as ultimate—can have rights. Second, the idea that (apart from artificial persons) rights are held only by those whose wellbeing is of ultimate value, is strangely disjointed from the fact that our rights often protect interests that are of very little, and mere instrumental, value. For example, as a faculty member, I may have a right to add a point to the agenda of the department meeting. It seems strange, to say the least, that my wellbeing must be of ultimate value for me to be able to have such a right. A criterion for the ability to have rights which avoids such oddities would—other things being equal—be preferable to Raz's.

We can illustrate one of the chief advantages of both Raz's and Kramer's proposal by considering another, much more straightforward suggestion.

For Interest Theorists, a natural way of explaining our refusal to construe blades of grass as possible right-holders would be to say that they have no interests. If rights protect interests, then beings that have no interests cannot have rights. Two obvious candidates for an explanation as to why blades of grass have no interests are (1) that they are not sentient[2] or (2) that they have no conative life (they do not desire their continued existence, have no urges, purposes, and so forth). However, neither sentience nor conation seems necessary for having interests. Organisations, companies and even states have interests, but they are obviously not sentient. Conation does not seem necessary either. Unborn children or members of future generations do not have any conative life (yet) but this doesn't prevent us from thinking of them as having interests.[3]

Even if we disregarded such entities as organisations and members of future generations, another problem with regarding sentience, or conation, as a necessary condition for being a possible right-holder is that we would be drawing a sharp boundary where there is none. Our intuitions regarding possible right-holders are simply not as clear-cut as any such criterion would make them out to be. That is not to deny, of course, that some people may draw sharp lines in their judgement regarding possible right-holders. But such lines—if they are drawn at all—are drawn in different places. And most of us, especially those who have not considered the issue as academic philosophers, do not draw a sharp line between possible right-holders and others. What we have, instead, is something of a spectrum with certainty on both ends and a good deal of uncertainty in between those ends. Almost no one doubts that sane adult human beings are possible right-holders. Conversely, few people think that it makes sense to ascribe rights to stones or mountains or buildings. In between those two ends, our confidence that a being is a possible right-holder typically diminishes the further we move away from the prototypical right-holder. Thus, we have both interpersonal disagreement and individual fuzziness. In such a situation, philosophers may well be tempted to generate clarity by stipulating some criterion, but if we are serious about capturing our actual usage of the term 'right' then we should resist this temptation.

Both the proposals of Kramer and Raz have the considerable advantage that they leave room for the relatively uncertain boundaries of our conception of possible right-holders. This is exactly as it should be. If our aim is to do conceptual analysis, we should avoid drawing sharp boundaries where there are none.[4] A new analysis of rights, then, should aim to explain why adult human beings are

[2] As Bentham famously wrote 'the question is not, Can they reason? nor, Can they talk? but, Can they suffer?' (1996: ch 17n).

[3] It seems plausible, though, that having either sentience or conation is sufficient for having interests. Feinberg (1974: 49) argues that future generations will—when they come into being—have rights against us that we not pass on to them a world that is a used-up garbage heap. Johan Brännmark (2016) argues that these rights should be construed as generational rights. But either way, one may argue, as Cecile Fabre (2009) does, that future generations have no interests yet, because they cannot be harmed before they are conceived.

[4] Wenar (2013: 22) affirms the same. Thanks to Mark McBride for reminding me.

uncontroversially considered to be possible right-holders. It should also aim to explain why our confidence in the appropriateness of ascribing rights to a being decreases gradually when we move from human adults to children, to the mentally disabled, to infants, higher animals, lower animals, other organisms, and inanimate objects. And, finally, it should do so in a manner that is as little ad hoc as possible.

B. Accommodating Liberties, Powers and Immunities

Often, the analysis of rights has focused on claim-rights—ie rights that are, in Hohfeld's terminology, correlative to duties of other people. So, Anne's claim-right not to be molested by Ben is correlative to Ben's duty not to molest Anne. As Hohfeld pointed out, however, sometimes we use the word 'right' to refer to a *liberty* (an absence of a duty). Upon acquiring a driving licence, I am relieved of a duty I previously had, not to drive a car on the road, and acquire a liberty to do so. Other rights, like the right of people to marry the partner of their choice, are legal or normative *powers* (the ability to change a normative relationship). Yet other rights are *immunities*. They correlate with a lack of ability of someone else to change your normative position. Your right not to be arbitrarily divested of your property correlates with a *disability* (absence of a power) of government officials to arbitrarily divest you of your property.

Since not all our rights are claim-rights, it will be an advantage for a conceptual analysis of rights if it can accommodate rights that are not claim-rights. This should be fairly obvious, but apparently it's not. There is a strong tendency to regard rights as somehow tied to *normative constraints* on the behaviour of others. Following George Rainbolt, we may call this the 'normative constraints thesis'. The thesis comes in several versions, some more thoughtful than others. The Interest Theory and some versions of Will Theory can be, and often have been, interpreted as primarily analyses of the direction of duties. Lyons' 'qualified beneficiary theory', for example, simply equates having a right with standing in some qualified sense to benefit from someone's performance of a duty (1994: 29–30). Other versions of the 'normative constraints thesis' equate having a right with one's interest being a *reason* for holding some other person to be under a duty (Raz 1986: 166), or having one's interest protected by the imposition of normative constraints on the acts of others (MacCormick 1982: 154).[5] Hillel Steiner—a Will Theorist—has no qualms identifying constraint on others' conduct as an uncontested feature of rights (1994: 59). George Rainbolt agrees that rights constrain the acts of others (2006: 27). And again, Kramer and Steiner have argued that Interest Theory and Will Theory are best understood as confined to claim-rights accompanied by immunities (2007: 295).

[5] Elsewhere, however, MacCormick does seem to allow for 'naked' liberties as rights (1977: 205).

None of these authors, I presume, would deny that we often recognise rights to do things (say, to drive a car after acquiring a driving licence).[6] The contention is rather that a liberty to do something only counts as a 'right' to do it if the action is in some appropriate sense protected by constraints on other people's behaviour. One seemingly obvious way in which one may be protected in the exercise of a liberty is if others have a duty not to interfere with your doing what you have a liberty to do. Call this a 'vested' liberty.[7] The question how many of our liberties are protected by duties of non-interference is not easy to answer, since the notion of 'interference' is much less straightforward than we are often led to believe (see, for example, Makinson 1986: 415–18). Consider my right to sit on a bench in the park. Suppose I walk to the park on a Sunday morning intent on exercising my right but I find someone is sitting on the bench (it happens to be a single-seater). If my right is only a Hohfeldian liberty, it does not entail a claim-right against other people that they get up to let me sit on it (after all, other people have a right to sit on the bench as well). In one possible sense of the word 'interfering' this person *is* interfering with my plan to sit on the bench. We would also agree, however, that if *this* is what is meant by interference, then my right to sit on the bench is not protected by duties to non-interference. The same goes for my right to drive on the road (traffic jams may block my way), a basketball player's right to score a three-pointer, a businessman's right to out-compete others. Thus, most of our liberties, even the liberties that we identify as rights, do not seem to be protected by specific duties prohibiting interference with their exercise.

This has not troubled those who think that rights constrain the acts of others. The standard response is that even if people may 'interfere' in several ways with my attempt to sit on the bench, there are certain things that they may not do to me (assault, harass, threaten, etc) and these general obligations will in some sense protect my attempt to exercise my liberty. When we recognise liberties as rights, we do so because they are protected by a collection of more general duties that are not correlative to the liberty,[8] but that constitute—in Hart's terminology—a protective perimeter that protects us from *certain kinds of* interference. Call these 'protected liberties'. The normative constraints thesis would then hold that liberties which are not *vested* must be *protected* by such general duties if they are to be recognised as rights.

[6] As recognised, eg, by Hart (1982); Simmonds (1998); Cruft (2004); and Wenar (2005). But see Steiner (1994: 74). Williams (1956: 1142), while deploring the use of 'right' for 'liberty' acknowledges that liberties are called rights 'even in statutes'. In the following, I will simplify the issue by leaving immunities and powers largely aside.

[7] Following Hart's exegesis of Bentham, though Hart makes it clear that Bentham's category of a vested liberty was ambiguous between this and what I shall call a 'protected liberty'. See Hart (1984: 167, 171–73) Different authors have subsequently used different terminology. Most have followed Lindahl (1977: 17–18, 70–72), whereas Steiner (1994: 75) uses the term 'vested' for a liberty that is not protected by a 'correlative' claim against interference but (only) by a protective perimeter of general obligations.

[8] If we allow for the use of 'correlative' in a non-Hohfeldian sense of a duty not to interfere with the exercise of a liberty.

Before we ask whether liberties must be protected in order to count as rights, we should note that Alessandro Spena (2012) has convincingly argued that the standard examples (such as I've given) fail to make the case that some liberties do not entail claims to non-interference. We may simply be mistaken in thinking that I have a liberty to sit on the park bench. Perhaps my liberty is in fact narrower—say, a liberty to take a seat in case nobody else is already sitting on it. That would account for the fact that we don't think of the person sitting on the bench when I arrive as infringing on my right. And again, the basketball player may not have a liberty to score a three-pointer (achieving his goal being a legitimate part the description of the liberty) but only liberties to do certain things which may result in the scoring of a three-pointer (ibid). Be that as it may, the examples below will show that some liberties (under any description) may be entirely unprotected and still be regarded as rights.

In order to fully test the normative constraints thesis, we need to enquire whether we would recognise certain 'naked' liberties—ie liberties the exercise of which is protected neither by obligations not to interfere nor by a protective perimeter—as rights.[9] The problem is that the notion of a protective perimeter is both vague *and* weak. This is because there is no conceptual link between a liberty and the duties that may constitute a protective perimeter, and because the notion of a perimeter does not require it to be impenetrable. A soccer player's liberty to score a goal is protected from certain kinds of interference, but it is not violated if the goalkeeper stops the ball in its course. Consequently, it seems that *any* duty that renders illicit a potential interference with the exercise of a liberty may be regarded as constituting (part of) a protective perimeter. And since we always have many such duties (moral and legal), we hardly ever have liberties that are not protected. The only way to put to the test the normative constraints thesis, then, is to look for unusual examples. Unusual though they may be, the examples will show that we will recognise liberties as rights even when they are not accompanied by any protective perimeter.

One such example is the right of a convicted criminal to (attempt to) escape death. Brian Tierney (1997) has discussed a *quaestio* of Henry of Ghent who wondered 'whether one condemned to death can licitly flee'. It might seem that the criminal could not, since Henry wrote, 'the body of one condemned belongs more to the judge than some other temporal thing'. However, even though the judge 'had the power of capturing, holding and killing it ... the criminal had the power of using his body so as to preserve its life'. Henry went on to argue explicitly that this power was not only equitable, but licit (permitted by the law of nature), and not only licit but a right (*ius*) according to the law of nature (Tierney 1997: 83–85). Hobbes and Pufendorf would later argue along very similar lines that, although a judge has the right to put a convicted criminal to death, the criminal retains the right to attempt to escape death (Tierney 1997: 81–82). The point here is relatively simple: neither Henry of Ghent, nor Hobbes, nor Pufendorf found it inappropriate

[9] My use of 'naked' is different from, eg, Steiner (1994: 75), who allows naked liberties to be surrounded 'by a rather more penetrable perimeter'. I will assume that a liberty is only naked when there is no perimeter of general obligations.

to describe the (naked) liberty of a convicted criminal to try to escape death as a subjective natural right. Nor, for that matter, do any of us encounter any conceptual shock when we read that this liberty was so described. Yet the liberty is not protected by any general duties that enhance the prisoner's prospect of doing what he has a right to do. How much less protected can a right to escape death be than when one can be licitly chained and executed?

Another example is that of two enemy soldiers who face each other in a combat situation. Imagine that both parties are fighting a just war, and because both are combatants in action, we may presume that each is morally and legally permitted to kill the other. I did an anecdotal test with colleagues and friends and most found it perfectly suitable to describe this situation as one in which each has the right to kill the other. Again, this right is not protected by a protective perimeter of obligations. Indeed, what could count as a clearer example of absence of a protective perimeter than others being permitted to kill you before you were able to exercise your right to shoot?

Certainly these are exceptional situations, but the conclusion that can be drawn from them is nevertheless significant. The fact that we do not experience a conceptual shock when reading Henry of Ghent's, Hobbes's or Pufendorf's description of the right of a convicted criminal to try to escape death shows that the normative constraints view is mistaken. A liberty may be a right even when it is neither vested nor surrounded by a protective perimeter. More importantly, this also throws into doubt the assumption that we recognise other liberties as rights *because* they are either vested or protected. It is of course possible that we identify different rights for different reasons, but it would be surprising, to say the least, if we found that we identify liberties as rights when they are unaccompanied by a protective perimeter *and* that we only regard them as rights because of their protective perimeter when they are accompanied by one.

We may conclude that, other things being equal, a conceptual analysis that can recognise 'naked' liberties as rights will be preferable to one that cannot. At the same time, the analysis should not ignore the fact that we more readily recognise normative incidents as rights when they are accompanied by relevant constraints on the behaviour of others. Hence, it will be a major advantage for a conceptual analysis of rights if it can allow us to understand why it has seemed to so many that rights constrain the acts of others *and at the same time* allow that rights do not *entail* normative constraints.

C. Identifying Necessary and Sufficient Conditions for Holding a Right

An analysis of rights should explicate the necessary and sufficient conditions for holding a right.[10] Interest Theory is often considered to have fared better in this

[10] But see Kramer's contribution to this volume.

respect than Will Theory, but there are significant differences amongst Interest Theories. Consider first Lyons' interpretation of Bentham, which may not, strictly speaking, be an analysis of a right, since it only considers necessary conditions. According to this interpretation, one has a right whenever one 'stands to benefit' from the performance of a duty.[11] This is rather unsatisfactory as an account of our ordinary notion of rights. It is easy to think of counterexamples. I certainly 'stand to benefit' whenever someone abstains from murdering any of the people I love. Nobody thinks, however, that I have rights against everyone that they abstain from killing any of the people I love. In the literature, we can find two significant attempts to improve this aspect of Interest Theory. The first, whose foremost representative is Raz, appeals to the reason for holding someone under a duty. The second attempt, undertaken by Kramer, is to improve upon a criterion first developed by Bentham.

Raz's proposal would at first glance seem to resolve such troubles. A right-holder, for Raz, is someone whose interest is a sufficient reason for holding some other person(s) to be under a duty. Now it may be in my interest that other people don't kill someone I love, but *that* interest is not a sufficient reason for holding other persons to be under a duty. My loved one's own interest in not having her life taken away, on the other hand, almost certainly *is* a sufficient reason for holding others under a duty. In more recent work, however, Raz has observed—quite correctly—that the weight or importance given to a particular right often bears little correspondence to its value for the holder (1995: 47–48). For many rights, the rights-holder's interests are only part of the justifying reason. In some cases, rights are justified at least as much by other people's interests or the general interest than by the interests of the right-holder. Crucial, however, is that the interests of others matter in such cases 'only when they are served by serving the interest of the right-holder' (1995: 53). So a police officer's liberty to make an arrest and his claim-right not be interfered with while doing so are grounded in the public's interest to safety and that is served by the police officer's ability to perform an arrest in certain circumstances. Many civil and political rights fall in this category: the importance we attach to them is due to their contribution to the common good much more than the extent to which they protect interests of the right-holders. Some of these rights are clear counterexamples to Raz's earlier theory: in some cases—such as that of the policeman's right to make an arrest or a journalist's right not to disclose his sources—the (chief) reason for the existence of the right is an interest of the public, rather than that of the right-holder. Raz's modified theory, then, allows for third-party interests to be counted alongside the individual's interest for the purpose of identifying a right-holder, but only if these third-party interests are served by serving the right-holder's own interest (*cf* section IV of Sreenivasan's

[11] See Lyons (1994: 27–30). As Mark McBride correctly observed, this is not—strictly speaking—an analysis of rights. Nevertheless, Lyons' interpretation of Bentham is sometimes considered as an early proponent of Interest Theory. Hart (1982: 165ff) interprets Bentham differently.

essay in this collection).[12] Sreenivasan has called this a piggy-backing solution (since the weight of the interests of other parties are allowed to augment that of the right-holder for the justification of someone's duty) and he objects that this instrumentalises the individual's status as right-holder (2005: 265–66). Another problem with Raz's account is that some rights—like the liberty rights discussed in the previous section—simply are not reasons (let alone sufficient ones) for holding other people under a duty.

Matthew Kramer has suggested that Bentham's criterion for identifying right-holders can be modified so that it provides the necessary and sufficient conditions for being a right-holder. Kramer wrote that 'any person Z holds a right under a contract or norm if and only if a violation of a duty under the contract or norm can be established by simply showing that the duty-bearer has withheld a benefit from Z or has imposed some harm upon him' (1998: 81). But this does not establish sufficient conditions for right-holding. If someone kills someone I love, they surely have withheld from me the benefit of being with my loved one, but we do not normally think that the murder of someone I love is a violation of my right. Later, Kramer has added that the interest of the requisite sort cannot be *wholly vicarious*: it cannot reside wholly in the furtherance of somebody else's interests (Kramer and Steiner 2007: 303). This doesn't yet solve our problem. My interest in not having my loved ones killed is not wholly vicarious. I may well have an interest in my loved one being alive over and above the pleasure of knowing that my loved one is doing well. Recently the formulation has been further refined: someone holds a legal right under a contract or norm if and only if one set of facts minimally sufficient to establish a breach of the norm or contract includes the undergoing of a detriment of this person at the hands of someone who bears a duty under that contract or norm (Kramer 2010: 36–37). This seems to solve the aforesaid problem: me undergoing some detriment is sufficient but not minimally sufficient to establish that someone has breached a norm by murdering my loved one. Unfortunately, the solution comes at a huge cost.

First, the criterion may apply to legal rights, but it does not apply to certain moral rights, especially human rights. Most of us do not think of a human right to subsistence, for example, as existing only if we have already identified the relevant duty-bearer. This may not trouble those who are primarily interested in legal rights, but it is easy to see that a criterion that applies equally to both moral and legal rights is superior to the one offered by Bentham as modified by Kramer. Second, the criterion only works when we have already agreed to limit the category of right-holders to that of persons (sane adult human beings). However, if we were to omit the reference to persons, then the criterion would allow for talk

[12] David Enoch has suggested that an interest in the right-holder might give rise to the right, while the interest of the public might explain the stringency, but this doesn't seem plausible to me (*cf* Kamm 2002: 485).

of the rights of lawns when the law forbids people to walk on the grass in order to protect it from being trampled. As I have explained above, neither limiting rights to persons, nor ascribing rights to lawns is in line with how we think about rights. Third, Kramer's proposal does not allow us to capture rights that are not the correlatives of duties. The right (liberty) that one acquires with a driving licence, or the right (power) to get married are not adequately captured by the description. A new analysis of rights should aim to identify such right-holders. Additionally, it should aim to identify right-holders when the rights are powers, liberties and immunities.

II. Intensional Adequacy

A theory of rights may adequately capture the instances that we regard as rights (and thus be extensionally adequate) but still do so for the wrong reasons. We may illustrate this with Wenar's Kind-Desire Theory of claim-rights, which solves some of the problems we found with Raz's and Kramer's accounts. Within a system of norms that refers to entities under descriptions that are kinds ('parent', 'journalist', 'human' etc), Wenar maintains, claim-rights correspond to enforceable strict duties that members of the relevant kind want to be fulfilled (2013: 218–19). This analysis solves the problem of piggy-backing in that it does not require that duties are justified by the interests of the right-holder. Thus, if a legal system supports a statement that police officers have a duty not to force a journalist to disclose her sources, and a journalist, *qua* journalist, 'wants' police officers to fulfil their duty, the analysis will correctly identify the journalist as having a right.

It is difficult to dispel the suspicion that the reference to the journalist 'wanting' the duty to be fulfilled is just another way of saying that the journalist (*qua* journalist) has an interest in the fulfilment of the duty. A more important point, however, emerges when we ask *why* journalists 'want' these duties to be fulfilled. Obviously, the journalist (*qua* journalist) would want the fulfilment of these duties because this will help her to carry out her function. This point can be strengthened if we look at the examples given by Raz in his discussion of the same issue. Raz argued that the interests of others play a role in the justification of rights 'only when they are served by serving the right-holders' interests, only when helping the right-holder is the proper way to help others' (1995: 51). It is striking, however, that all the relevant cases of Wenar's are cases in which the interests of others augment the interest of the right-holder in order to justify the right—in which those interests are served by the action of the right-holder. This is true for journalists. It is also true for the rights of parents to child benefits, for the rights of people who support invalid parents or spouses to reductions in their tax liability, for the right of free speech, and even for the rather unusual case of a pregnant women not to be executed until she delivers her child. So, I suggest that even if Wenar's account correctly identifies the right-holders in such cases, it does so for the wrong reason. A new analysis of rights should not only aim to identify such right-holders but also aim to identify them for the right reason.

This point can be generalised if we take a step back and look at the debate between Will Theorists and Interest Theorists from a broader perspective. In the last two decades, the debate has become so heavily focused on showing that one account does better than the other in terms of extensional adequacy that one might be tempted to believe that this should be the principal yardstick to determine the adequacy of either theory. That, however, would be to misconstrue the dynamics of the debate. Herbert Hart, for example, recognised that his Will Theory did not accommodate many of the normative incidents to which we ordinarily apply the word 'right'. Nevertheless, he was convinced that his characterisation of a right as involving an ability of a right-holder to exercise control over another's duty captured a fundamental characteristic of rights.

It is easy to see that it is the disagreement over the fundamental characteristic of rights that has allowed the debate to continue. Many Will Theorists may well concede that the Interest Theory better fits our linguistic intuitions regarding the reference of the word, or concept, 'right'. The fact that the debate has continued nevertheless shows that the debate is not only driven by a desire to fit these intuitions, but also by different ideas regarding the nature of rights. Interest Theorists think that it is not a mere coincidence that rights tend to protect interests. Will Theorists, on the other hand, may well agree that rights tend to protect interests, but they deny that this is their essential characteristic. Even if Will Theory and Interest Theory *did* identify the same normative incidents as rights, they would still disagree in their answer to the question *why* these incidents are properly identified as rights.

A new analysis of rights, therefore, should not only identify the appropriate incidents as rights, but it should do so for the right reasons. In my view, the persistence of the debate shows that both the Interest Theory and Will Theory capture some of our intuitions in this respect. Hence, it would be a major advantage for a new analysis of rights if it could accommodate the intuitions at the basis of both accounts, provided it can do so in a non-ad hoc manner. The qualification that it should do so in a non-ad hoc manner precludes simply combining Interest Theory and Will Theory without *explaining why* rights should do these two things: protect interests and provide the right-holder with some amount of normative control.

This list of adequacy constraints is not meant to be exhaustive, but it captures some of the main inadequacies that plague recent accounts. It remains to be seen if any account can satisfy them all, but progress on any of them relative to current accounts should count in favour of adopting a theory.[13]

[13] I would like to thank Mark McBride for his detailed comments which helped me improve the essay.

References

Bentham, J (1996) in JH Burns and HLA Hart (eds), *An Introduction to the Principles of Morals and Legislation* (Oxford: Clarendon Press).

Brännmark, J (2016) 'Future Generations as Rightholders' 19 *Critical Review of International Social and Political Philosophy* 680.

Fabre, C (2009) 'Preconception Rights' in S de Wijze, MH Kramer and I Carter (eds), *The Anatomy of Justice: Themes From the Political Philosophy of Hillel Steiner* (London: Routledge).

Cruft, R (2004) 'Rights: Beyond Interest Theory and Will Theory?' 23 *Law and Philosophy* 347.

Feinberg, J (1974) 'The Rights of Animals and Future Generations' in W Blackstone (ed), *Philosophy and Environmental Crisis* (Athens, GA: University of Georgia Press).

Hart, HLA (1982) *Essays on Bentham: Jurisprudence and Political Theory* (Oxford: Oxford University Press).

—— (1984) 'Are There Any Natural Rights?' in J Waldron (ed), *Theories of Rights* (Oxford: Oxford University Press).

Kamm, FM (2002) 'Rights' in J Coleman and S Shapiro (eds), *The Oxford Handbook of Jurisprudence and Philosophy of Law* (Oxford: Oxford University Press).

Kramer, MH (1998) 'Rights Without Trimmings' in MH Kramer, NE Simmonds and H Steiner, *A Debate Over Rights: Philosophical Enquiries* (Oxford: Clarendon Press).

—— (2001) 'Getting Rights Right' in MH Kramer (ed), *Rights, Wrongs and Responsibilities* (Basingstoke: Palgrave Macmillan).

—— (2010) 'Refining the Interest Theory of Rights' 55 *The American Journal of Jurisprudence* 31.

Kramer, MH and Steiner, H (2007) 'Theories of Rights: Is There a Third Way?' 27 *Oxford Journal of Legal Studies* 281.

Lindahl, L (1977) *Position and Change: A Study in Law and Logic* (Dordrecht: Reidel).

Lyons, D (1994) *Rights, Welfare, and Mill's Moral Theory* (New York: Oxford University Press).

MacCormick, DN (1977) 'Rights in Legislation' in PMS Hacker and J Raz (eds), *Law, Morality and Society: Essays in Honour of HLA Hart* (Oxford: Clarendon Press).

—— (1982) *Legal Right and Social Democracy: Essays in Legal and Political Philosophy* (Oxford: Clarendon Press).

Makinson, D (1986) 'On the Formal Representation of Rights Relations' 15 *Journal of Philosophical Logic* 403.

Rainbolt, GW (2006) *The Concept of Rights* (Dordrecht: Springer).

Raz, J (1986) *The Morality of Freedom* (Oxford: Clarendon Press).

—— (1995) Ethics in the Public Domain: Essays in the Morality of Law and Politics, rev edn (Oxford: Clarendon Press).
Simmonds, NE (1998) 'Rights at the Cutting Edge' in MH Kramer, NE Simmonds and H Steiner, *A Debate Over Rights: Philosophical Enquiries* (Oxford: Oxford University Press).
Spena, A (2012) 'The Strange Case of the Protective Perimeter: Liberties and Claims to Non-Interference' 31 *Law and Philosophy* 161.
Sreenivasan, G (2005) 'A Hybrid Theory of Claim-Rights' 25 *Oxford Journal of Legal Studies* 257.
Steiner, H (1994) *An Essay on Rights* (Oxford: Blackwell).
Tierney, B (1997) *The Idea of Natural Rights: Studies on Natural Rights, Natural Law, and Church Law* (Grand Rapids, MI: Scholars Press).
Van Duffel, S (2012) 'The Nature of Rights Debate Rests on a Mistake' 93 *Pacific Philosophical Quarterly* 104.
Wenar, L (2005) 'The Nature of Rights' 33 *Philosophy & Public Affairs* 223.
—— (2008) 'The Analysis of Rights' in MH Kramer et al (eds), *The Legacy of HLA Hart: Legal, Political, and Moral Philosophy* (Oxford: Oxford University Press).
—— (2013) 'The Nature of Claim-Rights' 123 *Ethics* 202.
Williams, G (1956) 'The Concept of Legal Liberty' 56 *Columbia Law Review* 1129.

10

Respectful Adjudication of Rights Conflicts

ANNA-KARIN ANDERSSON[1]

I. Introduction

The objectives of this essay are: (1) to advance the core components of an attractive account of what behaviour is required in order to show respect for persons; (2) to show this account's relevance for adjudication of particularly difficult rights conflicts; (3) to explain the concrete applications of the account for some central areas of political philosophy and bioethics; and (4) to defend the account against objections.

The main thesis to be defended is that certain particularly challenging rights conflicts should be adjudicated by considering to what extent individuals involved in the conflict have promoted certain values prior to the occurrence of the conflict. I am proposing a tie-breaking procedure for rights conflicts where neither of the rights in the conflict is already favoured somehow. The method is justified because it treats the agents involved in the conflict with respect in an important sense. The requirement to consider to what extent the individuals involved in the conflict have promoted certain values prior to the occurrence of the conflict is supported by the deontological account of respect for persons. Encouraging people to actively promote certain values is a way of showing all rights-bearers respect. If people who actively promote certain values enjoy advantage if they become involved in a rights conflict, they are thereby provided opportunities to affect the outcome of such rights conflicts. Surprisingly, this account is neither consequentialistic nor perfectionistic. It is entirely deontological.

After introducing and defending the account, I explain how this method is a fruitful complement to settling the conflict by means of a lottery. It is essential to note that I focus on defending the theoretical and intuitive appeal of the proposal. Implementation challenges, and tentative suggestions for approaches of meeting

[1] The author gratefully acknowledges very helpful written comments by Peter Vallentyne and Gopal Sreenivasan on earlier versions of this essay, and Mark McBride for help in finalising the essay.

these challenges, will be outlined, but developing solutions to these challenges fall beyond the scope of this essay.

II. The Normative Framework

By a 'right', I will mean a moral claim-right that correlates to an enforceable duty of an agent to engage in certain behaviour or abstain from engaging in certain behaviour (*cf* Hohfeld 1923). Although the directedness of a duty does not in itself imply that the duty has any specific weight (Sreenivasan 2010), I will here (controversially) assume that rights do trump (Dworkin 1984), or have lexical priority over (Rawls 1971), other moral values.

First, why is the protection that rights provide appealing? Rights understood in the aforementioned sense ensure that rights-bearers are protected from the risk of being exposed to certain types of arbitrary power exercise. Such protection allows people to plan and pursue certain projects of their own choice within the limits of predictable, systematically justified restrictions, without the insecurity of being frequently exposed to the risk of arbitrary interventions with crucial aspects of their lives. Respect for persons (at least) requires that we keep a certain kind of distance from the person, her possessions and her activities (Kant 1996). This interpretation of what is required in order to treat persons with respect is widely endorsed and plausible, though not necessarily the only plausible interpretation. The justification for this rights theory is deontological (Nozick 1974).

Second, how is the explanation of the appeal of rights relevant to the issue of rights conflicts? In order to respond to this question, I will discuss cases where exceptions (ie, infringements) are necessary because the rights of two different rights-bearers conflict. We are forced to make exceptions because respecting the rights of both rights-bearers is impossible. Although the existence of rights conflicts has been disputed, many commentators do hold that they exist. I will not attempt to settle this dispute here, but rather examine how rights conflicts may be adjudicated under the assumption that rights conflicts exist. Suppose that these rights conflicts are characterised by the following features: (1) both rights-bearers involved in the conflict have equal status as rights-bearers in virtue of their physical and mental properties; (2) both the conflicting rights are justifiably considered equally weighty; (3) there are no circumstances of the conflict that appear to be reasons for infringing on one conflicting right rather than the other. A common way of describing such a scenario is to say that two inconsistent obligations are each undefeated, even when all things are considered. Such obligations are commonly contrasted with 'prima facie' obligations (Ross 1930). Those are obligations that we are *ceteris paribus* required to fulfil. Some commentators hold that only conflicts between 'all things considered' obligations are 'genuine' rights conflicts. For the purposes of this essay, we do not need to determine whether *only* the aforementioned type of conflict should be considered 'genuine'. In cases of genuine conflicts, arranging something akin to a lottery is typically regarded as a fair method of resolving the conflict, or permitting an adjudicator to settle the dispute by exercising her own discretion. I will postpone discussion of the lottery solution until I have developed my proposal.

I will initially consider cases where the agents involved in the conflict have not agreed to allow the adjudicator to exercise personal discretion over the adjudication process. If both agents involved in the conflict have authorised the adjudicator to settle the conflict as she pleases, I hold it that the adjudicator does treat the agents with respect. This is because the adjudicator then acts on behalf of the agents involved in the conflict. Many, though not all, theorists within the moral rights tradition consider this a fair conflict resolving method (*cf* Steiner 1994; 1998).

In order to introduce the proposal, I will assume that agents involved in the conflict do not agree to a lottery or to letting an adjudicator settle the conflict at her own discretion. Once the proposal is introduced, I will argue that the proposal should be offered in combination with the lottery. Now, how can the rights conflict be adjudicated in a way that shows both rights-bearers due respect?

III. Implications for Adjudication of Rights

I will use the following case in order to introduce the proposal. Suppose that A and B are autonomous agents to the same degree. Hence, they both measure equally well regarding the properties that distinguish paradigmatic examples of rights-bearers. Their physical and mental properties cannot be referred to in order to adjudicate any rights conflict between them in favour of one or the other of these agents. Suppose also that neither of them is responsible for the occurrence of the rights conflict in question. Both A and B urgently need a new heart. Suppose that both are equally entitled to care according to whatever theory of social justice we endorse, and that neither patient is responsible for her predicament, or willing to step down from her claim-rights to receive care. Only one of the patients can be given priority.

I will now explain and defend three important adequacy criteria of an acceptable adjudication method. I will then very briefly outline my proposal of an adjudication method. In the next section, I will develop the proposal.

(1): A plausible adjudication method should adjudicate the rights conflict without unjustified bias towards either of the rights-bearers involved in the conflict. Also, the method should be neutral with regard to different conceptions of what makes people's lives 'go well'. This adequacy criterion rules out moral and political perfectionist adjudication methods. Such methods would adjudicate conflicts by considering to what extent adjudicating in favour of either rights-bearer would promote a certain objectively worthy moral value. The merit of moral and political perfectionism is a subject of dispute (*cf* Wall 2012; Aristotle 1984; Barry 1995;

Brink 2003). I defensibly but controversially hold that sound adjudication methods should not be perfectionist methods. Sorting out the merits of perfectionism in any of its many sophisticated versions falls beyond the scope of this essay.

(2): Adjudication processes should be *predictable* in a (possibly limited) sense for rights-bearers who might be subjected to such adjudication. Such predictability, however, is also an important aspect of respectful treatment of the rights-bearer because it allows her to plan her activities within her allocated sphere of discretion while being able to predict how potential rights conflicts will be adjudicated. Predictability contributes to an acceptable adjudication process. It is not sufficient in order for the adjudication process to be morally acceptable: adjudication methods can be predictable yet unjustified. Some degree of predictability, however, seems necessary in order for the adjudication method to be morally acceptable. We saw that this is one of several plausible interpretations of what is required in order to treat a rights-bearer with respect.

(3): Finally, the adjudication method should be exposed to *public scrutiny* and ongoing assessment of the adjudication method in question should be invited.[2] Making the adjudication method available for public scrutiny further prevents arbitrariness and influence of individual discretion in the decision process. This gives the public ample opportunity to exercise influence over the content of the principles that will guide their interactions with each other. It also encourages ongoing discussion of the proper principles for adjudication. The adjudication principle defended below should be exposed to regular scrutiny and could be replaced by another principle if, upon reflection, that other principle proves to be more plausible. This allows individuals who may be exposed to the adjudication principle in the future to affect the content of the extant adjudication principle.

I propose that the aforementioned interpretation of what is required in order to show rights-bearers respect, when applied to genuine rights conflicts, mandates that adjudicators of the conflict consider to what extent A and B have promoted certain values prior to the occurrence of the conflict. It is important to note that this is a question about morally acceptable methods for adjudicating rights conflicts *when nothing about the contents of the rights or the circumstances of the rights conflict leads us to conclude that one of the rights should prevail.*

IV. Elaborating on the Principle

Consider again the aforementioned agents, A and B, who both require life-saving treatment. An example would be a heart transplant. How should we settle this conflict in a way that satisfies the adequacy criteria of a morally acceptable adjudication method? The conflict could be adjudicated by considering to what extent

[2] A similar adequacy criterion has been advanced by Norman Daniels and James Sabin (Daniels and Sabin 1997: 323–25; Daniels 1994: 27–29).

A and B have engaged in activities that could be considered as promoting various moral values, broadly construed. Although this suggestion appears perfectionist, I will argue that it is not. All agents should be given a wide range of lifelong opportunities to realise different moral values. As developed in detail below, such opportunities might include various forms of voluntary work that promote, for instance, other people's wellbeing, capabilities, or physical security. If the selection of such opportunities is sufficiently large and diverse, each agent may choose to promote *her own* set of moral values. Any such activity is permissible provided that it does not violate anyone else's rights. The permitted methods of value promotion are restricted by the set of rights that the conflicting rights belong to.

The proposal is compatible with several deontological rights theories. Conclusively defending one rights theory against other rights theories or against other normative theories falls beyond the scope of this essay. In the case of a rights conflict, the agent who has been most successful in promoting *whatever values she endorses, without violating rights*, should be given priority. This account is justified because each agent has been given substantial equality of opportunity to affect the outcome of the adjudication process in case of a rights conflict. Although adjudicating the conflict by considering which agent has produced *more* value, the fact that the adjudication outcome favours the agent who has promoted *a specific value* is not what justifies the adjudication decision. Put differently, the fact that it favours an agent who has promoted *that particular value* is not what justifies the adjudication principle.

It is crucial to note that the method is not perfectionist: the justification of the method is that the agent has created more 'action space' for herself by engaging in certain activities. The justification is not that such activities promote a value that is finally or instrumentally worthy of realisation. The promotion of some value is a *mere tool* for offering agents opportunities to affect the outcome of adjudication of conflicts they might get involved in. It is equally crucial to emphasise that the justification for this method is not consequentialist: the method is not justified in virtue of aggregating any moral value. The method is justified because it does allow agents to exercise control over crucial aspects of their lives, within the limits of the rights of other rights-bearers. We could describe this as giving an agent opportunity to *pre-create* discretionary action space (*cf* Steiner 1994) that they can use in case they get involved in rights conflicts. Again, it is important to note that this is a question of morally acceptable methods for adjudicating rights conflicts *when nothing about the contents of the rights or the circumstances of the rights conflict leads us to conclude that one of the rights should prevail.*

In order to clarify this proposal, we need to systematically specify its content. Let's explore, in order, (i) the *contents* of the values that might be promoted, as well as (ii) *how* these values could be promoted.

Most or all rights theorists would agree that protection of physical integrity in some broad sense is imperative or at least permissible. Therefore, it is reasonable to claim that at least some rights conflicts of the aforementioned kind could be resolved by considering what rights-bearer has previously engaged in activities that promote the protection of the physical integrity of people other than the rights-bearers involved in the conflict. I will initially limit the discussion to protection of physical integrity simply for the sake of introducing the core of the account. I readily acknowledge that protection of wellbeing, capabilities, or something else again might play the same role. As mentioned, the pool of available values to be realised through various activities must be extensive and diverse in order for the adjudication method to be neutral between particular values in the aforementioned sense. Commonly discussed methods of protecting people's physical integrity are policing, neighbourhood watch activities, car-pooling for children, dissemination of information, intelligence activity, and so on. I will use such examples in order to explicate the proposal.

Suppose that A's and B's skill sets differ greatly. Their use of these skill sets may have different impacts on the level of protection of other people's rights to physical integrity. A might be a highly skilled computer scientist, who has exercised her set of skills to protect millions of people against devastating threats caused by potential attacks against core societal functions that depend on computers. Or, she might be an exceptional designer of security systems for residences. One tentative version of the proposed adjudication principle suggests that we should prioritise the agent whose skill set has previously been used to secure a higher level of protection of other people's physical integrity. One possible objection is that adjudicating in the favour of A because of her ability to promote the physical integrity of other people benefits A in an unfair way. She might have acquired this skill set entirely by her own efforts. However, it is possible that those skills may at least partly be due to inherent talent, access to material resources, or other types of endowment, for which she is not responsible. Contemporary debates on equality of opportunity[3] in different senses indicate that such favouring of A on the basis of her ability to contribute to the protection of others would be morally impermissible. Let us, then, instead assess the following proposal.

Maybe we should adjudicate the conflict in favour of A, if no factor that depends on A's congenital, or other undeserved endowments, produces the promotion of protection of other people's physical integrity. This adjudication principle does not favour either rights-bearer because of their congenital endowments. In order to assess this principle, we should consider the following version of the aforementioned hypothetical case. Patient A is a person who is actively and frequently promoting activities that contribute to the protection of other people's physical integrity. She is organising the neighbourhood watch in her community, volunteers in a car-pool to provide safe rides for children in the local sports club, and raises funding for organisations that inform teens about problems involving date rape and abuse. Let us suppose for the sake of the argument that none of these activities require any specific congenital abilities; they only require willingness to engage in them. Readers who do believe that these specific activities do require

[3] Influential contributions to the debate on equality of opportunity include Otsuka (2003); Vallentyne (1997, 2002); Steiner (1994); Arneson (1989); and Dworkin (1981).

some particular skills or endowments could easily think of other activities that do not. One particularly noteworthy example is the spreading of information about prevention of bullying in schools.

In the UK, it has been suggested that individuals who agree to be on the organ donation registry should be given priority if they themselves come to need an organ transplant. This could potentially be considered another implementation of the aforementioned adjudication principle. The value to be promoted would be wellbeing, broadly construed. Individuals who choose to promote the wellbeing of others might enjoy an advantage should they get involved in a rights conflict. Anyone is eligible to register, regardless of endowments. Mere registration would be sufficient in order to enjoy priority in case of rights conflicts, so even individuals with congenital diseases that would disqualify them from actually donating could earn the right of priority. It is important to note that this adjudication method may be inappropriate in settings where individuals with pre-existing health problems might feel more pressured to register than people with lesser health problems, or no health problems at all. And it is important to note that my proposal would not affect the practice of abstaining from harvesting organs from a dead patient who is registered as an organ donor if the family objects to harvesting. One major benefit with this adjudication method is the fact that determining whether an individual who is a registered donor should be prioritised in case of conflict is straightforward. Difficulties may arise, however, if both individuals involved in the conflict are registered donors. This adjudication method is predictable, transparent and provides opportunity for public scrutiny.

This adjudication method would encourage, but not coerce, people to engage in activities that would favour them if they faced a deadlocked rights conflict. There is an extensive debate regarding whether such willingness depends on congenital properties as well. Let us accept the reasonable but disputable claim that agents are, to some extent, able to develop such willingness, and that not all such willingness is determined by factors beyond the individual's control. Each agent can, then, at least to some extent, predict and affect how she may be treated in case of a deadlocked rights conflict. Providing individuals with this kind of prudential incentive to contribute to the rights protection of others is a form of 'nudging'.[4] However, the justification of the method is that it is a way of empowering individuals by providing them with opportunities to control, to some extent, whether their rights will be overridden or not in case of a deadlocked rights conflict. Hence, this adjudication method only applies to rights-bearers who are capable of agency. I do not exclude the possibility that there may also be rights-bearers who are not agents.

The proposal may, though, be challenged because it does, however non-coercively, 'push' people to engage in certain activities. People who choose not to engage in those activities might be disadvantaged in case their rights conflict with the rights of others. I do not deny that this aspect of the proposal is controversial. My response to this objection is that this implication is less objectionable than

[4] For detailed discussion of the concept of 'nudging' see Thaler and Sunstein (2008).

allowing the adjudicator to exercise personal discretion, or to force the involved rights-bearers to resolve the dispute by means of a lottery. I defend this claim carefully in section V. Offering the proposed account as an alternative is defensible, in the light of the other available alternatives.

This adjudication method satisfies the adequacy criteria outlined above. Since the method recommends that certain rights conflicts be adjudicated by considering the extent of the involved agents' promotion of some moral value, not the contents of these values, the method is unbiased and value neutral in the required sense. If the method and the justification for the method are made public in proper ways, the method is transparent. And the method could also be exposed to public challenge and be subjected to revision if this is called for.

Here, I will merely outline some of the challenges any implementation of the account must face. Implementation of the proposed adjudication principle would need to develop solutions to epistemological and pragmatic challenges. The account should be implemented *only if* agents can be provided with substantial equality of opportunity to promote values of their own choice prior to rights conflicts. I believe that it is realistic and valuable to strive to create such opportunities. We would also need to prevent any power abuse by the individuals responsible for conscientiously assessing the deadlocked rights conflicts and adjudicate in accordance with the proposed principle. We would need to work out fair ways of measuring and comparing the efforts of people who differ greatly in age and/or physical/cognitive ability as older and greater endowed people have had greater opportunities to pre-create action space. We would need to ensure that enough and sufficiently diverse opportunities for promoting the relevant moral values are in place, and that all agents get access to information about these opportunities.

These important questions cannot be fully answered here, as the objective of this essay is to establish that the idea has enough intuitive appeal to merit further scrutiny and elaboration. The account does not aspire to offer a completely uncontroversial solution, for no such solution is possible. Neither does it aspire to be universally applicable. Any attempted solution will be challengeable. The most we can hope for is to develop proposals with as many benefits and as few shortcomings as possible. Pointing out controversial aspects of my account does not suffice to disqualify it. In order to challenge the account, one must also produce an alternative account with more benefits and fewer shortcomings. Although I suggest that the method is applicable to a wide range of rights conflicts, its applicability should be assessed on a case-by-case basis.

V. Adjudicating Rights Conflicts by Means of a Lottery

Hitherto, I have assumed that A and B will not agree to settle the conflict by means of a lottery. We may, however, be able to arrange a lottery that satisfies the adequacy criteria. If we roll the dice, or arrange a simple lottery, we have arguably adjudicated the conflict in an unbiased manner. By publicly announcing the lottery method, its application to rights conflicts, and appealing to the justification for using a lottery as an adjudication method, we also secure the predictability and transparence of the decision process. The method can be scrutinised and challenged by the public. Hence, the lottery satisfies the adequacy criteria. Hence, I do not dispute that the lottery can be a sound adjudication method. Next, I will argue that my proposed method should be offered as an option in addition to the lottery.

A major benefit of offering my proposal *in addition* to a lottery is that offering both the lottery and the proposed adjudication method increases the chances that any two individuals whose rights conflict with each other could find an adjudication method that both agree to. Hence, offering both methods decreases the risk of a deadlocked conflict in the first place. Although offering the proposed adjudication method in addition to a lottery does 'push' people who prefer the lottery solution to engage in certain activities in case their rights conflict with an individual who prefers the proposed adjudication method, offering the method and a lottery is less biased than offering only the lottery or only the proposed adjudication method. Offering *only* the lottery or *only* my proposed method would be biased in favour of agents who prefer one of these methods over the other. Hence, offering both methods satisfies the requirement that an adjudication method should be unbiased and value neutral (in the relevant sense) and better than offering only one of these methods.

I propose that *any* genuinely consensual resolution of a rights conflict is respectful in the required sense. If both parties agree about a resolution, both have been given the opportunity to exercise control over the outcome, and resolution by agreement is not biased towards either party. The proposed adjudication method should be applied when no such consensus can be reached. Why is it morally permissible to settle such conflicts by applying my proposed method, even if neither rights-bearer agrees to it? The response to this question is the following. We assume that the involved rights-bearers have refused to adjudicate the conflict by means of a lottery, and that they do not allow an adjudicator to settle the conflict at her own discretion. The proposed method is a last resort. The conflict *must* be adjudicated in some way. Hence, in situations where the involved rights-bearers keep rejecting *all* available adjudication methods, we are forced to impose an adjudication method on them at some point. My proposed method is defensible because it satisfies the adequacy criteria: it is unbiased, predictable and can be exposed to public scrutiny.

Is it equally defensible to force agents who refuse to accept any available adjudication method to settle the dispute by means of a lottery? We saw that the lottery, too, satisfies the adequacy criteria. However, the lottery solution deprives agents of the opportunity to affect the outcome of the adjudication process. If some adjudication method *must* be imposed on rights-bearers who refuse to agree to all available adjudication methods, my proposed method rather than the lottery could be considered preferable because my method allows agents to affect the outcome of such adjudications. This argument has sufficient intuitive appeal to merit careful consideration. It is not conclusive, however. But neither is the suggestion that the parties should be forced to accept a lottery in such situations: as an alternative we could hold that deadlocked conflicts could be respectfully resolved by forcing the parties to accept a lottery *or* my proposed method. In sum, the aforementioned argument for the claim that my proposed method should be offered as an alternative to the lottery solution remains convincing.

I hope that I have done enough to show that the proposal has strong intuitive appeal and merits further elaboration and scrutiny. I now wish to demonstrate that the adjudication method is applicable to a fairly wide range of difficult rights conflicts in central areas of bioethics and political philosophy. In the area of bioethics, we frequently encounter discussions regarding situations where equally deserving people of equal moral standing need medical resources that are in short supply, including medicine, surgery, vaccines and vital organs and tissues. The issue of fairness in healthcare allocation is one core area of contemporary applied ethics. Similar problems can be found in political settings where political institutions face the challenge of distributing crucial economic and material resources to members of the political community. The proposed adjudication method is significant because it applies, possibly in combination with the lottery solution, to a wide range of difficult conflicts over rights that protect crucial aspects of people's lives.

VI. Objections and Responses

One might object that implementation of the proposed adjudication method might encourage individuals to manipulate certain events in order to place themselves in a favourable position whenever such premeditation is possible. It might be argued that public announcements regarding the adjudication methods for rights conflicts of the aforementioned kind encourages people to initiate chains of events that will secure the prioritising of their own rights if and when their own rights will conflict with the rights of others.

This objection could be responded to in two ways. First, if all citizens have substantial equal opportunity to get access to the information about adjudication principles and to adjust their behaviour accordingly, no one is disadvantaged. If no one is disadvantaged, it is not clear that such attempts to place oneself in a favourable position in case of rights conflicts are objectionable. Second, if some such attempts are in fact objectionable, we might be required to prevent any behaviour we consider misuse. Requirements to prevent misuse do not, however, discredit the adjudication method as such. In any case, if the argument is cogent, deontologists will be able to utilise a wider range of tools for resolving deadlocks than previously realised. The occurrences of deadlock situations are also sufficiently frequent to merit careful investigation into resolutions. The proposed adjudication method provides an additional level of systematic justification for settling the dispute one way or the other.

Implementation of the proposal must negotiate challenges regarding the possibility of offering all persons genuine equality of opportunity to promote values they themselves endorse, and challenges regarding how to secure predictability of the system. Equality of opportunity can be achieved, at least in some contexts, by offering a very wide range of opportunities to promote values, and predictability can be achieved by clear information about opportunities to promote values, and information about how such promotion will be measured. Decisions regarding how promotion of various values will be measured should be the result of a transparent, public deliberation process in order to satisfy the adequacy criteria.

These are application challenges, not objections against the intuitive attractiveness of the proposal as such. Even if this proposal is not perfect, offering it in combination with a lottery is better than offering merely a lottery: it decreases the risk of a deadlocked conflict in the first place. The permissible methods for promoting value must fit within the rights theory in question without limiting the range of methods for promoting value too much. These abstract parameters for demarcating permissible methods of promoting value must be made more precise in a fully developed theory. There are, however, 'values' that any estimable rights theory would exclude, namely: racism, sexism and physical or mental abusiveness. By contrast, activities that are generally beneficial to humans, broadly conceived, without breaking the law, and activities that are not human rights violations, are promising candidates for permissible methods. Filling in these abstract parameters, however, should be (at least in part) a matter of public discourse.

VII. Conclusions

I have argued that a plausible interpretation of what is required in order to treat an agent with respect mandates that 'deadlocked' rights conflicts be resolved by considering to what extent the individuals involved in the conflict have promoted certain values prior to the occurrence of the conflict. I ended by exploring implications of the account for some central areas of political philosophy and bioethics, though more work remains to be done on such implications.

References

Aristotle (1984) *Nicomachean Ethics* (trans WD Ross) in J Barnes (ed), *The Complete Works of Aristotle* (Princeton, NJ: Princeton University Press).

Arneson, RJ (1989) 'Equality and Equal Opportunity for Welfare' 56 *Philosophical Studies* 77. Reprinted in L Pojman and R Westmoreland (eds) (1997) *Equality: Selected Readings* (New York: Oxford University Press).

Barry, B (1995) *Justice as Impartiality* (Oxford: Oxford University Press).

Brink, D (2003) *Perfectionism and the Common Good* (Oxford: Clarendon Press).

Daniels, N (1994) 'Four Unsolved Rationing Problems: A Challenge' 24 *Hastings Centre Report* 27.
Daniels, N and Sabin, J (1997) 'Limits to Health Care: Fair Procedures, Democratic Liberation, and the Legitimacy Problem for Insurers' 26 *Philosophy & Public Affairs* 303.
Dworkin, R (1981) 'What is Equality? Part 2: Equality of Resources' 10 *Philosophy & Public Affairs* 283.
—— (1984) 'Rights as Trumps' in J Waldron (ed), *Theories of Rights* (Oxford: Oxford University Press).
Hohfeld, W (1923) 'Some Fundamental Legal Conceptions as Applied in Judicial Reasoning' in W Hohfeld, *Fundamental Legal Conceptions as Applied in Judicial Reasoning* (New Haven, CT: Yale University Press).
Kamm, FM (1993) *Morality, Mortality, Vol I: Death and Whom to Save From It* (Oxford: Oxford University Press).
Kant, I (1996) *The Metaphysics of Morals* (ed M Gregor) (Cambridge: Cambridge University Press).
Nozick, R (1974) *Anarchy, State, and Utopia* (New York: Blackwell).
Otsuka, M (2003) *Libertarianism Without Inequality* (New York: Oxford University Press).
Rawls, J (1971) *A Theory of Justice* (Harvard: Belknap).
Ross, WD (1930) *The Right and the Good* reprinted with an introduction by P Stratton-Lake (2002) (Oxford: Oxford University Press).
Sreenivasan, G (2010) 'Duties and Their Direction' 120 *Ethics* 465.
Steiner, H (1994) *An Essay on Rights* (Oxford: Blackwell).
—— (1998) 'Working Rights' in MH Kramer, NE Simmonds and H Steiner, *A Debate Over Rights. Philosophical Enquiries* (Oxford: Oxford University Press).
Thaler, RH and Sunstein, CR (2008) *Nudge: Improving Decisions about Health, Wealth, and Happiness* (Newhaven, CT: Yale University Press).
Vallentyne, P (1997) 'Self-ownership and Equality: Brute Luck, Gifts, Universal Domination, and Leximin' 107 *Ethics* 321.
—— (2002) 'Brute Luck, Option Luck, and Equality of Initial Opportunities' 112 *Ethics* 529.
Wall, Steven (2012) 'Perfectionism in Moral and Political Philosophy' in EN Zalta (ed), *The Stanford Encyclopedia of Philosophy*, available at plato.stanford.edu/archives/win2012/entries/perfectionism-moral/.
Wenar, L (2015) 'Rights' in EN Zalta (ed), *The Stanford Encyclopedia of Philosophy*, available at plato.stanford.edu/archives/fall2015/entries/rights/.

11

Corrective Rights

HILLEL STEINER

I. Introduction

The aim of this essay is critically to appraise a central feature of Ernest Weinrib's account of corrective justice, as advanced in many of his writings and especially in his deservedly highly acclaimed monograph, *The Idea of Private Law* (Weinrib 1995). Criticism of that account has, by now, become a small cottage industry. But, as far as I'm aware, its avowed Kantian credentials have not been challenged. Indeed, one reason why they seem to have escaped such challenge may be what I'll display as a key misstep in Kant's own reasoning about rights. Sympathetic as I am, to both the formalist spirit of Weinrib's argument and Kant's basic conception of rights and justice, I shall contend that the particular divorce of distributive from corrective justice advanced by Weinrib is ill founded.

Peter Cane introduces his long review of *The Idea of Private Law* with a particularly astute description of Weinrib's project. So, and for the sake of readers who may be less familiar with that project, I hope to be forgiven for quoting that introduction in (nearly) full.

> Ernest Weinrib's aim is to show how private law should be 'understood'. By 'private law' Weinrib means the law of contract, the law of tort and the law of restitution, which he calls 'the entire domain of liability' (20). For Weinrib the central feature of private law is correlativity. The term 'correlativity' refers to the fact that through private law we organize the world in terms of bilateral relationships between individuals. The correlativity of private law finds expression both in the bipolar nature of private law litigation and in doctrines, such as causation, which link the plaintiff's claim to the defendant's wrong. In private law, one person's right is always a function of another person's duty, and vice versa. Weinrib argues that in order to give a proper account of private law, we must explain this central feature of correlativity. This can only be done, he says, from an 'internal' perspective because correlativity is a structural feature of private law. In his view, this accounts for the failure of 'external' explanations of private law in terms of its social purposes. For instance, the idea that the function of private law is to compensate for losses suffered does not explain why one person rather than another should provide the compensation or why compensation is only payable when losses are caused in certain

ways. Conversely, the idea that the function of private law is to deter certain types of conduct does not explain why such conduct is often only actionable if it causes loss to another. The inadequacy of external explanations of private law is a major reason, according to Weinrib, why economic analyses of private law are bound to fail. Properly understood, says Weinrib, private law is an end in itself and not a means to some other end such as a particular political or economic or social state of affairs. Rather more rhetorically, he says that 'the [only] purpose of private law is to be private law' (5). What this seems to mean is that the purpose of private law is to encapsulate and give effect to the fundamental idea of correlativity (or reciprocity) in human relationships. Reciprocity is only one of the bases on which human relationships can be conducted, and Weinrib does not argue that it is normatively superior to other modes of human interaction. His basic point is that since private law expresses that particular mode of interaction, any account of private law which explains it in terms of some other form of human interaction or in terms of some function other than the 'internal goal' of reciprocity is bound to be inadequate. Weinrib calls his account of private law 'formalistic' in the sense that it seeks to explain private law solely in terms of its allegedly central structural feature of correlativity. The formalist does not deny 'that legal arrangements have political antecedents and effects' (25); but formalists do say that private law can and must be understood and evaluated as good or bad in terms of its own structure before it is evaluated in terms of some external goal. A rule of private law which is not consistent with the internal logic and morality of reciprocity lacks a sound justification regardless of how well or badly it serves any particular external goal such as compensation or deterrence. For instance, the fact that one or other of the parties to a tort action is insured against the loss which forms the subject of the action would not provide a sound basis for deciding whether or not to impose tort liability on the defendant, however desirable loss spreading by insurance might be as a social goal, because insurance is not based on a reciprocal relationship between the two parties (36–38). Furthermore, from a formalistic point of view, private law cannot be understood in terms of moral principles except those which underpin the structure of private law. For instance, contract law is not explicable in terms of the principle that promises must be kept because this is a unilateral, not a bilateral, principle which does not explain why contract law only enforces some promises (50–53). For Weinrib, the reason why correlativity is central to private law is that private law embodies the concept of corrective justice as expounded by Aristotle. Corrective justice requires that when one person makes a gain and another suffers a loss as a result of wrongful conduct by the former, the gain should be shifted back to the loser so as to restore the parties to the positions they were in before the wrong in respect of that gain and loss. Weinrib argues that corrective justice explains why private law is bipolar, and it also explains why the duty of one party under corrective justice is the mirror image of the other party's right. *Corrective justice is to be contrasted with distributive justice. The two forms of justice both concern the allocation of resources; but they differ in that under distributive justice individuals' entitlements are not correlative to other individuals' obligations.* For this reason it is incoherent to say, for instance, that loss spreading can be a criterion of tort liability, because loss spreading is a principle of distribution, not of correction (74–75). *The structure of private law is corrective justice; and principles which are not based on correlativity of right and obligation do not fit into that structure.* According to Weinrib, this exposition of corrective justice in terms of gains and losses presupposes that the former position to which the parties are to be restored was in some sense just or, as Weinrib puts it, one of 'equality';[1] otherwise restoration to that position would not be just. *When and why is correction just? Weinrib finds an answer to this question in the concept of 'Kantian right'. This concept provides a framework for assessing human conduct as right or wrong. The 'principle of right' governs relationships between individuals, and is that 'the free choice of the one must be capable of coexisting with the freedom of the other in accordance with a universal law' (104); that is, according to rules which apply equally to all. The principle is concerned with 'the sequence from one person's performance of an action to another's suffering of its effects' (98); or, in other words, with a person's external conduct and its impact on the exercise by others of their freedom of choice. The principle of right is not concerned with internal motivations for action but only with the actions themselves; and it is not concerned with the impact of those actions on another's internal wishes (or needs) but only on that person's freedom to act in the external world. This is because the essence of free will is to be able to choose not to give effect in conduct to one's internal motivations. Thus conduct cannot be criticized under the principle of right either because of the actor's internal state of mind; or because the actor did not fulfil another's wishes or needs: wishes and (according to Kant) needs are both internal and not aspects of a person's external relations with others, and failure to satisfy them does not interfere with the person's freedom of action. Beyond this, the principle of right has no moral content. The principle of right judges people according to their external interactions.* The function of private law is to enforce judgments of right against individuals. When embodied in law, the principle of right becomes a social or 'public' principle (105). Courts act as 'the institutionalized embodiment' (106) of the principle of right. By providing sanctions for breaches of the principle of right, the law gives the principle of right a 'juridical standing' (107); it also sets standards for human conduct and provides incentives to comply with those standards. To summarize so far: for Weinrib, the law of contract, tort and restitution are best understood as concerned with bilateral interactions between individuals. These bodies of law are based on the idea that in their dealings with others, individuals should act consistently with other people's freedom of choice according to rules which apply to all. This is the Kantian principle of right (conduct). If a person acts inconsistently with the Kantian principle of right ('wrongfully') and thereby causes loss to another and makes a corresponding gain for him or herself, private law gives effect to the idea of corrective justice by requiring the parties to be returned to the position they were in prior to the act in question.[2]

For purposes of the argument that follows, Weinrib's two key claims are (1) that corrective justice is independent of distributive justice, inasmuch as the former has its own distinctive non-instrumental normative standard—namely, reciprocity—which is absent from distributive justice, and (2) that this normative standard is best understood as Kant's principle of right. My contentions are: (a) that Kant's principle of right itself has distributive implications; (b) that the aforementioned misstep in Kant's account consists in his failure to perceive one of those implications; and (c) that this distributive implication is construable in terms of bilateral reciprocity or correlativity.

[1] Quoting Weinrib, Cane notes that '[T]he disturbance of equality in Aristotle's account [of corrective justice] is the defendant's wrongful infringement of the plaintiff's rights' (58). '*Equality is merely a way of representing the norm that injustice violates*' (61) (Cane 1996: 472, fn 1) italics added.

[2] Cane (1996: 471–73) italics added.

II. The Kantian Principle of Right

In *The Metaphysics of Morals*, Kant's first order of business is sharply to distinguish the domain of justice or 'right' from that of ethics or virtue, by differentiating two types of moral duty: correlative and non-correlative. The former, in bearing on only the *form* of the relationship between persons' wills, differ significantly from the latter which concern the *content* of persons' wills—their 'maxims', purposes, ends, or intentions in acting—and which are thus matters of virtue. Correlative duties, by contrast, govern the interpersonal distribution of what Kant calls *external freedom*.[3] And what they do is normatively to constrain their bearers' actions (whatever the intentions motivating those actions) to ones consistent with a particular distribution of that freedom: a distribution whereby it is 'possible for the free choice of each to accord with the freedom of all'. Actions that encroach on other persons' rightful shares of external freedom violate their just rights.[4]

Confirming this fundamental Kantian difference between ethics-based assessment of actions and its justice-based counterpart, Arthur Ripstein supplies its underlying explanation:

> Kant draws a series of sharp divisions between right [justice] and ethics. Ethical conduct depends upon the maxim on which an action is done: rightful conduct depends only on the outer form of interaction between persons. The inner nature of ethical conduct means that the only incentive consistent with the autonomy at the heart of morality must be morality itself; rightful conduct can be induced by incentives provided by others. Other persons are entitled to enforce duties of right, but not duties of virtue ... Each of these differences between right and ethics turns on Kant's representation of principles of right as governing persons represented as occupying space. The basic case for thinking about your right to your own person is your right to your own body; the basic case for thinking about property is property in land, that is, a right to exclude others from a particular location on the Earth's surface; the basic case for thinking about contract is the transfer of an object from one place to another ... [Kant's] normative arguments ... for the Universal Principle of Right ... work out the implication of free persons whose movements of their bodies can come into conflict (2009: 11–12).

[3] Analyses of external or negative freedom—as access, unimpeded by others, to the physical components of actions—can be found in Steiner (1994: ch 2); Carter (1999: chs 7 and 8); Kramer (2003: chs 2 and 3).

[4] *cf* Hart (1955: 177–78): 'The concept of a right belongs to that branch of morality which is specifically concerned to determine when one person's freedom may be limited by another's ... Kant, in the *Rechtslehre*, discusses the obligations which arise in this branch of morality under the title of *officia juris*, "which do not require that respect for duty shall be of itself the determining principle of the will", and contrasts them with *officia virtutis*, which have no moral worth unless done for the sake of the moral principle. His point is, I think, that we must distinguish from the rest of morality those principles regulating the proper distribution of human freedom which alone make it morally legitimate for one human being to determine by his choice how another should act; and a certain specific moral value is secured (to be distinguished from moral virtue in which the good will is manifested) if human relationships are conducted in accordance with these principles even though coercion has to be used to secure this, for only if these principles are regarded will freedom be distributed among human beings as it should be'.

The most immediate such implication is that 'there is only one innate right':

> *Freedom* (independence from being constrained by another's choice), insofar as it can coexist with the freedom of every other in accordance with a universal law, is the only original right belonging to every man by virtue of his humanity. This principle of innate freedom already involves … innate *equality*, that is, independence from being bound by others to more than one can in turn bind them; hence a man's quality of being *his own master* (Kant 1996: 30).

What we have here then, at the very core of the Principle of Right, is what amounts to a reciprocal *distributive* relation. Each person has an original right against each other person, who correlatively bears a duty not to diminish the former's external freedom to less than his or her own freedom. And this right entails ('already involves') the further distributive right of 'being one's own master', or what is currently referred to (notwithstanding Kant's misgivings) as a right of *self-ownership*. The furniture of the world includes, inter alia, persons' bodies, and what Kant is thereby ruling out is slavery: a distribution of body ownerships whereby some of these bodies are not, so to speak, owner-occupied. Each person has an original right against each other person not to be enslaved.[5]

Persons necessarily use their bodies to set and pursue purposes, within the limits of respecting one another's rights to equal external freedom:

> [The norms and institutions of justice] provide the only possible way in which a plurality of persons can interact on terms of equal freedom. Kant's concern is not with how people should interact, as a matter of ethics, but with how they can be forced to interact, as a matter of right. The core idea of independence is an articulation of the distinction between persons and things. A person is a being capable of setting his or her own purposes, while a thing is something that can be used in pursuit of purposes. Kant follows Aristotle in distinguishing choice from mere wish on the grounds that to choose something, a person must take himself to have means available to achieve it … In this sense, having means with which to pursue purposes is conceptually prior to setting those purposes. In the first instance, your capacity to set your own purposes just is your own person: your ability to conceive of ends, and whatever bodily abilities you have with which to pursue them (Ripstein 2009: 14).

But pursuing purposes also requires access to extra-personal things: material objects and the portions of physical space which purpose-pursuing actions occupy:

> Space is more than a useful metaphor for Kant. Its normative significance arises from the way in which separate persons who occupy space can come into conflict in the exercise of their freedom, depending on where they are doing their space-occupying activities and what others happen to be doing in the same location (Ripstein 2009: 12).

[5] The meaning of the term 'original', in Kant's phrase 'original right', is akin to that of 'initial' or 'foundational' or, in earlier doctrinal usage, 'natural': it is *not*, as we shall see, akin to 'primordial' or 'historically earliest'. An original right is one (a) that can be exercised to create other rights, and (b) that has not been created by the exercise of another right. Non-original rights are created or acquired by contract, by exercises of liberties to appropriate unowned things and to transform elements of one's domain, and by violations of rights.

The means to our ends are clearly many and various, reflecting the multifariousness of those ends themselves. But among these diverse means, there is one which is common to all ends and a necessary condition of their achievement: namely, external freedom. Persons are necessarily debarred from achieving an end if their overt physical behaviour in pursuit of it is obstructed by others.

An original right to *equal* external freedom implies, then, not only an original right to self-ownership but also an original right to some extra-personal things. It is these two rights that are jointly constitutive of each person's original domain of rightful action. And it is through exercises of those original rights, of rights successively derived from those exercises, and of liberties protected by those rights, that the normative contents of these individual domains are modified over time.

What, then, are the extra-personal things that permissibly compose persons' original domains? Kant's answer is that the

> [f]irst acquisition of a thing can be only acquisition of land … [and that] any piece of land can be acquired originally, and the possibility of such acquisition is based on the original community of land in general … The possession by all human beings on the earth which precedes any acts of theirs that would establish rights (is constituted by nature itself) is an *original possession in common* (*communio possessionis originaria*), the concept of which is not empirical and dependent upon temporal conditions, like that of a supposed *primitive possession in common* (*communio primaeva*), which can never be proved. Original possession in common is, rather, a practical rational concept which contains *a priori* the principle in accordance with which alone people can use a place on the earth in accordance with principles of right (1996: 50–51).

Since extra-personal objects are exhaustively classifiable as either natural resources or the artefacts persons make from them and their derivatives in pursuing their purposes, Kant follows Locke and others in claiming that persons' original domains can consist of only the former. But he rejects not only Locke's account of the necessary condition for those resources permissibly to be privately acquired, but also, and more pertinently, Grotius' and Pufendorf's accounts too: neither labour-mixing nor the consent of persons in primordial ('primitive') communal possession constitute that condition.

III. Unilateralism and Omnilateralism

What is the problem here? A person, in privately appropriating unowned natural resources and thereby establishing an *in rem* right with respect to them, is *unilaterally* imposing correlative obligations on all others.[6] And this obviously does not sit

[6] Hohfeld plausibly suggests that, contrary to prevailing jurisprudential usage, persons' *in rem* rights—as ones correlatively availing against every other person—are less perspicuously contrasted with *in personam* rights, are indeed fully reducible to a multiplicity of *in personam* rights and, hence, are more perspicuously labelled *multital* rights, in contrast with *paucital* rights which avail against only particular other persons; *cf* Hohfeld (1919: 75–76).

well with Kant's Principle of Right, the fundamental entailment of which is that each person is his or her own master. As Nick Sage observes:

> For Kant, private law is a system of equal freedom. No single person acting alone—unilaterally—can alter the scope of another's freedom. That would prefer one person's freedom over another's. Corrective justice requires that the explanation for a private law obligation be bilateral, rather than unilateral, in form: the explanation must show equal concern for both plaintiff and defendant. Here is an apparent problem about the original acquisition of property. It seems to be unilateral. A person originally acquires property in an unowned object by taking control of it. That action subjects every other person to new duties and disabilities: others must now not interfere with the object and can no longer acquire it themselves … So it seems that the acquirer has changed the scope of others' freedom. And the explanation for others' obligations seems to turn solely on the acquirer's action or choice … This problem is not new. On one interpretation, it troubled Kant himself (2012: 119).

As Kant's text suggests, the problem of reconciling private appropriation with each person's innate right to equal external freedom is indeed one which exercised him. And he sought its resolution in the concept of an *omnilateral will*. For him, the reciprocity required by justice consists in presupposing that private appropriations, far from being unauthorised unilateral acts, must be ones which are authorised by the will of each and every person. What those who form that omnilateral will are each doing, in authorising private appropriations of land, is waiving their respective rights of self-ownership that protect their *liberties to use* those sites, which are thereby permissibly appropriated: rights that correlatively entail duties in others not to treat them as trespassers, not to forcibly expel their bodies from those sites. In so waiving, they are voluntarily incurring enforcible duties not to trespass on privately appropriated sites. Their consent *transforms* appropriators' acts from impermissible curtailments of their freedom to permissible ones.

But the authorisation of this presupposed omnilateral will *cannot* be that of the empirically conjectured general will that Grotius and Pufendorf had claimed, for that will is insufficiently inclusive. It cannot be an authorisation by (merely) all the particular persons who, historically, enjoyed primordial communal possession (*communio primaeva*): such a will would be, at best, merely a multilateral one. Rather, since rights *in rem* endure through time and descend through a succession of owners, Kant's omnilateral will is conceived as the will of all humanity in an ahistorical *communio possessionis originaria* which, far from being the object of an empirical conjecture, is an *a priori* 'practical rational concept'. Only such a will can be constitutive of the universally instantiated obligations that correlate to *in rem* rights:

> For a unilateral will (and a bilateral but still *particular* will is also unilateral) cannot put everyone under an obligation that is in itself contingent; this requires a will that is *omnilateral*, that is united not contingently but *a priori* and therefore necessarily, and because of this is the only will that is lawgiving. For only in accordance with this principle of the will is it possible for the free choice of each to accord with the freedom of all, and

> therefore possible for there to be any right, and so too possible for any external object to be mine or yours (Kant 1996: 51).[7]

So, Kant rejects the appropriation accounts of Grotius and Pufendorf because their private appropriators, although not inconceivably authorised by all their contemporaries who enjoyed primordial communal possession, would nonetheless have been similarly exercising an unauthorised unilateral will, inasmuch those contemporaries' consent would itself have amounted to no more than 'a bilateral but still *particular* will'. The correlative obligations ostensibly created by those appropriations could not conceivably have been authorised by, nor therefore could they bind, non-contemporaries; nor therefore could they correlate to *in rem* rights. Only appropriations authorised by Kant's non-contingent, ahistorical omnilateral will can conform to the Principle of Right's core injunction, that the free choice of each accord with the freedom of all. And only such appropriations can generate sets of private property rights, by making it 'possible for any external object to be mine or yours'.[8]

How satisfactory is this, as a solution to the *unilateralism problem*—the problem of reconciling private appropriation, and the *in rem* rights that descend from it, with each person's right to equal external freedom? Is it sufficient to sustain free appropriative choices that accord with the freedom of all? As Sage notes:

> Recently, theorists of private law have re-encountered the problem and have adopted what they take to be Kant's solution. On this approach, Kant solves the unilateralism problem by mandating a 'civil condition' of public legal institutions, in which the 'omnilateral will' of everyone legitimizes original acquisition ... [Sage] scrutinizes the 'civil condition' solution, as construed by Ernest Weinrib and by Arthur Ripstein. Neither account solves the alleged problem of unilateralism (2012: 119).[9]

The argument that fails to solve the unilateralism problem is one invoking Kant's 'postulate of public right'. This universally vested right correlatively entails each person's duty to enter a 'rightful' or civil condition, whereby public legal institutions supply the omnilateral will that transforms any private-appropriation-based claim—which can be only provisional in their absence—into a rightful entitlement.[10]

Several difficulties beset this proposed 'civil condition' solution. Most immediate is the simple fact that, in the absence of *global* public legal institutions, the general will of only a *geographically local* set of public legal institutions—of a nation state—is no more constitutive of the requisite omnilateral will than was that of Grotius' and Pufendorf's *temporally local* primordial community. Both are insufficiently inclusive to supply the kind of appropriative authorisations which the Principle of

[7] This omnilateral will is thus somewhat akin to that emerging from a Rawlsian original position comprised of all members of all human generations—past, present and future; *cf* Rawls (1999: 256).

[8] *cf* Ripstein (2009: 156–58).

[9] '*Alleged* problem' because, in Sage's view, 'the real solution to the unilateralism problem [is] recognizing that it is not a problem' (2012: 119–20); the grounds for this view are assessed below: 223 ff.

[10] *cf* Kant (1996: 44–45, 84–86).

Right requires.[11] But even setting this difficulty aside, the 'civil condition' solution fails to overcome the unilateralism problem. Why?

That condition, inasmuch as it embodies an omnilateral will, is held to transform a unilateral act of appropriation into a rightful one by sustaining a common legal system in which (on Weinrib's view) all persons are reciprocally obligated to recognise that all such acts create valid rights, or (on Ripstein's view) legislation is solely for the public good.[12] The difficulty here arises from the fact that neither of these solutions implies, of any particular act of appropriation, that it is consistent with the freedom of all. Sage sees their failure to imply it as basically due to the limitations of Kant's system itself. He argues that, on the one hand, unilateral appropriation must count as a violation of others' freedom unless it enjoys their *actual* consent: hence what Weinrib and Ripstein offer are accounts that have 'the flavour of omnilateral actual consent'. But on the other hand, 'Kant must reject any account of [rightful] original acquisition that makes it contingent on every person's actual consent', rather than a necessary deliverance of *a priori* practical reason (Sage 2012: 129).

However, Sage's own 'solution' to the unilateralism problem—'recognizing that it is not a problem'—fares no better. His bold core claim is that, contrary to Weinrib and Ripstein, appropriative acts simply do not alter the scope of others' external freedom at all:

> [O]riginal acquisition is unproblematic because your taking control of an unowned object is just your own action ... You do not, in taking control of an object, choose any other person's action for them ... [T]he object is at most the target of others' *potential* action—in other words, of their mere wishes. That is irrelevant for Kant ... We might say, then, that prior to its acquisition an object—which does not have any normative standing of its own—is invisible to the Kantian right. An object appears for the very first time upon acquisition, *already* incorporated into some person's sphere of external purposiveness ... Original acquisition does diminish 'freedom' in one sense: it shrinks the domain of objects that could *potentially* be subjected to others' action. But that has nothing to do with Kantian freedom (2012: 132).

So, Sage's 'no problem' solution rests on the claim that one's Kantian external freedom consists *not* in one's unimpeded access to objects that could be subjected to one's action, but rather in not having one's action chosen by another—a freedom that is unaltered by another's appropriation. Only taking (damaging, secreting, etc) something that already belongs to another counts as diminishing his freedom.

Acknowledging that if freedom has its 'ordinary meaning', Sage agrees with Weinrib and Ripstein that one person's appropriative action 'means that a certain

[11] This, because the rightful boundary of each national legal jurisdiction presumably requires as much conformity with the Principle of Right—with the omnilateral will of the *communio possessionis originaria*—as does that of each privately appropriated site. Evidently, the general will of a set of particular persons, who jointly form a particular nation state, is very far from being identical with that omnilateral will.

[12] Sage (2012: 126–28). Weinrib's discussion is in Weinrib (2012: 276–79), and Ripstein's discussion is in Ripstein (2009: 148–59, 198–204).

object is no longer available for others to access. To that extent, the freedom of those persons is limited, they are under new constraints, duties or obligations, and their normative situation is changed' (2012: 131). But the reason why appropriative acts nonetheless do *not* limit others' freedom—why unilateralism is not, after all, a problem—is said to be that Kant is deploying a 'special' conception of freedom: '[F]or Kant, "freedom" means only that each person's action must be their own—it cannot be chosen by any other person' (Sage 2012: 131).

Is Sage correct in this contention? Recall Kant's own formulation of external freedom. The foundation of all just rights, he says, is each person's one innate right—a right to 'Freedom (independence from being constrained by another's choice), insofar as it can coexist with the freedom of choice of every other in accordance with a universal law' (Kant 1996: 30). Sage's conception of Kantian external freedom is clearly non-equivalent to Kant's own conception of it, since there is a significant difference between having one's range of chooseable actions *constrained* by another person and having one's actions *chosen* by another person. More precisely, those of one's actions that are chosen by another person form a proper *subset* of the set of those of one's chooseable actions that is constrained by another person: there are ways of constraining that set of chooseable actions without thereby choosing any of them (whereas the reverse is not true). And one of those ways consists in appropriating objects which might otherwise have been employed by those persons in pursuit of their purposes. If this were not so, then Sage's argument implausibly implies that one person's appropriation of the entire surface of the Earth would not count as a constraint on others' freedom.

So, it very much looks like the 'no problem' solution is itself problematic and, hence, that the unilateralism problem persists. That said, Sage's general approach to resolving the problem does point us in a fruitful direction. Excavating the presuppositions of Kant's key concepts here is, indeed, the way to make the needed progress. Sage's mistake lies in focusing on the concept of *external freedom* and interpreting it implausibly. I want to suggest that a more promising focus is the idea of the *omnilateral will* itself.

IV. Kantian Distributive Justice

We had already noted one dimension of the distributive character of the Principle of Right: each person's body is owner-occupied, and each therefore owes a correlative obligation to every other person to refrain from encroaching upon the various incidents of that ownership. What now seems clear is that this principle's distributive implications also extend to extra-personal things. Private property, Kant is saying, *necessarily* presupposes an ahistorically original community of land which, like the Principle of Right itself, he regards as an *a priori* deliverance of practical reason, as is the ahistorical 'general will of humanity'—the omnilateral will—which, Kant insists, is alone capable of authorising particular appropriations. Put simply, all persons—regardless of their temporal and geographic locations—are originally equal shareholders in the Earth's natural resources, in *at least* the minimal sense that all persons are equally vested with an original liberty (no original duty not) to occupy and use those resources. A private appropriation's conformity to the Principle of Right constitutes a just title only if it necessarily—rationally and non-contingently—enjoys the consent of each other person to relinquish that liberty.

Let's pause to take stock of this argument. For an obvious question to ask is whether the Principle of Right itself implies any distributive rule limiting *how much* of those resources any person may privately appropriate. Kant himself (like most of his commentators) suggests not. Or more precisely, and surprisingly, he seems to adopt a quasi-Hobbesian stance with regard to such limitation: '[H]ow far does authorization to take possession of a piece of land extend? As far as the capacity for controlling it extends, that is, as far as whoever wants to appropriate it can defend it' (1996: 52).[13] Two questions. First, is it *plausible* to believe that all persons, as members of a universally inclusive, ahistorically original community of land, and as participants in the formation of the authorising ahistorical general will of *that* community, would rationally accept *this* rule for private appropriation? Would all members of the third or fourth or fortieth human generation rationally accept an *unconditional* obligation to respect a set of property titles descended from the titles created by sites' first (undefeatable) occupants?[14] Second, given the nature of external freedom as unimpeded access to the physical components of actions, are the unencumbered and exclusionary property rights licensed by *this* appropriation rule ones that can be consistently derived from a principle enjoining each person's equal freedom—his or her 'independence from being bound by others to more than one can in turn bind them'?

I take the negative answer to these questions to be self-evidently correct. While '*might makes right*' may be an acceptable rule in some contexts, for example, certain athletic contests, it can have no obvious place in the determination of each person's rightfully equal share of external freedom. For such a rule would confer much greater freedom on only those members of historically earlier generations (and thence their successors) who possessed superior capacities to defend whatever they chose to appropriate. And conversely, it would vest fewer, if any, rights to freedom in others, many of whom might thereby incur unperformable duties of non-trespass.

So, while Kant does make telling points against Locke's labour-mixing account of appropriation (1996: 52), it is reasonably clear that he would have been better

[13] I leave it to the reader to ponder the consistency of this authorising norm with Kant's laboured insistence on the distinction between physical possession and rightful possession.

[14] Doubtless, considerations of the 'tragedy of the commons' and other collective action problems would rationally persuade them of the need for *some* private appropriation rule. But the very concern motivating those considerations—namely, an aversion to sub-maximal production of universally beneficial wellbeing—tells strongly against *this* rule: proficiency in defending one's control of a site in no way implies proficiency in using it in a maximally productive fashion.

advised to ponder what has come to be called the *Lockean Proviso*: a prohibition against appropriating more than would leave 'enough and as good' for others. For this is a rule that is transparently more consonant with the equal freedom enjoined by the Principle of Right, and one that is a far more plausible candidate for adoption by the ahistorical general will of humanity. In any case, I shall here assume that this rule is the one that Kant *should have* embraced, and that what this rule enjoins is each person's original entitlement to an equal share of natural resources.[15]

Such a rule is evidently a distributive one. Moreover, and contrary to Weinrib's contention, this distributive rule is perfectly capable of generating correlative relationships and, indeed, entirely determinate ones. Each person owes, to each other person, a duty of forbearance from appropriating more than an equal portion of natural resources. From this it can be inferred that any over-appropriator owes, to each under-appropriator, a determinate portion of her over-appropriated amount. A simple arithmetical illustration will suffice. Suppose that the number of persons is five and that the amount of resources available for appropriation is 200. Therefore, to avoid over-appropriation, each may appropriate no more than 40. If two persons nevertheless each appropriate 70, and the other three persons each appropriate 20, the former each owe 10 to each of the latter.[16]

What is important to note here is that, as Weinribian corrective justice maintains, the over-appropriators (defendants) are each bound to each of the under-appropriators (plaintiffs) by the bipolar relation of correlativity: they each bear an entirely determinate obligation to each under-appropriator, who is correlatively vested with the claim that each over-appropriator transfer 10 to him or her. And this *corrective* correlative relation is itself directly implied by the aforementioned *distributive* correlative relation. Hence, adverting to Cane's previously quoted review of *The Idea of Private Law*, it would appear that Weinrib's claim—that, unlike corrective justice, under distributive justice individuals' entitlements are not correlative to other individuals' obligations—is one that owes too much to Aristotle and too little to Kant (and Locke).[17]

Sets of legal property rights in persons and extra-personal things, and of the contractual rights derived from exercises of those property rights, are *just*—are in conformity with the Principle of Right—only if they derive from antecedent exercises of universally instantiated original rights to self-ownership and to an

[15] For defence of this assumption, see Steiner (1994: chs 7 and 8); Steiner (1997); Steiner (1998: 274–83); Steiner (1999); Steiner (2012).

[16] Calculation of the amount owed by each over-appropriator to each under-appropriator, when the amounts of over- and under-appropriation differ among respective members of these two groups, evidently requires the application of an algorithm. But that requirement is fully consistent with—indeed, presupposes—the existence of a determinate correlative relation between each over-appropriator and each under-appropriator. Transmission of these liabilities and entitlements, through a succession of generational cohorts, is accomplished by converting them into periodic payments (of rent).

[17] Thus, Weinrib (1995: 62), following Aristotle, argues that 'Distributive justice ... consists in an equality of ratios. In contrast, corrective justice features an equality of quantities'. But under the Kantian/Lockean conception of distributive justice advanced here, these two equalities are identical.

equal portion of natural resources. And it follows that legal rules of corrective justice that remedy violations of rights which are *not* so derived must lack the normative force that Weinrib says is invested in them by Kant's Principle of Right. For Weinrib:

> A rule of private law which is not consistent with the internal logic and morality of reciprocity lacks a sound justification regardless of how well or badly it serves any particular external goal such as compensation or deterrence ... [Weinrib's] exposition of corrective justice in terms of gains and losses presupposes that the former position to which the parties are to be restored was in some sense just (Cane 1996: 472).

The sense in which that former position was just must therefore be such that, in it, the plaintiff's and defendant's respective sets of private rights reflected their respective original entitlements to their own bodies and to equal shares of natural resources. In practice—that is, where natural resources have been fully and unequally appropriated—this latter entitlement becomes one to an equal share of current natural resource *value*, and it consequently entails corresponding correlative encumbrances on natural resource ownerships.[18]

References

Cane, P (1996) 'Corrective Justice and Correlativity in Private Law' 16 *Oxford Journal of Legal Studies* 471.

Carter, I (1999) *A Measure of Freedom* (Oxford: Oxford University Press).

Hart, HLA (1955) 'Are There Any Natural Rights?' 64 *Philosophical Review* 175.

Hohfeld, WN (1919) *Fundamental Legal Conceptions as Applied in Judicial Reasoning* (ed WW Cook) (New Haven, CT: Yale University Press).

Kant, I (1996) *The Metaphysics of Morals* (1797 ed and trans M Gregor) (Cambridge: Cambridge University Press).

Kramer, MH (2003) *The Quality of Freedom* (Oxford: Oxford University Press).

Rawls, J (1999) *A Theory of Justice* (1971, rev edn) (Cambridge, MA: Harvard University Press).

Ripstein, A (2009) *Force and Freedom: Kant's Legal and Political Philosophy* (Cambridge, MA: Harvard University Press).

Sage, NW (2012) 'Original Acquisition and Unilateralism: Kant, Hegel, and Corrective Justice' 25 *Canadian Journal of Law and Jurisprudence* 119.

Steiner, H (1994) *An Essay on Rights* (Oxford: Blackwell).

—— (1997) 'Choice and Circumstance' 10 *Ratio* 296; reprinted in M Kramer (ed) (2001) *Rights, Wrongs and Responsibilities* (London: Palgrave Macmillan).

[18] I'm very grateful to Andrew Halpin, Mark McBride and James Penner for their comments and suggestions about arguments advanced in this essay.

—— (1998) 'Working Rights' in MH Kramer, NE Simmonds and H Steiner, *A Debate Over Rights. Philosophical Enquiries* (Oxford: Oxford University Press).
—— (1999) 'Kant, Property and the General Will' in R Wokler and N Geras (eds), *The Enlightenment and Modernity* (London: Macmillan).
—— (2012) 'Left Libertarianism' in F D'Agostino and G Gaus (eds), *Routledge Companion to Social and Political Philosophy* (London: Routledge).
Weinrib, EJ (1995) *The Idea of Private Law* (Cambridge, MA: Harvard University Press, 1995).
—— (2012) 'Poverty and Property in Kant's System of Rights' in EJ Weinrib, *Corrective Justice* (Oxford: Oxford University Press).

INDEX

Note: Please be aware that 'Interest Theory' (IT), 'Will Theory' (WT) and 'Hybrid Theory' (HT) are abbreviated in this index.

www.ingramcontent.com/pod-product-compliance
Ingram Content Group UK Ltd.
Pitfield, Milton Keynes, MK11 3LW, UK
UKHW020806290926
15470UKWH00003B/982